Colonization as Exploitation in the Amazon Rain Forest, 1758–1911

Colonization as Exploitation in the Amazon Rain Forest, 1758–1911

ROBIN L. ANDERSON

University Press of Florida

Gainesville · Tallahassee · Tampa · Boca Raton
Pensacola · Orlando · Miami · Jacksonville

Copyright 1999 by the Board of Regents of the State of Florida
Printed in the United States of America on acid-free paper
All rights reserved

04 03 02 01 00 99 6 5 4 3 2 1

Library of Congress Cataloging-in-Publication Data

Anderson, Robin L. (Robin Leslie)
Colonization as exploitation in the Amazon rain forest, 1758-1911 / Robin L. Anderson.
p. cm.
Includes bibliographical references and index.
ISBN 0-8130-1719-X (cloth: alk. paper)
1. Land settlement—Amazon River Region—History. 2. Land settlement—Brazil, North—
History. 3. Amazon River Region—Colonization—History. 4. Brazil, North—Colonization—
History. I. Title.
HD469.A43A53 1999
333.75′13′09811—dc21 99-36929

The University Press of Florida is the scholarly publishing agency for the State University
System of Florida, comprising Florida A & M University, Florida Atlantic University,
Florida International University, Florida State University, University of Central Florida,
University of Florida, University of North Florida, University of South Florida, and
University of West Florida.

University Press of Florida
15 Northwest 15th Street
Gainesville, FL 32611–2079
http://www.upf.com

Graças a Deus

CONTENTS

TABLES AND MAPS

Tables

Maps

PREFACE

"Those who do not know history are doomed to repeat it." While not universally applicable, that statement can truly be applied to the history of the settlement of Amazonia. Promoters in the nineteenth century repeated the mistakes of the colonial officials before them. Developers today have ignored the errors of all previous generations. *Colonization as Exploitation in the Amazon Rain Forest, 1758–1911* examines those earlier attempts in detail and concludes that little has been learned. The knowledge that has been gained has been at huge cost to the human and environmental landscape. All attempts to settle large populations in the Amazon have essentially failed—those of the eighteenth and nineteenth centuries, and particularly those of the twentieth century.

The history described here is not a happy one. Students of environmental history, tropical history, or Brazilian history will see that the same erroneous assumptions and suppositions have led to the destruction we see today in Amazonia.

The indigenous peoples understood their environment and how to thrive in it. Their knowledge is reflected in the story of Curupira. According to Tenetehara lore, Curupira was a forest spirit, a protector of game. Those who angered him because of overhunting game or wasting food were led by him deep into the forest. His feet were placed backward, so the errant hunter, thinking he was headed for home, would be led deeper and deeper into the forest, where he would lose his way and die. The Tenetehara understood the penalty for poor stewardship of their resources. The Portuguese and the Brazilians have followed Curupira.

The author would like to thank the individuals, institutions, and foundations that have supported this research. Particular thanks go to the Fulbright Foundation and the Organization of American States, which financed two years of research in Amazonia and in Rio de Janeiro, and to Arkansas State University, which has provided the leave time for writing. To Rollie E. Poppino, Hilgard O'Reilly Sternberg, and Barbara Weinstein, I say "muito obrigada" for your valuable insights. Many thanks also to the staff of the Biblioteca Pública do Pará, the Biblioteca Nacional, Arquivo Nacional, and the Instituto Histórico e Geográfico Brasileiro for helping me locate so much valuable material. Finally, warm regards to all those who aided this research; your help and insight were essential to the project. Ultimately, however, I take full responsibility for the information and opinions that follow.

INTRODUCTION

The Place, the Time, the Setting

During the last quarter century, the Brazilian government has shown a considerable interest in the colonization and settlement of the Lower Amazon Valley. Huge sums of money have been appropriated for colonization projects, numbers of families and individuals have been persuaded to participate in these programs, and various government offices have been created to handle the logistical and administrative details of such plans. Yet such interest in settlement of the Lower Amazon is not simply a recent creation. Rather, the current emphasis on effective settlement of much of the vast emptiness of the Amazon Basin must be seen in light of a long-term historical concern with national sovereignty and occupation of the region.

The Amazon in Portuguese and Brazilian History

Although the actual discovery of the lower reaches of the river and the first serious attempts at settlement were separated by over a century, the Portuguese monarchy did see some limited value in holding onto the lands they claimed in the basin. The region was considered of only marginal value until the eighteenth century, to be claimed simply in order to prevent other nations from establishing a foothold. Radical change in opinion, and subsequently in policy, came in the 1750s as effective settlement and efficient exploitation of human and natural resources of the area took on new importance. The years 1758 to 1798 saw implementation and development of the first coherent, long-term, state-run policy of settlement in the basin, the Directorate system, which controlled a total of sixty-one Indian villages scattered along the waterways of the colonial province of Grão Pará.[1]

As the eighteenth century drew to a close, the Directorate system proved to be a cumbersome method of encouraging settlement and agricultural development, and it was abolished in 1798. For the next twenty years, interest in the Amazon ebbed to a new low as the Crown dealt with problems in Napoleanic Europe, the eventual exile of the court to Brazil in 1808, and the subsequent establishment of a Brazilian monarchy. During the 1820s and 1830s the basin experienced political unrest that eventually resulted in open warfare. When peace was restored in 1836, the imperial government in Rio de Janeiro again began to consider the need to occupy the Lower Amazon and encourage its development. Attempts at colonization resumed haltingly in the 1850s and were spurred on in the 1870s and 1880s by the influx of drought refugees from other parts of Brazil. By the early 1880s, the economic boom resulting from the export of rubber financed a parallel boom in immigration and colonization projects designed to populate the province.

The collapse in 1911 of the rubber export enclave also destroyed nearly all of the government programs, such as immigration and colonization, health, education, and land title legitimization. Between 1911 and 1930, efforts to settle more underpopulated land were sporadic and half-hearted, until 1929, when the Japanese began emigrating to Pará. By 1930, a total of forty-six colonies of all kinds and origins had been established throughout the 1,227,530 square kilometers comprising the state.

Thus, since 1758 there has been a varying degree of government commitment to the settlement of the state of Pará. The colonization programs of the period from 1960 to 1990, with the building of the TransAmazon and other highways and development of agricultural communities along their roadsides, have been simply the continued extension of attempts at settling one of the most complex ecosystems in the world. The problems that have accompanied such settlement have been legion, and few have been definitively solved. Yet, an examination of the historical antecedents of present programs may well provide clues to prevent the failure of future endeavors. The attempts at settlement during the colonial period of the eighteenth century, and the renewed efforts in the last half of the nineteenth century, showed that, while the humid tropics may be a difficult area to settle, the task is by no means impossible. In spite of incorrect perception of actual conditions and problems, and policies not always applicable to those conditions and problems, people can and will settle in the humid tropics.

The Environment

At first glance the Amazon Basin appears to be a remarkably homogenous area: warm, wet, and flat; dominated by rivers, streams, lakes, and swamps; and covered by luxuriant forest. Certainly most of the early descriptions of the area carried such images, along with the supposition that the soil was uniformly rich and capable of sustaining permanent agriculture. Such images can be often explained by the fact that travelers saw mostly riverbank ecology and climax vegetation. They rarely ventured away from the gallery forests along the rivers or saw large areas where the forest had been disturbed for lengthy periods of time. In fact, the region is anything but homogenous, with marked differences in soil types and fertility, landform, water quality, and rainfall. The variation of the myriad microecosystems is reflected in the tremendous variety of species of fauna and flora. In turn, human habitation has been selective, choosing sites suitable to agriculture or the gathering of various plants and animals.[2]

In terms of landform and soils, the Lower Amazon can be divided into two worlds, the floodplain, or *várzea*, and the uplands, or *terra firme*. The basically flat appearance of the Amazon is typical of the várzea, as the river drops only one hundred feet in the nine-hundred-mile journey from Manaus to the Atlantic. In such a broad flat basin, very small differences in relief, such as those found on the natural riverbank levees, can be of critical importance. Most rural inhabitants of the várzeas live on the levees, producing subsistence crops on the fertile soil deposited on the banks during annual floods and raising some livestock. Soil fertility depends heavily on such annual replenishment, and a low-flood year will cause lower agricultural yields, while a high-flood year will bring new soil and hardship for months until the water recedes.

Because of the limited availability of fertile soil in the basin, population has historically clustered along the riverbanks, giving an impression of dense settlement when viewed by the river traveler. Relatively few people in the colonial period chose to inhabit the uplands. The soil there is poor and fragile, a far cry from the assumed fecundity so glowingly described by visitors in the nineteenth century. Upland soils are largely sandstone and laterite, with a very thin humus layer that is quickly and easily destroyed by sunlight and heavy rain. The one notable exception to this statement is the anthropogenic "black earth," or *terra preta*, found in isolated patches on Marajó Island and near Santarem. These soils were formed from ancient kitchen middens and are extremely fertile. Unfortunately, they are also very rare. Continuous cropping has not generally been possible on most upland soils, and slash-and-burn agriculture has proved the only solution to the problem of low fertility, since fields used in this method are occupied for relatively short periods. In the colonial period almost all settlement was confined to the lowlands, while the Indians of the upland interior remained largely beyond Portuguese control. Only in the last 120 years has there been much interest in agricultural settlement of the terra firme.

Just as elevation and soils change regionally, so too there is a difference in the water found in the rivers that drain into the basin. Further, water type has had an impact on the location of human settlement in Pará. The "white-water" rivers, principally the Solimões and Amazonas, take their name from the vast quantities of dissolved and suspended solids and salts washed out of the Andes. The swamps in those areas are rich in nutrients and fish life since they receive the silty water during flood season; when the flood level drops, the silt is left behind in dry places and muddy lakes.

Most of the tributaries of the Amazon originate in the geologically ancient shield areas, crystalline formations and sterile soils that do not produce the silt of the younger Andes. The water from these rivers is called "black" or "clear" water and is comparatively low in nutrients. The "black-water" rivers such as the Xingú, Negro, Jarí, and others have tea-colored water resulting from tannic acid leached from upstream soils, while the "clear" rivers such as the Tapajós and Tocantins are crystal clear and deep blue. Floods on the black-water rivers produce no silt, while the clear river floods do bring some nutrients.

These nonsilty rivers have much less fish life due to a poorer biological chain; they also tend to be malarial areas because of lower salinity and acid soils, which affect mosquito population. The várzeas, where they do exist, are much poorer than white-water várzeas, thus inhibiting riverside agriculture. Thus, black-water rivers have not proved the most auspicious for settlement; the soils are poorer, protein sources less abundant, and disease more prevalent. In addition they are navigable year round only for limited distances due to rocky rapids relatively near their confluence with the Amazon. Very few eighteenth-century villages situated along black-water rivers were far removed from that juncture.

The regional variations in environment have been important enough to affect substantially the economic patterns in Pará. For that reason, the state/province can be divided into ten regions: Rio Amazonas, or Lower Amazon; Rio Tapajós; Rio Xingú; Rio Tocantins-Araguaia; Furos and Marajó uplands; Marajó lowland campos; Estuary; Rio Guajará; Bragantina; and coast.[3] Since colonial times differential development has characterized these regions, and the economic history of one was not necessarily similar to the others. For example, the Marajó campos have been the traditional locus of lowland cattle ranching, while ranching in the Lower Amazon developed more slowly and with somewhat different techniques. While the Tocantins is characterized by plantation agriculture near its mouth, its upriver region has been traditionally dependent on collection of Brazil nuts from the forest. Similar stands of Brazil nut trees (*Bertholetsia excelsa*) are located in abundance around Alenquer and the

Rio Jarí. The coastal area, now referred to as the Salgado, has long been dependent on subsistence agriculture with some cash crops and heavy dependence on fishing, as has the Estuary region. Daily tides rather than seasonal floods force a different approach to lowland agriculture along the coast and estuary compared to agriculture farther upriver. In short, it was precisely the regional variation that made possible the wide variety of forest products, fish, and other aquatic products, as well as agricultural goods that have traditionally formed the basis of the Pará economy.

Man, Technology, and Change

Thus, the physical environment of Pará offered a variety of ecosystems available for exploitation when the Portuguese arrived. The extent, however, to which the Portuguese occupied and organized settlement of the basin depended equally on the modest technology available to them. The Indians had developed their means of producing food, housing, weapons, and implements long before the Europeans arrived. Their technological advancement appears to have been made always within the context of balance with their ecological niches.

The Portuguese introduced some new elements of their own technology, forming an amalgam of traditional and more modern tools and attitudes toward their environment. Yet, in both the cases of transportation and agriculture, the comparative level of technology changed little in the colonial Amazon. The Portuguese simply adapted Indian knowledge and techniques to a system of gathering products for an externally oriented market economy. Real change in the technology of agriculture and transportation had to wait until the nineteenth century and the industrial revolution.

The field of transportation provides a case in point. The moving about of people and goods in the Lower Amazon Basin has traditionally taken place on water. The tremendous fluvial network of the basin made vast sections of land accessible without the need of terrestrial avenues of transportation. The Amazon River itself is navigable by oceangoing vessels up the Solimões as far as Iquitos, Peru. The Rio Negro is also navigable for some distance. The tributaries west of the Madeira are easily navigable into the Acre area, thus facilitating transport of rubber in the nineteenth century, but east of the Madeira navigation is stopped by rapids within 300 kilometers of the tributary mouths. The Tapajós is navigable for almost 300 kilometers, and the Xingú and Tocantins for roughly 200 kilometers each.

Travel within the basin in the colonial period was strictly by canoe, although that term covered a number of craft powered by sail, oar, poles, or a combination thereof. The largest were probably not more than eight or nine meters in length.[4] The collection expeditions from Directorate villages consisted of a number of such relatively small vessels, and the yearly transports of the collected goods were also moved in canoe convoy.

Because of the hard labor of rowing the heavy canoes against strong river currents, attrition among Indian rowers was high, and it was often difficult for the villages to supply enough rowers to staff canoes for official business. The European settlers were equally dependent on manpower to move their goods to market, and there was constant friction as they competed actively for the available labor force.[5] The royal service was given priority, and on at least one occasion collecting was suspended in order to make labor available to the royal expeditions.[6] Because of the difficulties in getting enough labor and the hardships of prolonged journeys, transportation was also an exceedingly slow process. Particularly during flood season it could take several months to make the journey from Belem upriver.

There was very little that could be done to alter the situation. It was simply an accepted fact that roundtrip communications between the governor in Belem and the directors of upriver villages took a minimum of six months. Moreover, losses in river and coastal traffic were frequent as laden canoes overturned or sank.[7] Small wonder that the directors enjoyed their high degree of autonomy, since there was virtually no way for central authority to communicate with them on a regular basis. The effort of moving goods and letters had to be confined to official correspondence and village production destined for Lisbon, thus discouraging short-run trade. Distance and isolation combined to force each town to be as self-sufficient and independent as possible, a trend which contributed to the relatively weak economic links between *municipios* in later centuries.

There was little interest in land transportation in colonial Pará. As long as water travel was feasible, and since no great riches were found in the occasional penetration to the interior, the building of roads was not considered essential. Given the knowledge then available about construction and maintenance of roads in the humid tropics, road building would have been nearly impossible in any case. A road was proposed to link Belem to Pastos Bons in neighboring Maranhão in order to provide more fresh meat to Belem. There were occasional comments about settling Indians along this road through the uplands, but nothing was done to develop colonization of the roadside, and the road itself subsequently was abandoned to the jungle. Without economic incentive to build such lines of penetration, and without the technical capability of rapid and efficient clearing and road building, the uplands were left for later development. Thus, in the field of transportation, the lack of available technology spared a fragile environment from human occupation for an additional span of time.

Technology also had a tremendous effect on agriculture and the agricultural potential of the land. Because of the variations in soils in the Amazon, agricultural technology in the colonial period in Pará was a critical factor in determining location of settlement. Although there have been cattle ranches and sugar and rice plantations in Pará since the seventeenth century, general land use in agriculture has focused primarily on subsistence cropping. On the floodplains, the levees, or the drier portions of the area behind them, crops are planted in semipermanent plots, or *roças*. In areas where problems of lack of dry land or continual infestations of leafcutter ants (*saúva*) are present, gardens may be maintained on raised platforms or in discarded canoes. The key point about lowland agriculture, particularly in white-water lowlands, is its continuity and stability, features not found frequently on the uplands.

The slash-and-burn method of agriculture found throughout tropical Latin America was, and generally still is, the most typical way of converting natural upland environment into plots of land on which to grow manioc and a few assorted crops to feed families. The method is relatively simple: all the trees are cut and left to dry until near the end of the dry season when the whole area is burned. Crops are then planted in the ash-covered soil amid the charred logs and blackened stumps. The ash provides some needed nutrients, and the first-year crop is usually fairly high in yield. By the second year the quantity and quality of yield drops, often dramatically, and usually after three to five years the plot must be allowed to revert to secondary forest (*caapoeira*) and a new plot cleared.

Such a system of semisedentary agriculture is practical where populations are small and widely scattered, but where constant cropping is required to support relatively dense populations and provide a marketable surplus, it can be devastating. The soil does not regenerate quickly, and return to climax vegetation may take fifty years or more. Thus with such a land-use system operated under relatively high population densities (over five persons per square kilometer), vast areas of land can be laid waste in a short period of time. Population densities in some regions of Pará, especially near Belem, exceeded five persons per square kilometer even in the eighteenth century.

During the Directorate period there was no pressure to move away from the lowland; the population did not exceed the carrying capacity of the land, and there were empty lands along the riverbanks. Thus the potential environmental destruction caused by overcropping with slash-and-burn techniques did not pose a serious threat to the Amazonian ecosystem during the colonial period. The agricultural techniques required under the optimal environmental conditions in the lowlands were minimal, and there was no pressure to develop them further. The environmental destruction of the uplands would not get under way until the nineteenth century.

1

The Context and Structure of the Directorate

Colonization is generally defined as the conscious effort of a government at any level to assure sovereignty over the land by putting people on it to occupy it and to develop and exploit its natural resources. The Directorate system, as set forth in the regulations of the *Directorio que se deve observar nas povoações dos indios do Pará e Maranhão emquanto Sua Magestade não mandar o contrario*, or *Directorio* for short, was the first concerted effort of the Portuguese government in Lisbon to apply such an effort in the Amazon Basin. It remained in force in Pará from 1758 until 1798 and was designed to control and organize a total of sixty-one villages scattered throughout the captaincy.

Settlement of the Amazon in the Context of Brazilian History

Portugal developed such aims of occupation and economic development for the benefit of the mother country as soon as the first footholds in Africa were established during the quest for a trade route to the riches of India. Pedro Alvares Cabral's discovery of Brazil in 1500 fell within Portugal's territory, as defined by the Line of Demarcation, but attracted little interest at the time. The Crown was occupied with plans to set up trade and diplomatic relations in Africa and India, not plans to administer claims on an entirely new continent.[1]

Nevertheless, King Manuel recognized the need to establish a Portuguese presence on this new holding. The native peoples had to be converted from their heathen—that is, not European—ways, and the search for gold had to be started. The earliest profitable product was brazilwood, extracted from the northeast coastal forests by local populations and sent to Portugal, where it was used as a valuable dyestuff. Thus the very first activity of the Portuguese in Brazil was to deplete one of the resources of the tropical rain forests—and to do so to the virtual extinction of the species. The first lesson to be learned about Portugal's colonial claim was that valuable products were to be stripped as quickly as possible from the land, without regard for future supply. The pattern of destruction of the rain forest predated even the discovery of the Amazon Basin.

Over the next few decades, Portugal began to set up occupation of coastal Brazil. The land grants of the captaincies were an attempt to put the cost and risk of colonial settlement into private hands. During the sixteenth century, forests were cleared, native peoples were enslaved, sugar became the most important export, and exploration of the interior continued. As Portuguese settlement moved southward along the coast, an added problem was encountered as the Dutch and the French began to assert conflicting claims on the land. Eventually, the foreigners were expelled from the Portuguese colony, and the next lesson of colonization had been learned: the claim of territorial ownership must be backed by strategic and effective occupation of the area.

By the mid-seventeenth century, exploration of the interior by individual initiative was well under way. The *bandeiras* from São Paulo were expeditions into the lands away from the coast in search of Indian slaves and gold. It was largely because of the bandeiras that the effective occupation and claim of ownership pushed well beyond the Line of Tordesillas. Penetration of the interior did indeed provide sources of Indian slave labor and the eventual discovery of gold in the 1690s. As the sugar industry began to decline, gold mining became the most important economic endeavor in Brazil and the greatest income producer for Portugal. It also sparked further exploration in search of new strikes, and additional areas of the interior became rapidly populated as news of new gold and diamond deposits spread. Thus, the entire early history of Brazil centered around exploration, exploitation, and occupation. The constant search for land, labor, and wealth spread Portuguese claim to areas far beyond the original discovery.

The story of the discovery and early colonization of the Amazon Basin follows those same themes. By the Treaty of Tordesillas, the basin fell within Spanish jurisdiction, but little attention was paid to the area by anyone beyond occasional slave-raiding bandeiras until 1637. Virtually the only organized activity by Europeans until then was the creation and expansion of mission fields by the Carmelites and Jesuits.[2] However, in 1637, two Spanish Franciscans arrived in the fortress-settlement of Belem at the mouth of the river, having traveled downriver from their missions on the east side of the Andes. Their journey was regarded by the Portuguese Crown as an attempt to reaffirm Spain's claim to the area. In response, Pedro Teixeira led an expedition of some two thousand men up the Amazon, Solimões, and Napo Rivers, ultimately arriving in Quito Ecuador. On his return trip, he formally laid Portuguese claim to the entire Amazonian watershed. From that point onward, the Portuguese

Crown had to direct attention to the effective occupation and control of the immense rain forests of the Amazon Basin.

Part of the problem was the scarcity of population. From the beginning of the European experience in the Amazon, labor was a far more valuable resource than land. It is difficult to ascertain the size of the pre-Columbian Indian population in Pará. Current estimates put the precontact population of the entire basin at somewhere around five million, allowing for variation in regional density depending on availability of protein sources.[3] At the time of the coming of the Europeans, there were essentially two types of indigenous cultures in the basin: sedentary agriculturists, whose economic base depended on both agricultural and aquatic products, and nomadic groups living on the interfluves, who were hunters and gatherers. The Portuguese concentrated on missionizing the riverine agriculturists at first, and did not work with nomadic tribes for some time.

History of the basin in the early seventeenth century was characterized by the continual attempts by the Portuguese to control the estuary of the river. The first Portuguese settlements were fortresses, as the Lusitanians sought to secure the basin for Portugal and drive the English, French, and Dutch from the area. The forts at Belem (1616) and Gurupá (1623) were the first, being the most needed to protect areas of greatest traffic from the Atlantic approach to the basin. In 1697, forts were established and garrisoned at Desterro on the north shore of Amapá, Santarem at the mouth of the Tapajós River, Óbidos near the mouth of the Trombetas-Cuminá, and Parú at the mouth of the Parú River, all of which controlled access to the Amazon via the tributaries.

The last major fort built was São José de Macapá in Amapá, begun in 1764 and finished eight years later, designed to further protect the northern mouth of the Amazon. Forts were also built in the Captaincy of São José do Rio Negro (present-day Amazonas state) at Barcelos and Tefé to protect the western approaches from penetration by the Spanish. The forts in Pará were not large, but they became poles of attraction for migration and would develop into towns in the next three centuries. The settlements that grew up around them were primarily populated by whites, with Indian villages annexed. Their economic development tended to differ somewhat also from the purely Indian towns.

The other form of settlement used extensively prior to the Directorate was the mission. Franciscans, Mercedarians, Carmelites, and especially the Jesuits established missions to group Indians in locations where they could be catechized, educated, and protected. The mission system was designed to spread the Holy Faith and teach the Indians the mores and culture of a European society in hopes of assimilating and protecting them from the white settlers in search of cheap and plentiful labor. The protection of the mission Indians had been necessary since the early seventeenth century, when Portuguese settlers began to move into the area, seeking a steady labor source to exploit the land, forest, and river. Under the mission system, the padres essentially controlled the Indian settlements, and therefore the availability of Indian labor to the settlers, and were thus capable of controlling much of the general economy. It was precisely the conflict between settler and missionary over labor supply which led to the rebellion of the former in 1684 and the eventual expulsion of the latter in 1757. The expulsion of the Jesuits from all of Brazil two years later, and from Spanish America in 1767, was in good part a response to the order's enormous wealth and power independent of the throne.

By the mid-eighteenth century, a revamping of the entire Luso-Brazilian empire was clearly necessary. When Sebastião José Carvalho e Mello, the Marquis de Pombal, assumed the position of crown regent in 1750, he recognized the immediate need to restructure, streamline, and modernize Portugal's imperial organization. An ardent nationalist who considered his mission to be the strengthening of Portugal both politically and economically, Pombal sought to restore royal control over the imperial economy. From his investigations, he came to realize that England's control over Portugal's economy was responsible for Britain's economic development, while restricting that of Portugal.[4]

Pombal focused most of his attention on the production of gold in Brazil and the dispersal of wealth out of Portugal and into the English economy. He clearly saw the unequal balance of trade in Anglo-Portuguese commerce, and he directed much energy to changing that pattern. Along those lines of thinking, he attacked the illegal traders and the credit system they utilized so well, and he totally reformed the supervision of gold production. He also set up closer inspection and oversight of the sugar and tobacco industries. His attack on the Jesuits and their subsequent expulsion centered primarily on their economic control of land and products and, above all, of labor.

Pombal's interest in the Amazon Basin reflected his concern about lack of royal control of the economy and about the strategic necessity of effective occupation of the region. By the Treaty of Madrid of 1750, Portugal claimed the basin by reason of prior occupation, mainly through the missions and forts. Yet Pombal was quite aware that the missions and the valuable Indian labor resident there were under Jesuit, not royal, control.

He entrusted the delicate job of increasing the Portuguese presence in the Amazon Basin and of wresting economic control of the region from the Jesuits to his brother, Francisco Xavier de Mendonça Furtado. His choice of leadership reflected his commitment to putting the riches of Amazonia firmly into royal hands.[5]

One of Mendonça Furtado's most important recommendations was the creation of the General Company of Grão Pará and Maranhão, usually referred to as the Companhia Geral.[6] Pombal founded the company in 1755, giving it a monopoly on Amazonian trade. Its most important task was to import African slaves in sufficient numbers to supply Portuguese plantation owners with abundant labor at reasonable prices. By providing African slaves, he expected to weaken Jesuit control of the labor market, which effectively meant control of the entire basin's economy. The company's monopoly on trade was also expected to destroy the free traders who marketed Amazonian goods in Europe. In its twenty-two years of existence, the company never completely achieved the goal of slave labor supply, and its effective control of commerce was never absolute. Nevertheless, its function of regularizing export of cacao and other river and forest products brought Amazonia more closely under royal control than ever before.

It was also during Mendonça Furtado's tenure in Pará that the Directorate system was established. In the aftermath of the expulsion of the Jesuits in 1757, the Directorate was designed to organize Indian labor to produce goods for Portugal to sell on the European luxury market. Creation of the network of Directorate villages was an integral part of Pombal's overall plan to regularize labor for the production of agricultural and extractive goods, and to lay effective claim to the vast territory by the fact of organized occupation of the region. Thus, the Directorate clearly reflected Pombal's overall goal of exerting firmer control of Portugal's Brazilian empire. It was also very much a product of contemporary philosophy about the American Indian, coupled with the mission experience that had just ended and designed to fill the power vacuum that had developed when the Jesuits were shipped back to Europe.

Goals and Ideals

Both Mendonça Furtado and Pombal had very definite goals for the Directorate. Probably the most important one was the control of Indian labor. The Directorate was designed to bring Indian communities under effective Portuguese control and make the individuals available for a variety of labor services to the Crown and to private settlers. Forced acculturation became a requisite corollary to such labor and settlement policy, since the Indians had to be taught to respond to the Portuguese values of labor and property. Nevertheless, acculturation was seen as a by-product of creating a free workforce to serve the needs of European settlers.

A second goal was to refine and organize much of the chaotic collection of a wide variety of forest and river products being gathered by the Indians. It was also under the Directorate that the first serious attempts were made to encourage agriculture, not only for export products but equally for food to supply a growing urban area, Belem. Such a policy is a major criterion in considering the Directorate as a conscious attempt by the Portuguese government at colonization and settlement, setting the Directorate apart from the earlier regulations, such as the "Regimento e leis sobre as missões do Estado do Maranhão e Pará sobre a liberdade dos indios" of 1724.[7]

The third clear goal for the Directorate was the effective occupation of strategic routes and areas in the Lower Amazon. Here it was possible to blend settlement policy into those goals. Royal officials in Lisbon considered the settlement of Indians in riverbank villages to be the most efficient means of accomplishing such an aim. Most of the settlements had been missions, so in a sense the decision on location was predetermined. However, officials opted to continue using those existing sites rather than build anew. By forcing Indians to remain in the Directorate villages, adopt European values, and provide a docile workforce, the Portuguese were also maintaining at least some stable settlement patterns.

There were sixty-one Indian villages in Pará managed under the Directorate, scattered from Faro at the present-day Pará-Amazonas border, to Turiaçú on the Maranhão coast, and several tiny, now extinct villages in present-day Amapá.[8] The size of these villages varied in the second half of the eighteenth century, but they generally ranged between 150 and 1,000 people each, nearly all of them Indians, with officials and their families, a priest in nearly every town, a few white settlers (moradores and agregados), and a smattering of slaves. There were a handful of towns created during the 1758–98 period, but in general the towns had previously been mission settlements. Thus, for the most part, the Directorate continued existing settlement patterns and only rarely established new centers of population.

There were several valid, if somewhat obvious, reasons for using the mission settlements for the new program. They were already established, with church, jail, and administrative buildings in use and with individual houses for the inhabitants. People were already settled there, available for labor in royal or private service, so there was little need to procure laborers from distant regions. There was also an administrative necessity for using the existing towns: a distinct lack of qualified personnel to serve as directors for each town. In fact the shortage was often acute, as Gov. Ataíde Teive noted in 1768, saying, "in truth it is difficult to find men of honorable conduct for a job of such circumspection."[9] Given the difficulty of finding enough acceptable administrators to staff existing villages, it is not surprising that creating new villages, and thereby new posts, was inadvisable. Finally, these villages already had some economic base, however shaky, centering on marginal agriculture and collecting.

The aims and regulations of the Directorate, made specific in the ninety-five sections of the *Directorio*, reflect primarily the philosophical framework of the time and only to a much lesser degree the realities of existence in the Amazonian portion of the Portuguese empire.[10] The overwhelming desire of the Marquis de Pombal, who made the decision to expel the Jesuits, was to secure the Amazon Basin for Portugal. There were insufficient manpower reserves for the job either in Brazil or Portugal, so Pombal found the precedent for his plan of settlement in the Roman experience in Portugal. The Romans had settled Lusitania by a union of conquerors and conquered, supposedly on a basis of equality. Pombal saw potential application of that solution for the Amazon.[11] The Jesuits and other orders that had been in charge of settlement of the area through the missions were removed and secular control of the Indian villages established through the Directorate.

The Directorate did create a major shift in direction with regard for the reason for congregating the Indians in the first place. The idea behind the mission system had been to isolate the Indian laborers from demands of white settlers. The Directorate, on the other hand, was designed to regulate commerce, making the Indian labor useful to the Crown, and to make a part of each village's population available for service to private citizens. Although theoretically regulated by law, such service was open to abuse, thus exposing Indians to exploitation by local settlers.

In order to provide information about their charges, each director was expected to send a variety of annual lists and reports to the governor, including lists of agricultural fields (*roças*) and those working them, tithes assessed, shipment of goods, a *livro de comercio* showing goods produced for export, men involved in the extractive industry, distribution of laborers, and those absent from the villages. Not all of these lists were kept, and a great many were amalgamated in various forms.

The basic philosophy of the Directorate centered precisely around the need to civilize the Indians who were not yet considered capable of self-government but who could be taught to be "useful to themselves, to the settlers, and to the State."[12] Such teaching was the duty of the Portuguese and was to be conducted in a spirit of mutual respect and honor, based on prudent and kindly guidance. Education in that manner would permit the Indians to learn and practice the political rights and responsibilities of Portuguese citizens. The philosophy of the Directorate was clearly one of straight assimilation of the Indian into a foreign, Portuguese culture, something the mission system was never designed to do.

The Indians were expected to give up most of their culture and acquire various cultural attributes regarded as essential social behavior by the Portuguese. The most useful vehicle for such cultural change was education and language. Thus, schools were to be established to teach gospel, reading, and writing, with the cost of that education borne by the parents of the attending boys and girls. Many of these schools were established but were usually empty for lack of teachers.[13] There were a few reports from individual villages of finding qualified men to teach, but reports of lack of such people were far more common. Matriculation lists that have survived indicate that boys and girls were educated in almost equal numbers, perhaps because boys were also in demand for service and could not attend regularly. Further, use of the *lingua geral,* a lingua franca based on the Tupí language, was prohibited, and Portuguese was supposed to be taught to all those capable of learning.[14]

More tangible measures of assimilation were also to be enacted. Indians were expected to live in single-family dwellings, "in imitation of the whites," an attempt to eliminate the indigenous social structures based on the *maloca* living style, whereby a number of separate families lived under one roof.[15] All Indians were to be given Portuguese surnames.[16] They were to be strongly encouraged to acquire and wear clothes, a requirement considered essential by European standards of morality but often foreign to the native cultures.[17] The director was expected to be constantly on guard against the use of alcohol in his village, to actively discourage its use, and not permit its entry.[18]

To bring the races together in union and harmony, the Directorate set forth regulations encouraging interracial marriage.[19] Ideally the directors were to improve relations between whites and Indians and were to persuade the former that indigenous races were not an inferior people.[20] That particular mandate raises some interesting questions, since the very nature of the *Directorio* emphasized the superiority of Portuguese culture and customs. The attitude inherent in the working of the document would seem to imply the inferiority of the Indian vis-à-vis the European.

Each village was to be administered by a director appointed by the governor or captain general of the state. The directors were supposedly responsible to the local judge and chief.[21] In theory, the director was supposed to function as an adviser for matters within the village and as an intermediary between his charges and the economic and political outside world, beginning in Belem and stretching to Europe. Thus, most towns were to have their own municipal officials, judges, and town councils, while towns too small for such an administrative structure were to be governed by their chief. The director was expected to show due respect to the Indian officials in their political apprenticeship and was enjoined to refrain from political coercion.

The rules concerning the salary of the director demonstrate two important points about the financial workings of the Directorate. The director was not paid on salary, but on a straight commission basis, a flat 16 percent of the value of all items produced or collected in common by the villages. Choice of commission rather than salary reflects primarily the dearth of colonial financial resources, as there was simply not enough money in the coffers to pay many officials. Secondly, the commission method was designed to encourage the individual directors to increase production from the town, thus profiting the Crown through increased tax and tithe revenues, the Indians through increased buying power, and themselves through a larger share of the profits. The same rationale was used over the question of payment of the men in charge of the collecting canoe expeditions. They received a 20 percent commission on all collected goods, again hopefully increasing the profit for Crown, Indians, and leader alike. In principle it was a very tidy and efficient way of handling the problem, but in practice it made possible a great deal of abuse.

Directors were supposed to work hard to consolidate and augment the Indian populations. Village size was not supposed to fall below a minimum of 150 settlers, and a policy of concentration of population into fewer large villages was to be followed.[22] The favored method of increasing the village population was to bring Indians in expeditions (*descimentos*) from the upper reaches of the Amazon tributaries and settle them in the established towns.[23] It was specifically forbidden to mix Indian tribes without consulting them first; but, in fact they were rarely asked.

It is worth pointing out that the descimentos, which were run by the government, had a private counterpart. European settlers in the 1780s were allowed to resettle forest Indians, paying all costs of such settlement. Indians thus settled were not supposed to begin work until they had lived through a one-year acculturation phase.[24] Such forcible relocation was similar to the Spanish practice of concentrating Indian population in mission villages, or "reductions" (*reducciones*).

The Directorate system bore some resemblance to the reductions and royal *encomiendas*. In Peru, the *encomendero* took over the role of leader-

ship within a village, reducing the local chieftain, or *kuraka*, to an intermediary between him and the villagers. Decisions regarding goods to be
produced were passed down from encomendero to kuraka to workers.
Such a role was already well known by those who had lived under Inca
control. The director served the same role as decision maker, operating
under orders from the governor general to produce more forest products
for sale in Europe and to encourage agriculture to meet needs of villagers,
expeditions, and the population of Belem. The Amazonian Indians were
less accustomed to producing goods for an external market than were the
Peruvians, but they did have the experience of taking orders from mission
priests. The demands for Peruvian *mita* labor to work in the silver mines
of Potosí bear a striking resemblance to the demands for Amazonian Indians to staff the annual collection expeditions, again under direct orders
from their local European leader.[25]

The practices of forced relocation and coerced labor were widespread
in the Spanish empire in the first century after conquest. Although occurring considerably later in the Portuguese Amazon, the same organization
was used in the similar context of claiming and conquering new territory
and its rather scattered inhabitants.

In Central America, the concentrations forced on the Indians re-
sembled the descimentos required by the Portuguese to replenish fairly
constantly the village populations. As disease took its toll and as Directorate Indians often fled into the forest to escape forced assimilation, it was
necessary to restock the populations, often bringing together Indians of
very different tribes. A major difference here seems to be the attitude toward land; in Central America the Spanish wanted to accumulate land
made vacant by concentrating surviving Indians. In the Amazon, Indian
labor was much more valuable to both the Crown and individual settlers
than was land. The result was the same, however—concentrated locations of Indians available for labor in activities demanded by Europeans.[26]

A great deal of attention was paid to tithing in the *Directorio*. Prior to
the Directorate, the mission Indians had been exempt from the tithe, a
situation that was altered after 1757. Directors were to inspect the fields
each year and assign tithes on the basis of estimated production, keeping
lists of people and amounts tithed.[27] Tithes would be paid in foods but
were nearly always paid in manioc flour *(farinha)* at the usual 10 percent
rate. Tithing on forest goods was paid in Belem; tithes on cacao, coffee,
cravo, and salsa were paid when the goods were sold and embarked for
Lisbon, while tithes on all other goods were paid when they arrived at the
General Treasury of the Indians *(Tesouraría Geral do Comercio dos Indios)* in
Belem.[28] The tithe became one of the most onerous levies on the Indians

during the Directorate. There were constant reports by directors that the assessed quotas of farinha they had assigned, supposedly on the basis of projected yield, could not be met due to lack of labor, or more commonly, destruction of crops by floods, drought, or pests.[29]

By far the largest portion of the regulations centered around the economic structures of the Directorate. It would be difficult to say that, even in theory, agriculture received a higher priority than collecting. The former was given "primary importance" in the regulations, but the latter was considered the "most important and useful" part of the region's commerce, which was to have official priority and to be constantly encouraged.[30] The concern about forest collecting centered around a desire to organize it so that only the most lucrative products were collected.

There appears to have been a change in economic policy after 1788 or 1789, with much less emphasis on the spices and other exotic products collected from forest and river and more attention given to agriculture, especially the diversification of crops and encouragement of planting of coffee, cacao, rice, corn, and cotton. By this time, forest collecting was becoming more difficult and time consuming as some products became increasingly hard to find. Prior to the late 1780s, most of the correspondence between directors and governors regarding economic matters was concerned primarily with forest products. Letters responding to the governors' orders for diversification do not appear in the collection prior to 1788, but are plentiful for the next ten years. The change in policy could also well have been in response to a population decline, as adequate manpower was less available to staff long-term collecting expeditions and also produce agricultural goods.

Agriculture was encouraged for two separate and distinct reasons. In addition to showing the Indians the value of producing agricultural surpluses for exchange for exotic imported goods such as tools, agricultural promotion was needed to supply manioc flour, corn, beans, and tobacco for Belem and the forts. The missionaries had been accused of inaction and irresponsibility leading to food shortages in 1754 and 1755, and Pombal was determined that such a situation must not recur.[31] Therefore, Indians were to be strongly encouraged to grow more food than they needed so that it could be sold in Belem. Honors and privileges were to be given on the basis of agricultural promise.[32] Again, the emphasis on assimilation becomes clear, as few of the Indian cultures had previously accumulated the sort of surpluses demanded by the Portuguese. In the humid tropics, accumulation and storage of surplus food was usually thwarted by spoilage. The Indians had serious trouble assimilating this new attitude.

The director was to inspect, classify, and distribute land in an equitable fashion, and each Indian was to have his own plot of agricultural land. On it he was to grow enough food to supply farinha and other foods for himself and his family, and for the troops and inhabitants of the Rio Negro, where there were food shortages.[33] Gov. Mendonça Furtado blamed the current misery in 1757, in spite of what was considered good land, on the congenital laziness of the Indians and the practice of using their labor for private service at the time when their absence from their own fields severely damaged their crops.[34] Besides planting manioc to make farinha, the basic foodstuff of the region, Indians were expected to plant beans, corn, and rice, again for local consumption and to supply the expedition canoes and thus benefit the collection of products from the interior. The Indians were also to be encouraged to grow cotton, thereby supplying a nascent textile industry to produce cotton cloth for subsequent use as the major unit of exchange.[35] Tobacco cultivation was also encouraged, and this crop would bring special attention and honors to its producers, since it was a labor-intensive activity.[36]

During the late colonial period, agriculture in the Directorate villages remained in an embryonic and precarious state. New land was used, new agricultural techniques attempted on a trial-by-error basis, and pests and natural disasters were serious problems that took substantial tolls on the crops. In the 1790s crops were also lost in attacks by Mundurucú Indians raiding the area west of Marajó and in the lower Tapajós Basin.[37] Protein sources were exploited primarily for trade; fish, manatee, and turtles were hunted, and their number near village sites had drastically decreased by the 1790s. And most Indian males did not have enough time to do hunting and fishing on their own at any distance from the villages, since their time was largely spent in service either to the Crown or to the settlers. With so many problems connected with the gathering of wild foods, planting and harvesting of crops, and use of protein sources, it is no wonder that most villages survived perilously close to starvation.

Organization and the Chain of Command

In the eighteenth century, the Directorate functioned with a very clear theoretical chain of command. Ultimate control of policy regarding the Directorate resided with the Overseas Council in Portugal, which in turn reported to the Crown. Decisions regarding changes were made on the basis of reports from the governor general in Pará, whose information in turn came from directors' reports and letters from military men and Portuguese settlers. The general aim of all Portuguese colonial policy under Pombal was that the metropolis benefit from the income and resources of

Portuguese colonies. Under the circumstances, the men in Portugal who would benefit most from the Directorate were the administrators who could manipulate policy to their own advantage. The merchants who handled the exotic products from the Amazon also undoubtedly made a considerable profit on the European market. Thus, much of the profit derived from Portuguese control of the Amazon came directly to those men in administrative and commercial positions in Portugal. While the final decision-making power belonged to the Crown, those men sitting on the Overseas Council certainly had ample opportunity to enhance their own fortunes. However, within the context of the entire Luso-Brazilian economy, the profits from Amazonian trade were negligible compared to the tremendous wealth in gold and diamonds coming from elsewhere in Brazil. It is unlikely that any major fortunes were made solely off of the trade with Pará.

At a regional level, the governor general sitting in Belem held the greatest power as absolute civil and military authority, since he was sole representative of the Portuguese Crown. He held the ultimate responsibility for making the Directorate system work and dealt with most of the ordinary problems that arose. At the same time that he was expected to handle the administration of a very large and difficult area, he had little voice in the formulation of policy. The Correspondencia dos Diversos com a Metropole and the other collections of correspondence are full of descriptions and events, and requests for instructions on particularly knotty problems, but virtually nothing of an advisory nature to improve the workings of the system. He was supposed to function as the chief civil and military administrator, relaying reports to Lisbon and implementing the policy changes handed to him from the Overseas Council. Although he had little theoretical power to make decisions, the governor general enjoyed enormous de facto authority and regional power. Given the time required to request a decision from Lisbon and receive a reply, anywhere from three months to over a year, the governor had to make many on-the-spot choices and hope that official orders would not vary much from them. Even where there was serious deviation, the Overseas Council had very few ways to impose sanctions effectively on the governor. However, the governors were apparently honest, and there were few serious complaints of corruption lodged against the governors of Grão Pará from 1758 to 1798.

The key individual in the Directorate was the director himself. With very little theoretical control, the directors demonstrated that in practice they ruled virtually unchecked. The governor had very little control over their actions, and the Overseas Council had none. According to regulations sent from Portugal, they had to be Portuguese subjects, and the governor general was instructed to search diligently for qualified and competent men. In fact, the posts were usually filled by soldiers from the lower ranks who had neither experience nor training in administration. Governor Coutinho remarked that most directors knew only enough writing to sign their names. The scribes were little better; their handwriting and spelling were abominable.[38] In many cases, their annual letters were simply signed with an X above an indecipherably scrawled name.

Although they had no voice in overall policy decisions, the directors had considerable local power and used and abused it frequently and flagrantly. Even if the somewhat idealistic aims of the *Directorio* had been feasible in other respects, the essentially unlimited authority of this group of untrained, nearly illiterate, self-serving individuals would have doomed such aims to ultimate failure. The directors were virtually ungoverned and ungovernable, and only in extreme and unusual cases was disciplinary action taken against them.

Because of the extreme isolation of most of the Directorate villages, particularly those not on the Amazon River itself, directors did have considerable power of decision making at a purely local level, which would not have been permitted had transportation and communication time been shorter. They handled problems in agriculture and village management, problems related to the collecting and shipping of goods, and problems of discipline and punishment.[39]

The directors, representing the lowest level of colonial administration, were very possibly the ones who benefited the most from the system. They received the share of the profits to which they were entitled by law, the director's one-sixth discounted from all goods produced. They were also assigned Indians for their personal workforce, and all labor and services of those Indians belonged specifically to the director. Much of the directors' income also was derived from illegal levies on agriculture and other illegal fees and commissions extorted from their charges. They also undoubtedly partook in the contraband trade that continued to flourish along the rivers, since their knowledge and consent would have been required when such trade touched the individual towns they controlled.

Thus, the chain of command that began with the Crown, down through the Overseas Council, transferred to the Amazon via the governor general, and ended at the director also reflected the accrual of profits. The men who apparently benefited the most were the ones on either end of the chain. Both were intended to profit, although strong evidence indicates that the directors did somewhat better than the Crown intended.

Aside from the political appointees, elites in colonial Pará also included numerous individuals who were in some way directly involved in colonial trade. The treasurers of the General Treasury of the Indians handled all trade from the Indian villages, receiving a 5 percent commission for their efforts. The potential for making extra profit was great, since these men had control over storage of extremely valuable export goods. Portuguese and Creole merchants in Belem acquired control over transportation, consignment, and sale of plantation agricultural goods, the only other source of wealth in the basin. The white settlers, mostly plantation owners and cattle ranchers, were also developing economic and political muscle, to the point that their demands for Indian laborers could not be ignored. These men continued to expand their economic power after the end of the Directorate and assumed political power in the newly created legislature formed at Independence in 1822.

Counting all levels of European influence, three areas of aspirations could be delineated: the need to provide a reliable and steady source of food for the Belem market and elsewhere, the need to provide a resident labor pool from which workers could be selected for a number of tasks, and the need for a Portuguese presence along the waterways of the region. The Directorate theoretically would have accomplished all three goals. The Indian villages scattered along most of the navigable rivers would effectively claim the area for the Portuguese Crown. The crops produced on their communal plots were expected to be well in excess of local need and could therefore be sold in Belem or used to provision the garrisons at Macapá and Belem, or the official explorations of Mato Grosso. The Indians so conveniently clustered in these pseudo-European settlements would make their labor available to private individuals and to royal officials for the good of all.

As a form of settlement policy, however, the Directorate fell far short of expectations. The villages remained small, rarely exceeding a few hundred people, and they did not attract new population. The communal plots often went untended due to scarcity of farmers; food shortages in the villages were not uncommon, and the Indians had great difficulty in adjusting to the concept of surplus production and distribution. As population declined and labor levies increased, it became more and more difficult to induce the inhabitants of the Directorate villages to submit to the labor pool. Such serious problems were compounded by the decrease in availability of valuable forest products, Indian raids, destruction of crops by pests, and the ever-present problems of distance and difficulty in communication.

The goals of the Directorate as suggested here were not necessarily inappropriate, or even inherently impossible. They simply were not feasible without a great deal of patience and flexibility, which were largely absent. The goals set by Pombal and those who followed him were not realistic in the Amazonian context, and the Directorate was therefore basically a failure as a settlement policy.

Basic Procedural Issues

In the eighteenth century the decision on where to settle was determined by several factors, including the preexistence of many towns, the state of transportation, the perception of the environment by the men responsible for the choice, and the economic advantages of specific areas. The fact that many of the Directorate towns were a continuation of previous mission settlements cannot be overlooked. By continuing to use those locations, the difficulties of relocation and building construction were eliminated. Since transportation was exclusively by water and was dependent on oar, sail, and manpower, village sites were generally confined to water's edge, in locations where nautical problems such as tidal bores and rapids did not inhibit travel.

Because of their strategic location, mission towns were useful militarily also. Since the towns were situated along the rivers and coast, particularly around the mouths of tributary rivers, they could be used as informal checkpoints. The towns were not armed, and directors could only report unusual activity, but the ability to check on movement all the way along the river was valuable to overall military control of the basin. A curious report was sent from Soure in 1773, saying, "At this moment the chief of Mondim, of the town of Chaves, arrived, and he brings news that the outskirts of the town was visited by a launch with six men aboard, all dressed in green, who travelled . . . those waters and who spoke to him in a language totally foreign to his knowledge."[40] Since Soure is located on the southern mouth of the Amazon close to the Atlantic coast, these foreigners may well have been English, French, or Dutch, making their way up the coast to the Guianas. They may have put ashore for food or water. No other towns reported their presence.

Penetration of the interior took place only along the larger southern tributaries: the Tocantins, Xingú, and Tapajós Rivers but not up the northern tributaries. The emphasis on settlement along the southern tributaries probably reflected a greater potential replacement population from upriver and perhaps a more varied and profitable collection of forest and river goods. Along the northern bank, towns at the mouth of rivers guaranteed Portuguese domination of the watershed, as in the case of Fragoso (Rio Jarí), Almeirim (Rio Parú), Monte Alegre (Rio Maicurú), Alenquer (Rio Curuá), and Óbidos (Rio Trombetas).

The reasons for not settling the northern tributaries themselves are not clear from the sources. Probably there were fewer large concentrations of Indians than on the southern tributaries, and the rapids near the river mouths made penetration to the north much more difficult. The lack of forest products along the watersheds was probably not the reason, since most of the collection from Almeirim, Fragoso, Outeiro (now Prainha), Monte Alegre, and other northern bank towns came from along those rivers. The towns on Marajó, in the estuary, and along the coast reflected less the economic importance of forest collecting than the dependence on fishing, which yielded vast quantities of dried and salt fish, turtles and turtle oil, and manatee meat and oil.

The nonmilitary reasons for settlement along the rivers were perhaps more important for an understanding of settlement patterns. The várzea had the advantage of being easily accessible by means of transportation based on oar and sail. Agriculture on the annually flooded lowlands required less sophisticated technology than on the uplands, so the várzea was the logical place to begin systematic agriculture. Along white-water silty rivers such as the Amazon itself, the annual silt deposits greatly enrich the soil. The black-water and clear rivers such as the Xingú, Tocantins-Araguaia, and Tapajós rivers, where only about a quarter of the settlements were found, did not have such fertile soil. The upland terra firme lands are very different from the várzea, being much less fertile and more easily damaged by removal of the forest cover. The principal reason for ignoring the terra firme was not only the relative inaccessibility and poor soils, but more particularly the lack of large populations of sedentary agriculturists who could be coerced into the available labor pool. Thus there was nothing to attract the founding of new towns on the terra firme in the eighteenth century.

A number of towns, several of them established well before the 1750s, were flourishing, and they presented a very different picture, economically, demographically, and politically. These towns can be divided into two general groups: fortress towns and nonfortress towns. The former were not fortified settlements but simply the villages that grew up near established Portuguese forts, supplying food to the troops and housing the nonmilitary population, such as families of soldiers, merchants, prostitutes, and camp followers. Such towns existed near the forts at Santarem, Óbidos, Gurupá, and Macapá. The population tended to be predominantly white, with some African slaves, although several towns also had Indian villages attached to them. By the 1790s miscegenation had made the racial distinctions less noticeable.

The fortress towns rapidly became commercial centers, primarily because of the Portuguese and Luso-Brazilian merchants who lived there and who became the middlemen between gatherers and Belem merchants. Another, perhaps obvious, reason for the commercial success of these towns was their location; their economic control of upriver areas matched the military control provided by the garrisons. Upriver inhabitants coming by boats, all of which had to stop at these checkpoints, often traded locally or brought goods specifically for local merchants, particularly after 1798, when the Directorate no longer controlled the Indians' trade.

The nonfortress towns were those that had grown up independently of the large Indian villages and the forts, usually near some good agricultural land, as in the case of Cametá and Igarapé Mirim. Others were at strategic points along the coast, as Vigia and Bragança on the Belem–São Luiz coasting route, or in conjunction with economic enterprises, such as the royal sawmills at Abaeté, the lumbering operations at Acará, and the salt pens at Salinas. Most of the independent towns tended to be near Belem, along the Guajará River, which borders the city, or in the Tocantins estuary, where soils are among the most fertile in the basin. There were also a few towns along the coast from Belem to Bragança, but there was virtually no penetration of the interior between those points. Nor were there non-Indian settlements on the island of Marajó or upriver except for the fortress towns.[41] The Directorate towns were not exclusively Indian, and there were white settlers living near every town, but all of the colonial upriver towns were under the jurisdiction of directors. Those whites living near the Indian villages were often holders of large land grants, dependent on the Indians for labor to tend fields and herds and to collect the lucrative goods from the interior.

The northern bank of the estuary, now the state of Amapá, was claimed and held by Portugal by virtue of the settlements established there in the mid-eighteenth century. The fort São José de Macapá, begun in 1764 and finished in 1782, was the strategic point to prevent access to the Amazon by the northern channel made dangerous by shoals and tidal bores. Near the fort, the town of Macapá was established to garrison soldiers until construction of the fort was complete and to provide food and services for the area. Further west along the bank were the towns of Mazagão and Vila Viçosa da Madre de Deus, both founded in 1769, and the hamlet *(lugar)* of Santana de Mutuaca, founded in 1771.

The question of who to settle the Amazon was handled as two separate but related policies. On the one hand was the Directorate, a system designed to settle and acculturate the Indians. On the other was encouragement of European settlers to live near Indian villages or to create whole new towns, as in the case of Mazagão.

There were specific provisions allowing white settlers to live in the Directorate villages, providing they were of good moral character, would not acquire land already given to the Indians, would keep the peace, and would behave themselves.[42] If such conditions were met, the colonial government agreed to help the settlers build a house by supplying the materials and giving them land. If the settlers did not meet the stipulations, they were supposed to be expelled.[43] A number of European colonists, attracted by the ready supply of workers, did settle in and around the towns. Their constant abuse of labor regulations for Indians in private service was one of the major criticisms of Governor Coutinho in 1798. Nevertheless, among the volumes of correspondence of directors with the governor, there was not a single case recorded of disciplinary action taken against a white settler for his abuse of the privilege of settling near a steady labor supply.

Other forms of colonization were tried during the Directorate years which emphasized the settlement of Portuguese and Creoles, with the labor force being primarily African slaves. The Companhia Geral de Grão Pará e Maranhão provided economic incentives for the Portuguese and Luso-Brazilians who had capital to invest in plantation agriculture, thus encouraging settlement in the Tocantins estuary and along the Guamá River.

The case of Mazagão was an interesting example of another way of trying to settle the region. It was a unique experiment in moving a town in its entirety from one continent to another, staffing it with settlers, soldiers, ex-prisoners, and their families, and setting it down in virgin territory. Portugal had maintained a garrison of troops at Mazagão in Morocco until 1769, when the troops were withdrawn and the installations abandoned to the king of Morocco. It was then decided to send the entire garrison, together with families and subsidies in cash and livestock, to the Amapá estuary to found a new town to defend that coastline. The first families arrived at the new site in 1770, while others remained in Belem until sufficient housing was built.[44] The village was built during 1770–71 using Indian labor levies from villages throughout the estuary, and requests were frequently sent to Belem for farinha, dried meat, aguardente for the Indians, butter, salt, pots and pans, powder, tar, writing ink, paper, and all the other paraphernalia required to set up a town.[45]

During those two years, African slaves were brought to Pará to be sold to families going to Mazagão; in March 1770 alone, two shipments of 225

Table 1.1. Population of Mazagão, 1772–97

1772:	458
1783:	1,839
1784:	720
1789:	955
1797:	725

Sources: (1) Letter from Mazagão 1772; (2) "Mapa de todos os habitantes e fogos"; (3) "Relação das familias"; (4) "Extrato do mapa geral da população e produção"; (5) "Mapa geral da populacão da Capitania do Para."

and 194 blacks were brought for that express purpose. Evidently the slaves were not for use in construction of the town, but for agricultural labor after the families had moved in. Settlers in Mazagão suffered just as badly for lack of African slaves as did settlers elsewhere in Pará.[46]

By 1772, 56 houses were complete, 61 more under construction, and 17 just begun; a year later 139 houses were reported ready for occupancy, and the rest of the families moved. Work evidently continued for some time, as Indian labor continued to be assigned there.[47] The swampy site was not a healthy one, as there were yearly epidemics of malaria, as well as gastrointestinal and respiratory diseases. The plea from Mazagão in 1797 was particularly poignant: "It is because the disease time of year which we experience every year is coming; already many people [are] down not only with malaria, but also coughs and mumps. We implore Your Excellency to take pity on these miserable people by sending them a surgeon named Vicente Leião and a barber *(sangrador)* named Joaquim José Villanova, both of them to be found in the town of Macapá, where there are more surgeons and barbers."[48] There were numerous reports also of the poverty of the village, noting particularly the lack of farinha and meat. The scanty demographic data indicate that disease and an undesirable location encouraged out-migration, some of it to Macapá, most of it back to Belem, between 1772 and 1797. One observer in 1784 noted many houses were abandoned at that time.[49] However, Mazagão did manage to survive as a town in spite of demographic decline, as the following figures demonstrate.

The 1783 figure is likely suspect by its deviation, though it may represent the early influx once construction was completed, followed by rapid decline in the face of poor soils, malarial mosquitoes, and unfamiliar agricultural techniques. The 1784 *relação* mentions that there were at that time 133 households but that there had been as many as 351 households in previous years. If the average number of people per household had not changed radically, being 5.4 in 1784, that many households would have given a population of nearly 1,900. As substantiation, a letter in 1775 mentioned that conditions were much improved, new houses going up, old ones repaired, 207 houses occupied, and crops of rice and cotton doing well.[50] As people died or moved to a healthier spot, new settlers came in from surrounding areas or from Portugal. Mazagão was neither prosperous nor bustling, but it remained a nucleus of population in an otherwise very empty part of the basin.

A good deal of government activity and interest in bringing European colonists to Pará in the eighteenth century centered around the introduction of soldiers and their families, as well as *degredados,* ex-criminals who chose life as colonists rather than remaining in Lisbon prisons. In the year 1776 alone, at least two shipments of degredados arrived, some 132 men from prisons all over Portugal whose sentences had been commuted upon promise to settle and remain in Pará.[51]

Soldiers who went to Pará with their families received subsidies from the Crown, sometimes in money but more often in livestock, the numbers varying according to the rank and the number of family members. Thus, a lieutenant with wife, three sons, two daughters, one slave, and four other family members, received twenty cows, four bulls, and two mares; the *capitão mor* received forty cows, two bulls, and four mares. Single men and married foot soldiers without children each generally got three to five cows, one bull, and a mare. The ship lists which arrived with the new colonists indicated that livestock were sent with the families to facilitate quick settlement.

From 1763 to 1769 at least 348 families arrived in Pará for settlement near Belem and Macapá. The average household size was about four people, giving a rough approximation of nearly fourteen hundred persons; the families tended to be young, with heads of households in their early twenties and often including cousins, brothers, and parents.[52] Thus, besides the Directorate system other means were tried to attract settlers. Europeans did not come in large numbers, but some did come to the Lower Amazon to make a permanent home.

The towns of the Directorate formed a settlement network in Grão Pará, with channels of transportation and communication between the individual towns and Belem but with little contact between the towns. The analogy would be to an unfinished spiderweb with all strands radiating from the center and no interweaving strands. Even in cases of need for aid after crop failure, epidemics, and Indian attacks, such aid was requested from Belem, entailing perhaps several months' wait, rather than from neighboring villages. Thus, the colonial period set the patterns of trade and assistance within the basin, resulting in virtually no intermunicipio trade throughout the nineteenth and early twentieth centuries.

The most obvious and permanent aspect of such trade patterns was the maintenance of Belem as the commercial capital of the state and the prevention of growth of competing regional centers. There were no towns with individual spheres of influence, but rather many towns, each with ties directly to the capital.

Problems, Realities, Abuses

The Directorate was an enlightened and idealistic attempt at a new Indian policy coupled with a coherent plan to settle the Amazon Basin. However, the stresses placed on the system by the physical setting, the population decline, and the conflict with settlers over apportionment of labor meant that little of the Directorate program was feasible in the eighteenth-century reality. The conflict of ideal and reality created an atmosphere where dishonesty and abuse of power were commonplace.

Much of the abuse, which was decried periodically and was definitively exposed by Governor Coutinho in 1797, was related to the administration of the villages. The institution of the director was a prime example. Envisioned by the creators of the Directorate as a benevolent tutor of his innocent charges, he was admonished to act with "prudence, suavity, and tenderness" and always with the best interests of the Indians as his guiding principal, an unrealistic expectation at best.[53] However, in reality such humanitarians were sorely lacking if not downright impossible to find. The post did not pay well, which meant that prosperous, well-educated men did not care to serve, while less well-to-do men, usually soldiers, served in order to make their fortunes through legal or extralegal means. Governor Coutinho remarked in 1797 that "if the European is overcome by a voracious hunger for gold, he respects nothing in order to satisfy his greed," and that once transplanted to Pará, he becomes a different man, making the analogy to a ferocious jaguar (onça feroz).[54]

The director, through the local judge and council, was supposed to try minor infractions and mete out punishment. However, the reports from the directors themselves indicate that consultations with judge and council were rare, and most directors handled crime and punishment directly. Cases involving major crime such as murder, rape, and kidnap were beyond the jurisdiction of the directors and were sent to Belem for judgment.[55] At the local level, however, the directors wielded virtually unlimited power. Such power in unscrupulous hands encouraged abuses, and Governor Coutinho considered that most directors were veritable tyrants in their domains, extremely cruel men who used a variety of severe punishments for minor offenses. He specifically mentioned the chaining of people over fire ants' nests, leaving them for days without food.[56] He felt that the directors were trying to keep the Indians in a state of subjugation, thus perpetuating their own power, and he strongly recommended that the Indians be removed from their not-so-benevolent tutelage.[57]

Abuses of regulations were common. In fact, Governor Coutinho managed to condemn practices that violated nearly every major article of the *Directorio*. Regulations concerning the ban on sale of alcohol, assignment of labor levies, apportionment of proceeds from the sale of collected goods, length and distance of service, and many others were regularly and openly disobeyed. The Directorate system had to function within the reality of administrators, who had no face-to-face contact with their superiors and who were there principally to increase their own wealth. All the directives in the world charging them with benevolent tutelage of the Indians have to be seen in that context. It is unlikely that many better administrators could have been found for the villages when the overwhelming desire of the Europeans was to extract the greatest possible wealth from their positions.

Other colonial administrators, treasurers, priests, and soldiers were equally grasping and corrupt, witness Coutinho's remark concerning the destination of the proceeds from the collecting expeditions which had been assessed various deductions, "as well as the stealing done in as many hands as through which they pass."[58] The whole colonial administrative structure seemed to be riddled with graft, corruption, and theft. Further, the problems of adjustment among the newly arrived Indians from the descimentos was probably inevitable, since they were expected to renounce almost their entire cultural heritage and rapidly assimilate new, totally foreign mores and habits. Even under the best of conditions, the administrative role was almost predestined for abusive situations.

Forced assimilation was a problem in physical survival, not philosophy. Add to the cultural shock of such adjustment, the serious problem of acute infectious disease, ranging from smallpox to measles and the common cold, and clearly the Indians were fighting a losing battle for survival. Under more propitious direction, conditions might have been somewhat better, but the directors' behavior was not the sole cause of the dismal condition of most villages at the turn of the century.

The assignment of labor and management of salaries was the most common area of abuse. The directors controlled all of the economic activities of the Indians. They held the salaries of those men in service, were to act as intermediaries in all financial transactions, and were specifically instructed to make certain that their charges bought only necessary items for useful purposes, a clause which made possible the director's total control of the local economy. There were several control regulations preventing directors from buying the Indians' goods for resale in Belem, encouraging intervillage trade, and especially encouraging the Indians to sell their goods to Belem, but they evidently were frequently ignored.[59] Such admonitions could accomplish very little when the directors already held complete control over the Indians' commerce. It is interesting, however, that something akin to the *repartimiento de mercancías* in colonial Spanish America, by which goods were distributed to the Indians who were forced to pay for them, often regardless of need for such items, did not develop.

The regulations regarding salary were ambiguous and apparently conflicting, if not deceitful. Directors were supposed to explain to their charges that all goods they collected would be divided amongst them.[60] However, other regulations set aside one-sixth of the total production of all goods for the director. Further, when the goods finally arrived at the General Treasury of the Indians in Belem, payment of tithes, the cost of the expedition, the fee for the canoe headman *(cabo de canoa)*, and the director's share were all to be paid before the Indians received their share, paid in cotton cloth. In the three years 1759–61, the total income from the Indian villages amounted to 83:405$423, while total expenditures assessed on the villagers' production amounted to 95:816$287. The Indians pocketed a little over half of those proceeds, when according to regulations they should have only been tithed the usual 10 percent. Since there is a discrepancy of some 12:400$000, it may be reasonable to assume that the Indians did not receive the amount listed in the accounts. No mention was made of deficit operation during the Directorate. Governor Coutinho noted that after the usual deductions, not to mention wholesale graft, the Indians involved in commerce rarely received more than 20 to 30 percent of the profits, so presumably the deductions increased measurably after 1761.[61]

The expeditions, which frequently lasted four to six months, consisted of several canoes, usually one very large one, manned by Indians and commanded by a canoe captain who was supposedly appointed by the director with great care. These expeditions traveled to various areas, often at some distance, to collect specific goods. When they returned to their villages, the Indians rowed their canoes in one annual expedition to Belem to deliver the total annual production to the Treasury there. If the goods were perishable, as with mullet, turtles, and fish, they were not stored in the villages to await export but were shipped as soon as possible. In an effort to encourage local chieftains and officials to participate in the collection, they were allowed to send two to six men to collect for their personal accounts.[62] All other Indians on the collecting expeditions were supposed to be working for their own profit while in service, but the situation seemed far more characteristic of laborers working for the state and paid a flat wage.

While Directorate regulations about the use of Indian labor were detailed and explicit, there was virtually no way to enforce them. Distance made communication extremely slow, so that complaints could not be heard promptly, and isolation made flagrant abuse of the system very easy. Further, the Indians had few legal rights or recourse to petition. Most documented cases of directors' abuses and corruption came from visits by other colonial officials.

The desire of directors to further their own or friends' and relatives' interests meant that labor levies became increasingly heavy as the Indian population declined. Reports in the late 1760s and after frequently noted that there were not enough men to tend their own fields and provide local service, since most available labor had been siphoned off for royal service in building the Macapá fort, cutting wood for shipbuilding, or for rowing expeditions into Rio Negro or Mato Grosso. Those tasks had especially high desertion and mortality rates, so that new labor had to be constantly forthcoming, necessitating the use of young boys. In 1780, the governor suspended collecting throughout Pará in order to reserve enough labor to meet the needs of the state.[63]

A very large part of the problem of conflict between ideal and reality was the conflict between government officials and European settlers over labor. Europeans who moved into the villages did not do so for altruistic motives of helping to civilize the Indians. Rather, they sought to acquire fertile land near a steady supply of labor that could be used either for agriculture or the more profitable extraction of the *"drogas do sertão,"* the innumerable forest products that commanded such high prices on the European market. Their motivation was so different from that elaborated in Lisbon that local Europeans saw the Indians in a very different fashion from distant government officials.

The settlers wanted labor, and since they could not afford imported slaves, they wanted to use local Indians. The Europeans simply were not concerned with converting the Indians into Portuguese citizens, even if such conversion meant eventual free wage labor. They needed labor for their enterprises at the moment, not in the future.

Thus, it is not at all surprising that, caught between official orders to protect the Indians and apportion their labor equitably and local pressure by the settlers, who could not afford to follow normal procedures to get Indians in private service, the directors yielded to local pressure. Indians were therefore assigned where they were not necessarily supposed to have been assigned—to private individuals living at some distance from the villages, and for excessively long periods of time. The situation was not of the directors' making, but they responded to it in a spirit of aid to settlers and disregard for royal regulation.

If the plan of Pombal had been simply to enslave the Indian and make him into a laborer with no decision-making power in the economic process, the Directorate could be seen as an extension of the overall market economy culminating in Lisbon. The use of Indian labor would have simply been the means by which goods were produced for European markets. However, the issue was a bit more complicated. The ultimate goal of the Directorate, at least on paper, was to transform the Indian from a forest savage into a useful and productive member of Portuguese overseas society. Therefore, simple enslavement and coercion of labor was not consistent with those aims.

The only way that Pombal and the Overseas Council envisioned involving the Indians in the market economy and teaching them the value of their land and labor was by encouraging them to work. Encouragement was supposed to be a gentle method based on imitation of the Europeans who gained wealth from collecting and agriculture and on gentle persuasion to get the Indians to perform similar functions. The designers of policy in Lisbon, basing their thoughts on the philosophy of the time and on reports of the level of indigenous civilization in the Amazon, decided that the Indians would not be sophisticated enough to respond to profit incentives as they began their emergence as Luso-Brazilian citizens. Such thinking was fully consistent with the overall attitude toward the Indian throughout Ibero-America. The Directorate was not an isolated case of forced labor and acculturation of the Indian but was part of a much larger picture including Spanish American policies. Therefore, the Indians would have to be told how to organize their economic life until some time in the future when they would be capable of making those decisions for themselves.

The directors were given power to designate assignment of labor, but the orders governing their decisions were handed down from the colonial officials in Belem. Thus, the decisions concerning which goods to encourage were based on market conditions in Europe, refined by knowledge of local conditions in the Amazon and passed on to the Directors for implementation. Such an official structure did not take into account the effective autonomy of the individual Directors who could with impunity ignore such orders if they chose.

In any case, Indians had no decisions to make on what they were to collect, since all such choices were made at higher levels. They were simply expected to produce what they were told by their Directors, always with the knowledge that the decisions were made with their own welfare of paramount importance. In fact, the economic benefit to the Indians rated rather low on the scale of priorities and profits.

The Indians could not be considered simple laborers in the pay of the government or private settlers in this process but were supposedly free, even though under benevolent tutelage. The economic structure functioned to persuade the Indians, who were thus technically free, to perform tasks in a fashion much more akin to slave labor. Profit incentive did not play a role because it was felt by the Portuguese to be inappropriate to the Indians' situation. Command was the only mechanism they were supposed to understand. If coercion and force had to be applied to make the Indians work, it was unfortunate, but the end was felt to justify the means. Eventually, it was hoped by the Portuguese, the Indians would not need to be told to produce but would do so for reasons of personal profit. In the meantime, they had to work within an artificial system of coercion that functioned at the very bottom of the market economy, where the goods were being produced.

Problems and Living Conditions

Land tenure and ownership, health, and education were among the issues dealt with during the Directorate. In the villages, land ownership provided an excellent example of decisions being made for the Indians. Each village had its communal field (roça comum) in which all inhabitants were expected to work but the production of which was exported for consumption elsewhere. Physical coercion remained the sanction, and Directors were empowered by law to make the Indians work the fields. Milder incentives were also offered: promises of a share, albeit a small one, of the profits of the sale of production from the common field. The state, which was the principal buyer, did not pay competitive prices for that production, but the Indians were not free to sell on an open market.

In addition, individual families were apportioned private plots by the Director, which were to be cultivated for family use and the production of which was liable for tithing. Little information exists on the size of the individual plots, but they were probably at least a hectare each. When the Directorate ended in 1798, the private plots became legal property of those who had worked them, but the distribution of common land was unclear.

In the colonial period land was allocated to white settlers by royal grant (sesmaria), though even larger holdings were effectively occupied by illegal squatting (posse). The sesmarias on Marajó were classic examples: large, normally two square leagues, with ill-defined borders delimited in terms of natural topography, usually rivers and creeks. Because such boundaries were unclear, particularly during flood season, when much of the land is under water, sesmarias came to be described in terms of numbers of corrals or estimated herd size rather than in terms of area. Sesmaria grants in the Lower Tocantins were somewhat smaller than on Marajó, and were primarily farming rather than ranching properties. Boundaries were somewhat better defined, and holdings were described in terms of area, not production from the land.

Health care was a serious problem in the eighteenth century, partly because of the prevalence of disease, and even more importantly because of the state of the medical arts. The Directorate articles made no provision for any sort of medical personnel to be assigned as part of the staff. There were generally barber-surgeons attached to the forts at Gurupá and Macapá, and they would care for people in the immediate area, but only a very few people could ever be served. Had it not been for the Indians' owns healers, local populations would have suffered even more than they did since native lore supplied a number of local products used as salves, ointments, teas, and the like.[64] However, native lore was virtually useless in the face of epidemic diseases introduced by the Portuguese and their African slaves. The most commonly reported major diseases were smallpox, measles, and malaria, with dysenteries and respiratory complaints ranking close behind.

Smallpox was the single most deadly disease. Repeated infection from the slave ships meant that Belem was an almost constant pesthole from which contagion spread as boats arrived from towns and villages to deliver cargo and returned laden with germs. According to lists of slaves brought by the Companhia Geral in 1775 to 1777, an average of 4 to 8 percent of the slaves died either en route or during the sale, and most deaths were due to smallpox.[65] If accurate, the mortality figures are not unusually high in comparison with those from other Brazilian ports. In 1759, Gov. Mello e Castro reported slaves to have died of fevers and *bexiga* (smallpox). He went on to say that many of those deaths had occurred after disembarkation and after sale.[66] Infected slaves sold to sugar planters and other white settlers as far away as Mazagão quickly and easily infected large numbers of people. There was little difference in the mortality rate between Portuguese and Indians, since few had acquired immunity, vaccination was as yet unknown, and there was no cure available.[67] Jenner's pioneer work on vaccination was published in 1798, but it was some time before it was accepted and longer before vaccination became common in the Amazon. Vaccination was mentioned in 1804 in an effort to control smallpox, which had been particularly severe in the 1790s, but the trial was confined to Belem and had very little success.

Reports of an outbreak of smallpox or measles in a town ensured its isolation, which might have helped to check the spread of the disease, except that apparently healthy residents would flee the town. Since many were already infected, flight guaranteed the further dispersal of the disease. Óbidos in 1761, Pinhel in 1770, and Melgaço in 1772 all filed reports of people fleeing the outbreak of an unspecified disease and the subsequent lack of laborers and food. Similar reports were received from Pombal, Ponta de Pedras, Abaeté, Outeiro, and Marajó, most of these cases being due to smallpox. In 1774 the Commercial Intendent arriving in Vigia refused to land because of the outbreak of an unknown disease that reportedly killed rapidly.[68]

The Mazagão-Macapá area proved to be a staging ground for the spread of smallpox and other contagious diseases during the construction of the Macapá fort (1764–82). Indians were brought from all over the captaincy to work on the fort; in close contact with infected slaves and Portuguese, they died by the hundreds. The list of Indians serving at Macapá in 1769 showed a mortality rate of one-third, 93 of a total of 283, and most of the deaths were due to disease and overwork.[69] Again, many of those who survived the period of service may have unintentionally carried disease back to their homes.

Malaria was a common problem, the worst outbreaks occurring in the summer months during low water, when stagnant pools provided excellent mosquito breeding grounds. The northern bank of the Amazon from Macapá to Esposende and the Xingú River seemed to have had outbreaks most frequently. Cajary suffered so badly from malaria in 1794 that the director there requested that labor levies be made from Fragoso, since there were no able-bodied men in his village.[70] In Arraiolos, thirteen people died in one week from malaria. Statements were filed by councils in Veiros, Souzel, and Pombal in 1799 referring to a particularly severe outbreak of malaria that was causing daily deaths.[71] One of the long-range problems of malaria was that once afflicted, people would suffer recurrent attacks that weakened their resistance to other diseases and their ability to do the required labor.

Even though epidemic disease was widespread and virtually uncontrolled, little or nothing was said or done about the problem. A case in point, Mazagão was afflicted with serious malaria epidemics every year, and settlers there begged for medical aid from nearby Macapá. There was no mention that such aid was ever received. Officials were aware that the area had a severe malaria problem, but did not consider the matter serious enough to warrant attention. It was reported in 1784 that Mazagão was a bad area for malaria, "but in the summer only." After receiving that report and a lengthy report by a visiting surgeon in Mazagão, Governor Albuquerque reported to the court that people in Mazagão "intend to leave under the pretext of continual epidemics and scarcities that they suffer there."[72]

The apparent lack of concern with health matters was largely due to the perception of the problem. Disease was considered an act of God, unpredictable, uncontrollable, and virtually irremediable. The fact that innocuous European diseases such as the common cold or measles could be killers in the New World was not recognized by colonial officials. Furthermore, any material aid would probably have taken so long to reach the afflicted villages that people would either recover or die before help could arrive. Even though the officials of the Directorate were not concerned about providing aid, they were perturbed by the population decline. Yet they did nothing to alleviate the problems of disease in the villages.

The colonial government's attention to education was on a level with its involvement in medical assistance: uneven and ambivalent. The Directorate rules called for the establishment of schools (doutrinas) for the children as part of the general aim of the system to establish Portuguese as the official language, spread the gospel, and minimally educate the Indian children so they might make useful future citizens. The boys were to learn reading and writing and the girls to learn sewing and lacework, and both were to receive religious instruction.[73] The schools functioned in a very limited fashion for short periods and were frequently closed for lack of teachers; for lack of funding, which was to be supplied by the parents, presumably from their share of the forest collecting; and for increased need for the children's labor. Gov. Souza Coutinho said in 1797 that neither the Fazenda Real nor the parents were able to support the schools in the numbers requested by the Directorate.[74]

The age bracket for children attending school was six to ten years. After that age they were expected to work in the communal fields or do small jobs in the village. As the population declined it became necessary to use boys in the forest and river expeditions, and the schools gradually lost their pupils. Boys did accompany the collecting expeditions; as many as a quarter of the people involved in collecting were officially listed as boys (rapazes). In 1773 Gov. João Pereira Caldas reported that so many men had died in Macapá service that they were having to use boys taken out of school.[75]

Education did not have a high priority rating during the Directorate.

The feeling seemed to be that a limited amount of education was a good means of acculturating the Indians through language and religion, but that education was not to interfere with the Indians' provision of labor service and goods from forest collecting and agriculture. The matter of acculturation, for all the lip service paid it in the *Directorio*, was secondary priority in comparison to the need to pull profits from Indian labor. As part of the acculturation and colonization program, education received virtually no attention.

The policies of the Directorate and other attempts at settlement of the Lower Amazon enjoyed minimal success. Although the regulations sounded good on paper, they proved impractical in the face of an unfamiliar and often hostile environment, cultural baggage of those people involved, and other problems of such magnitude. Settlement policy for white settlers suffered nearly as badly as did the Directorate. Problems facing inhabitants of the basin, such as land tenure, were not immediately visible but would cause difficulties later, while disease posed an insurmountable obstacle from the very beginning. Attempts at "civilizing aspects" such as education proved impractical in the face of other, more pressing economic needs. About the only positive thing to be said about Directorate policy was that it prevented total dispersion of the Indian population after the end of the mission system. In all other respects, its policies basically failed to help populate the Lower Amazon Basin.

In terms of settlement and colonization, the Directorate had some measure of success in that it set the spatial, psychological, and methodological patterns for the future. Growing out of the mission system, the Directorate managed not only to maintain and enlarge existing settlements, but also to start a few new nuclei of population. Further, it tied these outposts of civilization together in an economic network centered in Belem and based on the only workable economic activity—gathering wild products while simultaneously encouraging agriculture.

Despite population decline, food shortages, epidemics, runaways, natural disasters, faltering agricultural beginnings, and many other serious problems, the Directorate did settle the basin to a degree not previously attained. Those towns would experience stormy years and hard times ahead in the nineteenth century, but nearly all of them managed to survive, some even to thrive. Their survival despite physical destruction and demographic catastrophe in the Cabanagem revolt, through economic boom and subsequent bust, and then during the continued struggle with disease, poverty, isolation, and natural disaster, can be credited in large part to their solid grounding in the late colonial period.

2

The Economic Basis of Settlement
in the Eighteenth Century

Economic exploitation of available goods from forest and river has been at the root of all penetration and colonization of the Amazon Basin. Thus, a study of colonization and immigration cannot be thoroughly understood without an examination of the economic basis of such settlement. Further, as Stephen Bunker succinctly put it, "each human intervention in the environment transforms it in ways which limit the possibilities of subsequent interventions."[1] Thus, each wave of settlement must deal with the resources depleted by previous generations. Nowhere is this pattern more evident than in the economies of the eighteenth and nineteenth centuries in terms of forest and river gathering and agriculture. At the same time that the social, political, and cultural systems encompass greater potential to attract people to the Amazon, they must face a dwindling supply of natural resources. Such resources range from availability of fish, fauna, and exploitable flora, to scarcities of arable land and problems of drainage.

Indeed, the earliest attempts to conquer and settle the Amazon depleted its most precious resource, the human populations who had lived in basic balance with the ecology for hundreds of years. The decimation of the indigenous population went hand in hand with seventeenth-century attempts by the Portuguese to conquer and claim the region. Despite a multitude of laws sent from Lisbon designed to protect the Indians, the few settlers (*moradores*) managed to raid and enslave whole neighboring populations. Such laws were overlooked with impunity, even as they were constantly rescinded and rewritten.[2] Occasional attempts to befriend local Indians in order to assure a steady supply of plantation labor served only to confuse the situation even more. Add to the casualties of overwork and enslavement the high rate of mortality due to introduced European diseases, and it is easy to see why the Indian population virtually disappeared from areas originally well peopled.[3]

The early settlers primarily focused their attention at first on plantation agriculture near Belem do Pará, founded in 1616 as an outpost against foreign incursion. Such agriculture depended heavily on slave labor, nearly totally supplied by Indians. In fact, there were never enough workers to provide a workforce sufficient to give sugar the foothold it enjoyed on the northeast coast, where planters were able to maintain a steady enough cash flow to be able to import African slaves on a regular basis. Although the Companhia Geral was supposed to import African slaves at reasonable prices, the local planters simply did not have the financial resources to develop a flourishing slave trade in the Amazon. Sugar declined in importance in Pará, and the moradores had to find supplemental sources of income to survive. The answer was cacao and wild clove *(cravo)*, which were gathered as consistently as possible, given the ever-present dearth of labor.[4] Such gathering represented the first concerted effort to extract the lucrative spices and other products from the forest, and in the process depleted easily available supplies.

Another early depletion was that of soil fertility. Although there was an immense amount of land available, even around Belem itself, that fact did not ensure a steady food supply for the European colonists. Because of the fragility of tropical soils, no land could remain in production for any length of time. Slash-and-burn methods of agriculture had served the preconquest populations well because they were not geared toward creating a surplus. When applied to provide food for the small settlement of Belem as well as the local colonists themselves, such agricultural practices began to claim more forest area than ever before.

Labor Problems in the Eighteenth Century

Labor policies set forth in the Directorate were complicated, ambiguous, and observed more in the breach than the compliance. Availability of labor was the most sensitive topic in Portuguese Indian policy, since native inhabitants were somehow expected to exist in a dual role of Luso-Brazilian settlers, near equals with the Europeans, and as a resource exploitable by the Portuguese to perform necessary services to make the fragile economy work. The inherent conflict between those goals meant that the philosophy of benevolent despotism behind the Directorate gave way before the increasing demands of settlers for labor and the need for men to work in royal service.

To solve the labor problem, Indians were to be divided into two groups, one to stay in the village and one to be given to the European settlers for stipulated periods of time for use in agriculture or forest collecting.[5] Thus, half of the able-bodied men aged thirteen to sixty years were to be available to the settlers, while the other half were to perform all other labor and services. The actual selection procedure was left to the discretion of the director, who was supposed to keep updated lists of all males in that age bracket, from which the parceling out of labor levies would be done.[6] The men in service, as listed in the annual reports from each town, were categorized into the following groups: service to local settlers; royal service; fishermen of the officials; men in the *canoa de negocio*, or collecting expeditions; miscellaneous occupations; and those men potentially available for service. All but the first were to be furnished from the 50 percent of the labor force remaining in the villages, which was supposed to furnish the local foodstuffs as well.

The actual number of men assigned in the different types of service varied a great deal, depending on region and period. Based on reports of service sent from directors of individual towns during the 1758–98 period, the "average" village labor list showed nearly one-third of the men serving on collecting expeditions; another quarter in royal service, most commonly rowers on exploratory trips to Mato Grosso; about 15 percent serving Portuguese settlers; and the rest being fishermen or doing miscellaneous duties.

The most confusing and ambiguous regulations in the *Directorio* dealt with payment to Indians for services rendered. For those who worked in royal service on the collecting expeditions, payment was to be made in rolls of cloth, since the Indian was considered incapable of handling money.[7] Wages were usually quoted in terms of cash, then converted to cloth, based on a figure fixed in 1751 and revised in 1773 by Governor Caldas, and salaries were to be held by directors until service was completed.[8] The rate of exchange was set by the General Treasury of the Indians and was skewed to the advantage of the Portuguese rather than the Indians. When the value of the cloth was lowered, the Indians had to produce more cloth than before, as well as work longer periods of time to acquire a small wage.

Settlers were supposed to pay in other goods rather than cash or cloth, though in fact cloth was the usual medium of exchange. They obviously did pay in cloth, as was pointed out by Gov. Souza Coutinho in his 1797 report on the abuses of the Directorate system.[9] Since cloth was the usual form of payment, such a prohibition was nearly impossible to enforce, as other trade goods were hard to acquire and rarely desired by the Indians. Such a system is certainly again reminiscent of the *repartimiento* system in the Spanish New World, where labor was often paid in goods that had no value to the Indians. In any case, it was never made clear just what barter goods were to be used. In fact, trying to prevent settlers from paying either in cash or cloth was probably a way of enforcing the official high rate of exchange, thus limiting the existence of a free wage scale.

Table 2.1. Indian Population, 1777–97

Year	Males	Females	Totals
1770	9,981	10,812	20,794
1773	8,971	10,152	19,123
1783	10,304	11,545	21,849
1784	10,225	11,527	21,752
1791	9,882	10,618	20,500
1792	9,617	10,343	19,960
1793	9,597	10,308	19,905
1794	9,279	10,137	19,416
1797	9,225	10,375	19,600

Sources: Statistical analysis of village reports and following completed censuses: (1) "Mapa de todos os indios e indias, fogos, e de todas as circumstancias que . . . observou o Dr. Intendente geral fez nos anos de 1783 e 1784"; (2) "Mapa de da população dos indios aldeados em todas as povoações da Capitania do Grão Pará no año de 1791"; (3) "Mapa geral da população dos indios aldeados em todas as povoações das Capitanias do Estado de Grão Pará . . . no años de 1792," in J. A. Pinto Ferreira, "Mapa geral da população . . . 1792," V International Colloquium of Luso-Brazilian Studies: Atas (Coimbra, 1963, 1:281–85); (4) "Mapa da população dos indios aldeados em todas as povoações da Companhia do Grão Pará no año de 1793"; (5) "Mapa da população dos indios aldeados em todas as povoações da Companhia do Grão Pará no año de 1794"; (6) "Mapa geral da população do Pará . . . no año de 1797."

The majority of Indians available for labor assignments were most commonly put to work in the *negocio do sertão*, forest and river collecting expeditions, the single most important economic activity within the Directorate. The directors often had trouble getting enough men to staff the collecting expeditions. The Indians were understandably reluctant to work in lengthy laborious expeditions from which they received little compensation. Further, as with most precapitalist peoples, as long as they had access to food and simple necessities, they saw little reason to work the long months involved in the collecting expeditions. Gov. Mello e Castro referred in 1759 to the Indians' "almost unconquerable lack of confidence, [thinking] that the negocio of their village is not theirs."[10] The Indians did not receive the share promised in the Directorio regulations and might have to wait as long as nine years before getting the payment they were allowed.[11] Such delay and neglect was one way of simply not paying the Indians for their labor. Their lack of confidence in promises of a share of the profits from collecting appeared to have been fully justified.

Decline in the Indian labor supply was an economic fact of life between 1757 and 1798. In 1796, near the end of the Directorate, it was estimated that there were only some 19,000 Indians being ministered, in comparison to estimates of roughly 30,000 in 1757.[12] The rate of decline becomes even more significant when considering the *descimentos* that had refilled the downriver villages periodically. The original population of the towns was shrinking, and even the constant arrival of forced migrants could not slow the rapid decline. Table 2.1 shows the results of the few completed censuses and annual head counts.

The general censuses of 1773, 1783, and 1797 showed the total population of all racial groupings, while data are available on the Directorate Indians for several other years. Despite the requirement of yearly population counts, directors were apparently lax in filing such reports as those required on population. There are no general census figures before 1773, although educated guesses are possible when enough individual reports were collected and saved. Using any census material from the Amazon is risky, except as a basis for some generalizations, because population was extremely scattered. The major problem with the Directorate data was not the scattered people but the deliberate hiding of individuals, particularly children, to avoid their being counted.[13] The director of the village of Pombal informed the governor in 1772 that he could not send a population list as he could not count all his charges "because these people have sons and daughters hidden away."[14]

Evidently the most precipitous population decline among Indians occurred before 1770, since the 1770–97 period showed only a gradual drop in numbers, only about twelve hundred people of an estimated decline of eleven thousand. The total population of Pará fluctuated but grew steadily after 1773, although the rise was not due to an increase in the numbers of Indians, but rather among the African slaves and, to a lesser degree, those classified as whites. Both groups showed increases at precisely the time that the Indian population of the Directorate villages was in decline.

It is not too difficult to find evidence for the decline of the Indian population, primarily because depopulation was a matter of some importance to the colonial officials, and superiors expected explanations. Migration in one form or another was a major cause of fluctuation in village size. Because of the importance of the descimentos, directors of individual towns regularly reported the arrival of new groups, the size of which ranged from a single family of less than ten members to some groups as large as thirty-eight people.[15] The governors also sent reports to Lisbon of even larger descimentos, sometimes over a hundred people.[16] Not all descimentos were successful, as was noted from Portel in 1771, when a large group being brought to that town fled and could not be found.[17] Sometimes bad weather, floods, or attacks of disease prevented the conquering troops from bringing new Indians to the towns, but the descimentos remained the principal method of settling new populations where the supposed benefits of Portuguese civilization could reach them.

However, migration flowed in at least two directions, and forced migration had its logical counterpart in desertion and flight, not only of individuals but often whole families and even entire towns. The most common desertions were those from the most onerous tasks assigned to the men in royal service: construction of the fort at Macapá, the woodcutting expeditions, work in the sawmills and shipyards, and the expeditions to Mato Grosso, for which great numbers of rowers were required.[18] The principal causes for desertion were ill treatment, overwork, no pay, no release at the end of the stipulated contracts, and the rampant diseases that swept the camps. The problem of filling vacancies at the same time that the adult labor pool was shrinking was detrimental to the economy of the entire basin, as Gov. João Pereira Caldas pointed out in 1773, "The work at Macapá, the other infinite and heavy services practiced in the time of my predecessor, and the repeated expeditions to Mato Grosso have completely ruined the villages, contributing also to this end [is] the desertion of the Indians, who, dissatisfied and burdened with so much work, easily plunge into the forests, and because of all this there are not enough of them to distribute to the settlers for collecting the spices and goods of the interior, so that only the Indian canoes from their own villages enter into that business."[19] As the situation worsened, it became necessary to draft young boys, and even women, into service in order to meet quotas.

Most of the large-scale desertions (fugas) took place from villages where disease had broken out, whereupon the inhabitants fled into the forest, spreading the contagion far beyond the village itself. Such refugees rarely returned. Either they died in the forest or they elected to remain beyond the direction of colonial administrators.[20]

Reports of individual departures and wholesale flight were far more common than reports of the capture of refugees. Often directors' reports mentioned that certain Indians in their villages were known to be from other towns, but little action accompanied such knowledge.[21] Directors occasionally requested permission to organize hunting expeditions to bring back groups within striking distance.

Once the runaways were returned to their villages, there is little information on their fate, except for those recalcitrants who "come fastened to tree trunks because it is the only means by which one can manage to get them to come."[22] In general, nobody made efforts to capture the refugees unless their numbers were large and were concentrated in one location. Both descimentos and desertions continued throughout the Directorate period.

When Indians fled from the established villages, they did not usually drift into the forest to live a solitary existence but joined one of the many fugitive refuges in the basin.[23] These *mucambos,* usually located deep in the forest and composed of runaway slaves, deserters from the military, and runaway Indians, offered security and community to the escapees and were a constant source of frustration and concern to the colonial officials. The largest and most notorious mucambos were reported on Marajó Island near its center, southeast and east of Bragança near the present Pará-Maranhão border, east of Santarem, and along the borders with the Guianas, especially Cayenne. The Guiana mucambos seemed to worry the Portuguese the most, since the border was unsurveyed and vague. Organized, armed, and unfriendly villages in that area could pose a serious threat to Portuguese hold on the territory.

Mucambos began with only a few families but often grew as large as 150 members.[24] Often they began as one man who provided refuge for fleeing Indians and in turn became hunted himself.[25] In any case, the mucambos were less notable for their size than for their number; there were mucambos reported near almost every settlement having slaves.

Once a mucambo had been identified, especially if its members were raiding crops and villages, efforts were made to capture it. Usually the government received requests for troops in order to return the illegally absent Indians and blacks to their formerly useful existence.[26] Sometimes local Indian officials were enlisted to bring the "mucambados" down in a descimento, as was the case in 1760 when Gov. Mello e Castro described a descimento of sixty-two persons from a mucambo near Cintra, brought by an Indian, "to whom I ordered the title *(patente)* of chief given as reward for his loyalty and the promise of bringing a larger descimento, and I also dressed him at my own expense."[27]

The mucambos, despite their attraction to runaways, did not develop into permanent settlements. Often within a few years a mucambo would disappear because of attack, disease, or simply the migration of its inhabitants. Thus, they were not a form of spontaneous colonization and settlement, but rather served a purpose of temporary sanctuary for the dissatisfied.

Migratory patterns, and desertions in particular, were an important cause of population decline, but reduction of population in the villages occurred for other reasons as well. Disease was a severe problem. The great epidemics that ravaged the basin began shortly after initial contact of European with the indigenous populations, and continued throughout the colonial period. The Directorate system proved an unintentionally fertile ground for germs. Highly susceptible Indians were crowded into towns, in fatal contact with the whites and slaves who often carried diseases to which they were themselves immune. The increasing numbers of slaves brought many cases of infectious disease, particularly smallpox. One epidemic of smallpox in the 1740s reportedly killed thousands of Indians.[28] Smallpox struck all, regardless of ethnic type, but it seemed to have been particularly virulent among the Indians. Malaria, measles, and various respiratory and gastrointestinal illnesses were major diseases that debilitated and killed.

Had the Indians had proper nutrition and not been overworked, they might have better withstood the ravages of disease. However, such was not the case. The directors' reports frequently begged for shipments of *farinha* to prevent famine, but farinha alone is a poor food, being almost entirely carbohydrate, with few vitamins, minerals, or proteins.[29]

Because of declining numbers of Indians and the problems in getting them to perform assigned tasks, alternative labor sources had to be considered and reconsidered. Portuguese settlers were demanding labor for their ranches and their collecting trips, and they were not overly concerned about the origins of that labor. They had wanted to use Indians prior to the Directorate, but the Jesuits had tightly controlled the numbers of laborers available to settlers. Officials of the Overseas Council stated that African labor was the best suited to the situation, but that Indians could be used as a short-term solution until enough slaves could be brought to Pará.

The conclusion implicit in such a policy was that as soon as there were enough slaves to meet the demand for labor, the use of Indians in private service would cease. In fact, the numbers of slaves imported from Africa were never sufficient to meet demand, and the allocation of Indians for private service continued throughout the Directorate period. The Companhia Geral do Grão Pará e Maranhão was given a royal contract to supply African slaves to those provinces, but probably no more than ten thousand slaves were ever destined for the fields and ranches of Pará.[30]

The naturalist Alexandre Rodrigues Ferreira summed up the situation succinctly in 1784, noting that the insufficient quantity and extraordinary prices of slaves made it impossible for most settlers to get the slaves they needed. Consequently, agriculture was suffering greatly because of the shortage of labor. Further, even though slaves were so valuable, they were mistreated severely. Gov. Mello e Castro described various abuses including chains and imprisonment, semistarvation, and severe corporal punishment.[31] Many slaves died shortly after arrival, and the slave population required constant importation to maintain even minimal levels.

Purchase of slaves required a large amount of ready capital in order to be able to outbid the gold miners of Mato Grosso, and therefore only the wealthiest planters and ranchers were able to buy slaves. The men working on a smaller scale, but with aspirations to affluence and influence, were effectively priced out of the slave market. It was a vicious circle, since without slaves they could not produce enough agricultural goods to be able to afford the high price of slaves. Such a situation thus drastically widened the social and economic gap between the two groups. Much of the violence directed against person and property during the Cabanagem revolt in the 1830s had its roots in the antagonisms caused by a small group's increased monopoly on wealth, land, and slaves established in the colonial period. That revolt was one of a number of regional rebellions that broke out in the decade after independence. It began with political squabbling among the Belem elite throughout the 1820s and broke into open race and class warfare in 1835. Most of the action in and around Belem and the few larger towns, such as Cametá and Santarem, was finished within a year, but sporadic violence in the interior lasted until the early 1840s.[32]

Eighteenth-Century Economic Sectors

Throughout the period of 1758 to 1911, one of the most outstanding features of the economy of Pará was the uneven development of its various sectors. The primary sector, divided into forest product gathering, fishing, and agriculture, remained by far the most active part of the overall economy. The secondary, or manufacturing, sector was most notable in its near-total absence. The tertiary, or service, sector developed somewhat briefly during the rubber boom but otherwise remained underdeveloped throughout the period.

The case of the Lower Amazon in the context of Portugal's eighteenth-century empire must be seen as an example of an interface between a parallel set of economic systems. On one hand was a local subsistence economy based on hunting, fishing, gathering, and agricultural activities and reinforced by official directives from Portugal. This subsistence economy provided the basis for settlement and survival of the small clusters of population in the Directorate villages. Additionally there existed an externally oriented economy operating within the larger context of the mercantilist Atlantic world. Given such an emphasis on the primary sector, Portugal never mandated development of the manufacturing sector, and indeed actively discouraged it. Further, the development of services reflected only the need for infrastructure so that Pará could provide its marginally useful products to the mother country.

In keeping with the economic structures of the Portuguese overseas empire, and with the guidance of the Marquis de Pombal and the Overseas Council, economic activity in Pará was primarily oriented toward maximum production for metropolitan luxury markets in Europe. Because of the lack of vast, easily used agricultural lands, such production centered on the extractive sector and only to a lesser degree on agriculture. The table below indicates the amounts of various forest and river products exported from 1773 to 1797.

Agriculture in the eighteenth-century Amazon was sharply divided into two sectors: the plantation and the subsistence farm. The former consisted of large holdings owned by European settlers who produced crops such as sugar and rice for export to Belem, with a labor force composed primarily of African slaves. The latter sector represented the Directorate villages, where individuals raised manioc and other basic crops for local consumption and the villagers tilled a community plot to provide an exportable surplus.

The extractive sector was not so sharply divided. Both villagers under the Directorate supervision and European settlers using Indian labor were collecting products from forest and river. The Directorate Indians worked in a forced labor system; they were told by their directors what economic activities they were to perform, what goods they were to collect, such as salsa, *cravo*, and Brazil nuts, and what their wages would be.[33] There is no evidence to suggest that Directorate Indians had any concept of the marketability or profit margin of the goods they were producing. They could not really be considered to be functioning within a market economy, responding to market incentives, even though the market mechanism for export was functional in Pará at a higher level. Rather, they worked in a simple but limited barter system and rarely if ever saw coined money.[34]

The Indians living in Directorate towns engaged in the export of agricultural products on a much smaller scale than the European plantation owners, both in terms of the crops produced and the markets for which they were intended. The Indians were expected to produce manioc flour (farinha), corn, tobacco, and other crops for the expanding urban market in Belem and for the military outposts. Here, too, management decisions on what to grow, how much to plant, and how much time to allot to agriculture were made by the directors, not the people actually working the fields. The Indians functioned as simple laborers, not as independent small farmers. Local need was often poorly calculated, and frequent food shortages were a major reason why people fled into the forests.

The entire economy of colonial Pará obviously depended on the import-export trade. Even though the financial structures within the captaincy were usually operating on a very limited budget, Pará was not poor

Table 2.2. Export of Extractive Products from Pará, 1773–97

Year	Salsa (arb.)	Brazil Nuts (alq.)	Cravo (arb.)	Tar (arb.)	Cupaiba (alm.)	Sumauma (arb.)	Urucú (arb.)	Andiroba (can.)	Turtle Oil (pote)
1773	2,308	600	2,445	—	—	—	744	—	—
1774	1	920	843	—	—	—	—	—	—
1775	1,147	—	5,032	—	—	—	51	—	—
1776	3,310	—	1,171	—	—	—	75	—	—
1777	3,019	—	176	—	684	—	111	—	—
1778	4,100	44	196	—	1,194	56	103	18	—
1779	3,500	569	1,927	212	307	51	53	2	—
1780	2,788	113	1,121	200	155	33	67	17	—
1781	2,815	39	1,102	—	296	12	41	—	—
1783	2,719	212	1,464	—	200	10	20	—	—
1784	2,789	265	3,075	—	174	101	9	30	—
1785	1,980	46	2,831	—	365	28	28	18	—
1786	1,311	617	1,941	—	494	26	24	6	—
1788	2,335	58	2,691	—	1,861	48	74	—	—
1790	2,946	481	1,696	—	462	44	79	6	24
1792	3,354	406	627	—	188	35	42	—	—
1794	2,296	243	1,514	—	36	10	36	6	—
1796	642	198	1,343	80	64	25	6	—	20
1797	2,160	12	2,375	—	141	3	60	6	—

Source: Statistical Program PARA8N.
arb.: arroba
alq.: alqueire
alm.: almude
can.: canada

in terms of balance of trade. The values of exports from Pará generally exceeded that of manufactures and wines, the principal imports from Lisbon, and of foodstuffs imported from other parts of Brazil. Cargo lists of individual ships calling at Belem in the 1780s and 1790s, though incomplete, give some indication of the types of goods imported. The provincial economy obviously did not supply enough food to feed its urban population in Belem. Sugar was the most common import because local production was far below demand, while tobacco, dried beef *(carne seca)*, and cloth were also frequently imported. In addition the import lists included grinding stones, crockery, heavy-duty cordage, chains and hawsers, leather, salt, iron, and "works of gold"; one ship in 1783 even carried eighty "holy images of saints," presumably for distribution throughout the captaincy.

Lists from the Companhia Geral's ships showed the value of imports broken down into categories. Three such lists provide some insight into relative values. The lists illustrate several points about importation of goods to Pará. By far the greatest value carried was in cloth *(fazenda)*, which in 1775 amounted to more than 75 percent of the total value. Despite the efforts of Pombal to restrict foreign participation in the Brazilian trade, the bulk of the cloth imported to Pará, primarily for use by the Portuguese settlers and soldiers, undoubtedly came from England, sold by British merchants in Lisbon.[35] It would appear that foreign cloth was reappearing in the Pará trade as the company ended its activity in 1778, although later lists do not mention the origin of the cloth. The necessity of importing dried beef underlines the concern in Belem that Marajó ranches could not supply sufficient meat to the capital, a situation still true today.

Salt was a constant item of import despite the fact that there were royal salt pens *(salinas reais)* at Salinas and other salt pens at Cintra and Bragança. The local production of sea salt was in no way capable of supplying enough salt for regular table use, let alone for the important task of salting fish. For example, an average basket of dried fish weighed six to eight *arrobas* (90–120 lbs.), while an average basket of salt fish weighed nine to eleven arrobas (135–165 lbs.). If it took approximately three arrobas (45 lbs.) of salt to process about seven arrobas of fish (105 lbs.), consider the amount of salt required to process the two to three thousand arrobas of fish being produced in Directorate villages each year. Salting was done either by Indians in service to the Crown or by those on the service lists who were supposedly tending their own crops and nets. In 1797 a report from Altar do Chão states that fourteen men and ten boys had finished salting 180 arrobas of fish that was then ready for export. Although the length of time required for the work was not stated, salting fish was clearly a labor-consuming task.[36] In addition to larger fish, the Portuguese also used salt to process mullet, manatee, and beef. Even on the basis of export production alone, obviously large quantities of salt were needed each year.

Gov. Mello e Castro pleaded for greater imports of salt in 1761, referring to "the miserable condition which some villages were in for lack of the staple," which made life hard and restricted commerce. He noted that Portugal had a great abundance of salt, but so little was sent to Pará that it had to be rationed, and he requested that all ships carry a "larger portion of that ballast which sells for such a good price here."[37]

Eighteenth-Century Extractive Economy

Collection and production of certain goods from the Directorate villages were the cornerstone of the export economy. One of the more striking aspects that emerges from export lists from the individual villages is the regional diversity of forest and river goods, reflecting the varying ecosystems of the area. Villages in some regions specialized in forest goods, others in river products, and several had very little extractive industry but seemed to devote more attention to agriculture. A classification of the regions revealed that the forest extractive areas were those of the Amazonas, Xingú, Furos, and Tapajós; river extractive regions were Marajó and the Estuary, and the nonextractive areas were the Tocantins, Guajará, and the coast.[38]

Directorate Indians collected vast numbers of extractive products, and the manner of collecting varied little during the colonial period. In any case, extractive products provided the economic base for settlement in several areas of the province. The products most often found in the annual negocio, or collecting, reports were: salsa, Brazil nuts (castanha), and cravo fino and cravo grosso, the "fine" and "coarse" designations referring to the extent to which the clovelike spice had been reduced from rough bark to finished spice. Also included under forest extractive goods were ship caulking materials (estopa), from various tree barks, most notably the Brazil nut tree, and tar for ships (breu). There were also many other products found less frequently, such as aromatic oils from the andiroba (Carapa guyanensis), cupaíba (Copahifera officinalis), and sumaúma (Ceiba petrandra) trees, miscellaneous oils (azeites), and wild pork (carne do porco do mato). Skins of the spotted jaguar (onça) and deer were rarely mentioned and were usually sent as special gifts to Lisbon, along with occasional live monkeys and birds. The turtle oil was sent in pots (potes) officially measuring 15.7 liters. The export of cupaíba oil was in almudes, another prestandardization unit of liquid measure, equal of roughly 32 liters. The andiroba oil, rather than being consolidated, was broken into smaller units and shipped in *canadas*, roughly 2.5 liters each.

As would be expected in a water-dominated area, fish and other aquatic animals made up an important part of the regional economy. Fish were either dried or salted (*peixe seco, peixe salgado*, or *peixe de salmoura*), except for the smaller fish, such as mullet (*tainha*), which villagers sent to Belem fresh by the basket. Turtles were usually shipped live; more rarely the meat was dried or salted locally. Most of the turtles were the large aquatic *tartaruga*, although there were reports of *jabutí*, a land variety. A major article of commerce was turtle oil (*manteiga de tartaruga*), made from the yolks of turtle eggs and used for cooking and lighting. Meat and rendered fat from the manatee (*peixe boi*) were occasionally sent, as was fried fish and *mixira* (fish, turtle, or manatee meat preserved in its own oil). Baskets of live crabs were sent to Belem for local consumption only. Because of the basic orientation of the extractive activities, little attention was ever given to the danger of overexploitation of any species involved in export. The Amazon was regarded as a gigantic and inexhaustible warehouse of wonders, and very few people seemed concerned about species extinction.

In fact, three economically valuable species in eighteenth-century Pará were placed in serious jeopardy: salsa, cravo, and turtles.[39] The Amazonas region exported the greatest portion of salsa, with the Tapajós River villages and the Furos settlements close behind in production. Somewhat less was taken from the Xingú region, but enough to indicate that salsa was extensively exploited in black-water and white-water river areas alike. Normally only the berries were collected, but with constant demand for the refreshing and supposedly curative powers of the drink made from them, the root was also used. Since taking the root involved killing the plant, the species became increasingly hard to find. In 1785 the following report was filed from Almeirim: "As the collectors from the interior tell us, this salsa is not the fruit of a tree as in other years, but rather the root of a plant. It is necessary to pull it out to take the root. . . . It seems to me that the same collectors said that the next year's collection will be small, if they can even find the plant, because the forest is well cleared of it, except on the Rio Jarí, where they say there is great abundance, because the area is large and confusing, and one cannot go there without a guide."[40]

The export figures after 1782 show a pronounced drop in the quantities of salsa from Amazonas, while the other three regions do not show a corresponding drop. It would seem likely, therefore, that the primary area of salsa production declined in favor of other areas where the plant grew but had not been exploited quite so efficiently. In areas where forest collection was relatively unimportant, no salsa collection was reported, leading to the tentative conclusion that its distribution was essentially limited to the forest-extractive regions. Cravo was the only forest product that figures even minimally in areas where extractive industry was not the principal activity.

Cravo was exported in greatest quantity from areas where salsa was not collected, the Furos and Tapajós and Xingú Rivers. Amazonas did not produce nearly as much cravo as other regions and frequently reported no export of the article. It too was subject to excessive collecting; the product itself was made from the bark of a tree, and when care was not taken to leave enough bark on the tree, it died from girdling. Cravo was a valuable product, with the bark much in demand, so that the most common inclination was to strip the trees. As in the case of salsa, each year the collection expeditions had to go farther and farther in search of cravo, thus leading to longer expeditions and less labor available locally for agriculture. There was no pronounced downward trend in cravo export in any region, as there was with salsa, so perhaps the elimination of the species did not proceed as rapidly.

The unrestricted exploitation of turtles was the most notorious case of species annihilation in the Amazon Basin. What the bison was to the North American Indians, the fifteen or more varieties of turtles were to the Amazonian Indians.[41] The river turtles furnished a nutritious and tasty meat, fat for cooking, shells for containers, bones for utensils and decorations, and myriad eggs for making turtle oil for light and cooking. It was the fine quality of the fat and oil that caused the overexploitation of the species. A naturalist traveling in the area in the 1780s, Alexandre Rodrigues Ferreira, noted that slaughter of the animals for their fat resulted in considerable waste of the meat, which was thrown into the water for "sustenance of buzzards, alligators, and fishes such as the piranha," a squandering reminiscent of the slaughter of the bison for their hides on the North American plains.[42]

Slaughter of adult specimens was extensive, but the collection of eggs for oil was far more damaging to the reproduction of the species. In October, the canoes would set out for the beaches along the Amazon and its southern tributaries in Pará, where the turtles laid their eggs. By far the greatest turtle beds were upriver in the Capitania de São José do Rio Negro, but turtles, their meat and oil, were also exported in quantity from Pará towns. Each turtle would lay one hundred to two hundred eggs in a sandy nest, which would be completely emptied by the adept hunters. It took about eleven nests to furnish one pot of oil. According to Ferreira, an average collection from one canoe of hunters in the Rio Negro captaincy was a thousand pots, with the amount doubled in good years.[43] In Pará the quantities were probably not quite that high, but several hundred pots were exported annually from the Amazonas and Furos and only a little less from the Tapajós and Xingú regions. Very little turtle oil or meat was collected from the other regions, although numerous live turtles were shipped from Marajó to Belem in the late 1760s and early 1770s.

Alexandre Rodrigues Ferreira was one of the very few who recognized the need for at least a minimum of protection of the turtles, but his advice went unheeded. In 1796 he pointed out the need for some protection since the eggs and offspring were used so wastefully and it took several years for a turtle to reach maturity.[44] He foresaw considerable decline unless such rampant overexploitation ceased, although from the available data it appears that the decline was already precipitous by the 1780s. No action was taken to control turtle slaughter, and today turtles are extremely scarce where once they numbered in the thousands.

Overexploitation was not recognized as a dangerous economic practice, for all forest and river products appeared to have been considered as renewable resources no matter how much they were exploited. Village directors were aware, however, that overdependence on one product was unwise, since it drove prices down and meant that a village concentrating labor in only one endeavor would not be able to supply food in times of emergency. Thus, to a limited degree the law of the marketplace operated to provide minimal protection, but in general, the economic policy of the Directorate did exploit some resources beyond their ability to reproduce.

It is somewhat difficult to ascertain definitively the amounts of different goods that were sent from the Directorate villages to Belem, and from there to Lisbon. Turtle oil, caulk, and tar were all used within the state, since there was a royal shipyard in the estuary and they were not articles of export. In an area where transportation was by water, manufacture and repair of boats could well have used all the tar and caulking that could be provided. Caulking materials came from all four extractive areas, with a slight emphasis on Amazonas, and each year showed some export, even if in small quantity. Most of the tar used in shipbuilding and repair came from Amazonas and only rarely from other regions.

Species distribution of both fauna and flora contributed to the regional diversity of the economy. In the colonial period nearly all Brazil nuts came from along the Amazon and the northern tributaries, the Rio Jari and Rio Trombetas.[45] Average yield of a tree was estimated at six to eight *alqueires* of nuts, an alqueire being roughly 13.8 liters. Since collection of the nuts did not involve destruction of the tree, Brazil nut production did not require increasingly long expeditions, nor was it as environmentally harmful as other forest gathering. In the case of salsa, Brazil nuts, cravo, and cupaíba, all were articles of export. Salsa export greatly exceeded Directorate production, and because of the consistency of the figures, it seems likely that the discrepancies resulted from the fact that other settlers were collecting over half of the salsa. The bulk of cupaíba oil came from the Xingú and Amazonas. With cravo, Brazil nuts, and cupaíba oil there was no pattern to the export figures in relation to the figures from the villages.

All of the Indians' export production was supposed to be delivered to the General Treasury of Commerce of the Indians, where it was listed and stored until ships were available to transport it to Lisbon. Since fairly extensive storage facilities were available, the most logical explanation for the fact that the export figures were often lower than the volume of incoming goods would center around storage. Perhaps dependent on space on outward-bound ships and on market demand and price in Europe for specific articles, some of the incoming negocio goods were stored until the following year. Brazil nuts, cravo, and cupaíba were all relatively durable products that could withstand storage if conditions were not too wet. Warehousing could thus explain the fluctuations, with exports exceeding incoming goods and vice versa in different years, since in the latter case the goods were stored and in the former case the annual production plus the stored surplus was shipped.

Fishing was probably the single most important economic activity that supported settlement throughout Pará. Salted and dried fish were exported from Directorate villages all over Pará, but the bulk of it came from Marajó, with its excellent interior fishing waters in the area around Lake Ararí, the innumerable channels of the Furos, the estuary between Belem and the coast, and the Tapajós River. Export from the Amazonas and Xingú was moderate and highly fluctuating, but the Guajará and Tocantins regions showed very limited export. Evidently ocean fishing was not a developed activity, because only a few arrobas of fish were exported from coastal areas. A number of different species of fish were sought, but the most prized and sought after was the giant *pirarucú* (*Arapaima gigas*, Cuvier, 1829).[46]

Fishing was a seasonal activity, since yields were much higher when the water was lower, the "*estação de vazante*," when the pirarucú were plentiful. Towns usually had fishing beaches (*ribeiras*) and the unlucky village which did not have easy access to good fishing could experience serious difficulties in supplying adequate protein sources for its residents. There were also royal fisheries (*pesqueiros reais*), one in Rio Negro on Carirí Island just downstream from the confluence of the Rio Solimões and Rio

Negro, and one in Vila Franca in Pará. The Vila Franca fishery was created in 1783 to meet the needs of the area, where there was reportedly an abundance of fish to catch but a shortage of fish for sale.[47] The fisheries were sometimes run by the government using Indians in royal service; at other times they were contracted out to Europeans who used Indian labor in private service (serviço de moradores).[48]

Collections from rivers and lakes varied regionally according to species distribution. Manatee meat and oil came from white-water areas, primarily the Amazonas and Furos, with several hundred arrobas exported in some years. Only minimal amounts came from the Tapajós and Xingú, and none was exported from other parts of Pará. Crabs and mullet distribution was almost the exact opposite from that of manatee. The only significant areas of export of crabs were Marajó and the Estuary, each region exporting 500–4,000 cofos, or baskets, each year. Mullet production was also centered on Marajó and the Estuary, with a few cases of export beyond those areas.[49]

Undoubtedly part of the reason for the strong regional affiliation was species distribution, but equally important was the mode of preparation; crabs and most mullet were shipped fresh to Belem in small amounts. Because of the rapid spoilage rate, the fresh meat could be kept only a short time, definitely restricting the travel time and distance that could be covered. Villagers fished "in common," and there was relatively little private export of fresh fish. The 1777 report from Monsarás listed the export from the village's fishing as 11,000 dried mullet, 13 baskets of fish, 19 baskets of salt fish, 240 baskets of crabs, and 28 alqueires of ash. This list was a representative sample of output from the villages on Marajó.[50] The basket, like the pot, was a unit of varying size. The average weight of a basket of fish was five to ten arrobas, depending on whether it was salt, dried, or fresh. A basket of crabs was roughly equivalent to three cofos.

Eighteenth-Century Agriculture

Both Directorate officials and the European settlers used Indians to participate in the extractive economy, and there were no noticeable differences between goods collected by those two groups. In the agricultural sector, however, there were marked contrasts between the crops and animals raised in Directorate villages and on the plantations and ranches. The Indian villages focused on production of basic foodstuffs such as farinha, the dry lumpy flour made from the root of the poisonous manioc (Manihot utilissima), and rice, with perhaps a bit of cotton or tobacco as a cash crop. The plantations were oriented strongly toward monoculture of export crops such as cacao, coffee, sugar, and rice. The ranches provided some beef and a steady supply of hides for local use and export. Table 2.3 indicates quantities of agricultural goods exported from Pará from 1773 to 1797.

Land held by the Portuguese and Creoles was usually assigned by grants of *sesmaria*. These grants consisted of large blocks of land measured by frontage along a watercourse and extending back for a stipulated distance. Sesmarias were granted primarily around Belem, on Marajó, along the coast from Belem to Vigia and near either fortress towns or Directorate villages.[51] The rich bottomland soils were put into plantation crops, but the uplands were generally unused except for gathering of forest products. On Marajó, land grants were used almost entirely for extensive cattle ranching. Many ranches were created out of the division and sale of the enormous Jesuit properties confiscated after expulsion of the Order in 1757. In general, there does not appear to have been much subsistence, small-plot farming by the Europeans. Belem was dependent on food from the Indian villages and the large ranches and farms and on the importation of foodstuffs from Portugal. It was an unstable market situation at best, and during years of bad floods or farinha shortages it became exceedingly difficult. The governors' letters constantly referred to the lack of food, particularly meat, for the capital.[52]

Cacao was without doubt the most important agricultural export item.[53] The value of cacao in total exports between 1730 and 1822 rarely fell below 50 percent. Some of the cacao exported was wild (*cacao bravo*), but no distinction was made in the export lists. It was grown largely by the European settlers, although references to cacao groves (*cacoais*) in Directorate villages indicate some production there. One likely reason for the relative unimportance of cacao in Indian villages was that it required constant care in weeding, tilling, and general care. The labor force allowed to remain in the villages was probably too small to be able to devote intensive care to such a crop. For whatever reason, of the 117 agricultural reports filed by directors in the 1770s, 1780s, and 1790s only 6 are on cacao plantings. After 1770, when government officials were encouraging its cultivation, production remained relatively higher, perhaps indicating greater cultivation in Directorate villages.

Cacao production was definitely regionally oriented. No cacao production was recorded from the coast, estuary, or Guajará, and only minute amounts of wild cacao on Marajó and the Tocantins. The Furos was definitely the most important region, exporting almost twice as much cacao as that sent from the Tapajós, Xingú, and Amazonas Rivers. In the 1760s roughly half of the cacao collected from Directorate villages came from the Furos, although the relative share dropped sharply after 1769. Marajó

Table 2.3. Export of Agricultural Goods from Pará, 1773–97

Year	Cacao (arb.)	Rice (alq.)	Farinha (alq.)	Sugar (arb.)	Molasses (alm.)	Liquor (alm.)	Coffee (arb.)	Cotton (arb.)	Indigo (lb.)	Hides (unit)
1773	58,784	935	—	—	—	869	4,273	—	—	—
1774	4,112	7,163	—	—	—	55	141	60	—	—
1775	72,908	19,480	—	—	—	1,479	4,468	21	18	4,700
1776	58,407	27,872	—	—	—	1,987	5,792	889	23	6,607
1777	69,007	40,346	—	9	—	1,675	3,542	2,053	66	8,840
1778	60,152	29,473	284	28	856	1,588	6,579	3,422	33	4,577
1779	57,884	89,236	718	64	580	423	4,513	5,158	5	14,711
1780	60,396	107,253	190	18	835	48	3,122	4,912	—	12,350
1781	40,490	96,761	117	5	166	—	2,838	8,572	—	11,647
1783	42,710	72,177	73	—	354	47	1,676	7,126	—	11,974
1784	100,777	118,605	40	6	331	334	1,796	6,608	—	16,102
1785	67,425	84,681	77	4	236	413	1,684	4,909	65	14,765
1786	84,129	83,849	51	12	152	84	1,282	3,795	—	16,525
1788	66,353	85,521	79	4	273	180	2,250	5,718	1	17,610
1790	77,611	68,807	224	4	137	374	3,539	7,060	7	23,714
1792	52,524	120,539	46	27	346	1,360	3,392	8,569	69	41,351
1794	79,722	103,503	37	4	155	8	2,812	7,832	—	22,450
1796	54,906	44,383	7	5	72	—	3,754	6,535	58	21,112
1797	122,526	90,171	37	—	66	181	3,576	8,233	59	13,887

Source: Statistical Program PARA8N.

arb.: arroba
alq.: alqueire
alm.: almude
lb.: libra

and the Xingú were producing a greater share until the late 1790s, when the Furos resumed first place.

Coffee was first planted in Pará, and for that matter in Brazil, in 1727 with seeds brought from Cayenne, with first export to Lisbon in 1732. The Pará fleet in 1750 carried 4,835 arrobas of coffee to Lisbon, about one hundred tons.[54] The level of exports varied considerably after 1773, indicating that coffee was not a booming, expanding crop but simply one that remained in steady production. The Directorate villages provided a small part of that export after 1773, but most coffee came from groves owned by Europeans.

The agricultural reports from the Directorate villages indicate more instances of coffee groves than cacao groves, with the number of trees varying from 400 in Ourem to 15,600 in Vila Franca. Most of the coffee was planted on uplands and was generally interplanted with shade trees.[55] There were very few references to trouble in growing the crop, so probably coffee was a moderately profitable crop that could be cultivated fairly easily. The coffee produced in Pará was used primarily for local consumption, however, and relatively little of the coffee sent from Brazil to Lisbon ever came from the Amazon.

Rice was grown in village and plantation alike. Native wild rice was used for local consumption, but serious export began after introduction of Carolina White rice in 1772.[56] The first year of export in 1773 showed only a small quantity, but in two years the export of rice had increased twentyfold. Much of the exported rice came from the plantations of the Lower Tocantins, where daily flooding due to tides provided an ideal growing situation. Rice was also strongly favored as a subsistence and export crop in the Indian villages, and a great many villages had separate rice fields *(arrozais)*, or grew rice in the community plot *(roça comum)*. Governor Caldas had high hopes in 1777 that rice would come to replace farinha as a staple, which was habitually in short supply.[57] He noted in passing that the Macapá area was producing 20,000 alqueires of rice that year.

Substantial amounts of rice were also produced in the Furos, Tapajós, and Amazonas regions. Marajó and the Xingú River also exported rice, although not on the scale of the Furos. Along the upriver section of the Tocantins there was some export from Directorate villages, but only a very little from the coast and estuary. The years 1774, 1782, and 1784 were evidently good harvests, and the exports for those years were high.

Farinha was, and still is, the basic staple of the Amazonian diet, and it was a major article of internal trade in Pará. Its export was never important to Europe or elsewhere in the colonial period, since it commanded a

Table 2.4. Tithing and Farinha Production in Alqueires by Region, 1758–98

Region	People Tithed*	Average Tithe Per Person	Total Individual Tithe Paid	Roça Comum Tithes**	Total Tithes Paid (Yr. Avg.)
Amazonas	390	1.0677	416.1	240.9 (22)	657.0
Tapajós	455	1.0147	461.7	275.5 (11)	737.2
Xingú	393	1.4062	552.8	171.3 (15)	724.1
Tocantins	450	1.1667	525.0	no data	insufficient data
Furos	377	1.0405	392.6	366.7 (03)	759.3
Marajó	379	1.2089	458.3	78.3 (06)	536.6
Guajará	233	1.4145	330.0	40.0 (01)	370.0
Estuary	396	1.0182	402.9	225.0 (08)	627.4
Coast	300	1.2883	386.1	293.3 (03)	679.4
Pará	375	1.1868	434.2	211.4 (69)	636.4

Source: Statistical Program PARA6N.
*Average number of people tithed per year per region for selected years.
**Numbers in parentheses refer to number of observations.

relatively low price, had virtually no market in Europe, and was produced for local consumption almost everywhere in Brazil. Further, production was frequently insufficient to supply local needs and demand
from Belem. Governor Caldas reported a severe shortage of farinha in
Belem in 1773, and the 1773–74 year was particularly bad as reports of
similar shortages came in from widespread areas.[58]

There is little if any correlation between areas of high production in
private plots and high production in the community plot. The wide fluctuation in figures could be due to variations in yield or, more likely, the
whim of reporting officials. Yields on private plots were remarkably similar, regardless of what region the plots were located. Much of the time,
Indians were barely producing more than that required for minimum local consumption.

Production from the community plot was not generally used for local
consumption. It was assessed the tithe and the director's one-sixth, and
the remainder was used for provisioning collecting expeditions, the Mato
Grosso explorations, and the garrisons, with any surplus being sent to
Belem. People who had to depend on their own plots therefore had little
emergency surplus stored away, and a bad year could bring famine un-
comfortably near. Table 2.4 shows farinha production from the different
regions of Pará during the Directorate years.

Communal efforts in agriculture centered on the community plot and
the rice field and cotton patch. Mixed cropping in the communal plot was
normal, the most common crops being at least two varieties of manioc
(designated as maniva and mandioca, sweet and bitter manioc respec-
tively), rice, corn, cotton, and more rarely beans and tobacco. Most such

plots were of medium size, from 100 to 200 square *braças* (roughly 50,000 to 200,000 square meters). Most plots would produce in six to eight months from planting time.

Clearing, planting and cultivation, and harvesting were clearly divided on the basis of gender roles. Men invariably did the clearing and burning, after which the women did the rest of the work, often divided into separate teams for planting and harvesting. With such a division of labor, men could be more easily be diverted to labor in the collecting expeditions. In thirty-four reports on agriculture, men composed only 39 percent of the labor force involved in the community plot and rice field. One report from Alenquer gave an approximation of the man days required to bring a medium plot to harvest; it took 72 man days to clear the plot and 248 woman days to plant and tend it.[59]

Both floodplain and upland were used for cropping, and each presented problems. The most serious difficulties facing those farming the uplands were drought and pest infestation. Drought occurred if there was insufficient rainfall, since plots were located away from riverbanks. Pests included rats, lizards, wild pigs, and especially saúva ants.[60] Because of the persistence of such problems, the Indians preferred to concentrate agricultural efforts on the várzea.

Floodplain agriculture was not exempt from pests; moreover, there were problems of drainage and shortage of space, since available land was determined by water level. In low flood years, yields would be lower due to decreased fertility.[61] Raids by marauding tribes were detrimental to agriculture no matter where it was located. The Mundurucú raids in the 1790s made it almost impossible for directors to get their charges to plant crops or collect forest goods.[62]

Corn and cotton were planted in the community plot, but they rarely appeared in the production records. Corn production was spread thinly across all regions, with the exception of the Tocantins. The estuary and Amazonas had the largest and most constant exports, but even there the export lists showed many years without any corn to send to Belem. Most of the cotton, which was exported in the bole, with or without seeds, came from the Tapajós, Xingú, and Furos, with only small amounts from other areas. There was also some export of cotton thread and, of course, the rough cotton cloth used to pay the Indian wages.

African slaves cultivated sugar on plantations owned by white settlers, and sugar was not found elsewhere. Earlier experience had taught Europeans that Indians were ill suited to large-scale agriculture, frequently fleeing whenever possible. Directorate Indians grew no sugar and were rarely drafted to work in the cane fields. Production of raw sugar had increased until export from the province was interdicted to eliminate competition with Bahian producers.[63] Most local production of sugar in Pará was converted to molasses or alcohol, which was then occasionally exported or more commonly consumed locally. Sugar consumption in Pará was generally confined to imported sugar from Bahia. Sugar plantations tended to be self-sufficient units involved in production of various foodstuffs and exports. Plantations on Marajó also produced bricks and tiles, pottery, cotton, farinha, rice, beans, corn, and alligator oil, in addition to sugar, molasses, and liquor *(aguardente)*.[64]

Cattle ranching fits into nearly identical patterns with sugar. Cattle ranches were not connected with Indian villages, even when located nearby. Indian villages rarely contained any large livestock such as cattle. Beef was important in local markets, although it was never sufficient to supply Belem, and hides were the only item of export of any quantity or value from the ranches. As noted earlier, nearly all the cattle ranches of any size were on Marajó. The *contemplado* grants awarded after expropriation of the Jesuit ranches and the later dissolution of the Mercedarian *fazendas* in 1794 added numerous privately owned fazendas to the rolls.[65] The herds were vast, widely scattered, and largely untended. The Jesuit herds at the time of confiscation were estimated at 134,465 head. The Mercedarian herds were estimated at 70,000 head at the time of confiscation in 1794. Their value was dependent on the market for meat, hides, and tallow, and on low labor costs.

The labor force on the ranches was composed of both African slaves and Indians supplied in private service. Two sets of fazenda reports in 1762 show that most fazendas using Indian labor had between two and nine Indians working, with only a few instances of greater numbers.[66] The principal work performed was the annual roundup *(vaquejada)* and slaughter of animals for dried and salted meat. Evidently dried beef was preferred, but in times of extensive flooding, salt beef was made, probably because of the inability of the workers to dry meat under very humid conditions. When flood conditions were bad, as they were in 1794, cattle were simply abandoned to their own resources, and roundups, tally, and branding ceased.[67] Under such conditions, the cattle industry could not, and did not, profit and grow. Hides could be taken, and their export would increase after bad years, particularly droughts, but dried and salted beef, which would have commanded better prices, were not produced.

Aside from the cattle fazendas, there was relatively little livestock production in Pará. Indian villages reported pigs and goats, and occasionally a few cows and horses, but in numbers rarely exceeding a total of one

hundred head for the entire village. Thus, whereas there were some substantial herds of cattle and hides were a bulky part of the area's export,
ranching and small-scale livestock production were not closely tied to the
economy of the Directorate.

As should be obvious from the description of the principal economic
activities and resultant exports, Indian males living under the Directorate
were engaged chiefly in the collection of forest and river products, and
their women contributed much less income from agriculture. Indian labor
was thus confined almost exclusively to the primary sector of the economy, and there was not much delving into home industry. Any existing
manufacturing was controlled by royal monopoly. The sawmills and
boatyards, the spinning of cotton thread and weaving of cotton cloth, the
manufactures of pots, bricks, and tiles were all worked by Indians in royal
service and managed by overseers. Although part of the general regional
commerce, such goods were not generally included in negocio reports but
were shipped separately to Belem, from where they were distributed
within the captaincy. There was virtually no regional specialization in
manufactured articles, nor were competing attempts at manufacture in
the private sector encouraged.

The organization of the economy during the Directorate years functioned efficiently and would have some longstanding effects. The economy of the colonial period after the end of the Directorate in 1798 continued in the same fashion for a few years until independence. The ending of
economic directive from an outside source, formerly Lisbon, combined
with the unrest and eventual destruction during the Cabanagem revolt in
the 1830s, disrupted the economy of Pará until the 1850s.

When signs of economic stability reappeared in the mid-nineteenth
century in the form of increased production and a rising population, there
were still vestiges of the extractive and agricultural economy that would
form the basis for a similar system during the rubber boom. Those economic bases in the nineteenth century both functioned as components of
a market structure but as polarized entities with relatively little interaction. The colonial patterns of emphasis on export and import rather than
the development of local competition with imports, and of a priority put
on the extractive economy as more profitable than the agricultural economy, would both be continued in the national period.

3

The Elites and Their Role in Colonization

The makeup of the elite class underwent a major structural change at the beginning of the nineteenth century. Because of those changes and the concomitant adjustments in their special interests, particularly economic concerns, the elite of Pará also took on new activities relating to settlement of the province.

The Nineteenth-Century Context of Immigration and Colonization

For half a century after the abolition of the Directorate in 1798, neither Portugal nor Brazil had an effective settlement policy for the Amazon Basin. Shortly before Brazil's political independence in 1822, the Belem elite began a heady orgy of political temper tantrums, pitting Portuguese against Creole in petty politicking that eventually broke into the open warfare known as the Cabanagem revolt.[1] The political rhetoric and vitriol did not reflect fundamental social or economic differences between the participants but simply questions of political method and the spoils of office. However, by engaging numbers of the semifree peasants and detribalized Indians of the region (known as *caboclos*), workers, and marginal small farmers to do the physical fighting, the elite foretold their own destruction. In 1835, when the lower class eventually rose in rebellion against the men they perceived as authority figures, a good many individuals of the ruling class died violent deaths.

Most of the fighting and destruction during the Cabanagem took place in and around Belem, but outbreaks of violence occurred all over the basin. It was a localized rebellion over local issues, with limited ideological scope that spread over an immense territory. It was not a revolt with a clear agenda or purpose, but the violence was often a matter of personal grudges and vendettas. The caboclos struck out against those individuals whom they saw as having wealth and power over them, most often being those of European ancestry. Although not clearly defined enough to be called race and class warfare, the Cabanagem was definitely a war between the haves and have-nots. The elite class suffered serious losses, as many died during the shelling of Belem or disappeared after fleeing the city.

When most of the fighting had ended by 1836, the survivors from the elite class slowly reestablished their economic control of the basin. In time, they would again guide the reins of economic growth, but they remained extremely cautious about their relationship with the caboclos. As the issue of colonization and settlement of new areas became a major topic of debate, the residual fear of the violent potential of the caboclos may well have been one reason for the decision to bring foreign immigrants rather than resettle and subsidize the native *paraenses*. The elites had no intention of allowing the caboclos any opportunity for advancement.

The situation during the 1830s was not unique to Pará. The years of the First Empire, under the rule of Dom Pedro I (1822–31), were politically tumultuous. Regional revolts like Pará's Cabanagem were widespread, some of them, like the Faroupilha in southern Brazil, requiring years to suppress. Those years were also economically uncertain as a newly independent country learned its position within the Atlantic community. Thus, it was not surprising that Pedro I spent very little attention or money on the issue of settlement policy, least of all in the Amazon. Those few settlements established in southern Brazil prior to 1831 were all created in response to specific situations and not as part of any long-range government plan to encourage immigration.[2] For example, immediately after independence was declared, the government made plans to bring Germans to settle in southern Brazil to secure its occupation and provide troops to prevent incursions from the Rio de la Plata region. Through the 1820s, more such mercenary soldiers/settlers arrived from Germany, Switzerland, and elsewhere to settle in southern Brazil, but local resentment of the foreigners and a mutiny among the troops put an end to the experiment. The halfhearted efforts to attract immigrants to Brazil had provoked considerable criticism both in Brazil and in the donor countries, and in 1830 the imperial government abolished all expenditures on foreign immigration.[3]

Under the regency (1831–40), even less attention was paid to immigration and colonization. The primary concern of the imperial government was to hold the empire together during a period of severe political and economic disruption and civil war in numerous, widely separated provinces. In the case of Pará, the worst of the violence and destruction of the Cabanagem occurred during the regency, along with the final subjugation of the rebels. During the regency, Pará's elites were more concerned with survival than settlement.

A trickle of immigrants did continue to arrive in Brazil during the regency, but their numbers did not even approach those of the First Empire.[4] The regency government passed a few laws and decrees to facilitate immigration, should it become economically and politically feasible when peace was restored in the empire. The new legislation included a naturalization law (1832), authorization for provinces to finance immigration separately from the imperial government, a rebate on anchorage fees for ships bearing immigrants (1835), and permission for formation of patriotic societies for purposes of encouraging immigration (1835).[5]

The political situation became much quieter after the ascension of Dom Pedro II to the imperial throne in 1840, but immigration to Brazil did not markedly increase until the 1850s. In Pará, by about midcentury enough recovery had taken place that interest in settlement had begun to rekindle among the local elites. The demographic losses during the Cabanagem were extremely heavy, as much as 20 percent of the population; the labor pool had shrunk noticeably; and food supply to Belem had become a continual problem.

As yet, there was relatively little movement at the national level to encourage immigration aggressively. Nor were foreign governments particularly interested in encouraging their citizens to depart for Brazil. The continued existence of slavery and the absence of a land law delineating areas for colonization were frequently cited as the principal causes for the lack of interest in emigration from Europe to Brazil. Further, until civil war and internal conflicts were over, Brazil did not look very attractive as a new home. Finally, until midcentury there was little in the way of "push factors" present in Europe that could dislodge population and make them willing to emigrate.

Government involvement in actively promoting and assisting both immigration and colonization became more evident during the Second Empire under the leadership of Dom Pedro II. However, throughout almost the entire period, commitment of the national government to settlement programs remained limited in terms of financial support and regional concentration. Little was done until after abolition of the slave trade and passage of the Land Law in 1850 and the 1861 law regularizing Protestant marriages and making it possible to register non-Catholic births and deaths. The first monies for immigration were made available in 1842, but the imperial government made it clear from the beginning that it would not bear the burden of bringing people to Brazil. In time that attitude softened a bit, but free passage for potential citizens was not part of the package.

An increasing interest in immigration and colonization at the national level was focused on settlement in southern Brazil, but in Pará programs to settle and effectively occupy the forest only limped along for many years. The guidelines established in Rio de Janeiro served as the basis for much of the provincial legislation regulating immigration and colonization in Pará. Yet, because of the high cost of immigration and settlement programs during the empire, only programs financed by the imperial government could hope for success. Individual provinces, even increasingly wealthy ones like Pará, simply did not have sufficient revenues for such undertakings. Rising export revenues from rubber shipments did not add much to Pará's coffers anyway, since most of the money went to the central government.

Much of the interest generated in Pará over immigration and colonization during the empire was due to the "demonstration effect" from southern Brazil, which provided the impetus to develop such policies. However, for roughly thirty years the Amazon remained a peripheral area regarded by imperial authorities as of little value. The shift of central power from Lisbon to Rio de Janeiro did not affect attitudes concerning the importance of the Amazon. The national government did not want to relinquish the area to foreign control, nor did it see any reason to spend any money on it either. Change in that attitude would not come until the 1880s, when rubber began to command real respect as an income producer for the government. Even then, the imperial government appeared to be far more interested in collecting their export tax revenues than in helping develop the area.

The revolution of 1889 had a greater impact on colonization in Pará than had independence or the ascension of Pedro II. The constitution of 1891 put in place a federalist government intended to decentralize power and decision making. As in other states, most noticeably Minas Gerais and São Paulo, in Pará there was more control from the state capital then ever before, thus making it possible for local elites to tailor policies to their specific desires. Further, control of export tax revenues by the state of Pará meant that there was a great deal of money available from the sale of rubber that could be channeled into local and regional colonization projects.[6] There was also a greater stability in the executive branch of state government and thus potentially greater stability and continuity in programs until 1911. Finally, the "demonstration effect" was multiplied several times over by the massive Italian immigration to the coffee fields of southern Brazil during the first decades of the republic.

The fiscal change that accompanied the revolution of 1889 was enhanced by the tremendous economic spurt from rubber export that had begun earlier in the 1880s. Coupled with the liberal positivist attitude of three governors in a row, financially flush times made development of settlement programs possible at greater levels than ever before. However, the heyday was short lived. A major shift in government attention to funding colonization programs took place in 1902 with the election of Augusto Montenegro as governor. Coming from a cattle-ranching family, he was firmly a part of a political machine run by Antonio de Lemos. Controller of Belem politics, and thereby the politics of the whole state, Lemos dominated the political scene during the peak and sudden demise of the rubber boom.[7]

Montenegro began dramatic slashing of all programs encouraged by the previous Historical Republican administrations, including colonization. Earlier administrations' interest in colonization and other programs of health, education, and transportation as a solution to the need for economic diversification and development came to a grinding halt. The ostensible reason given for closure of programs was the 1901 drop in rubber prices, but apparently that was a handy excuse in view of further expenditures to beautify Belem.[8] For whatever reason, however, the result was a cessation of all activity in colonization programs and the end of assistance to those people already settled on the land.

The catastrophic economic change that came in 1911 caused the whole rubber economy to implode. In that year, Malaysian rubber production first entered the world market in significant amounts, and in less than one year it successfully challenged the Amazonian monopoly. The cost of production in Malaysia was significantly lower than in the Amazon, and world prices tumbled to a level that made the Brazilian rubber noncompetitive. The resultant collapse of the entire basin's economy destroyed personal fortunes and government revenues nearly overnight. The 1911 crash also completely destroyed any vestiges of government interest in attracting and settling a rural population. The effects of the 1911 crash provided the classic example of the effect of an external economic change on local policy making.

Thus, outside stimuli, or lack thereof, had an important influence on attempts to settle the Lower Amazon. Independence did not bring any new interest in this area, nor did the first two central governments in Brazil. In fact, it was not until midcentury that colonization received much attention anywhere in the country. Even then, provincial governors in Pará were severely hampered by lack of revenues to implement any long-term plans. The fall of the empire did bring about enough decentralization of revenue collections to correct the problem, and colonization programs proliferated for a short time until complete economic collapse in 1911 halted any further development.

Composition of the Decision-Making Elite Class

While it is difficult to overestimate the importance of external conditions in policy formation, they essentially provide only the backdrop for actual policy. The next important factor to consider is the elite class in Pará, the control they maintained over policy, the goals they held, and the benefits that accrued to them. Those considerations played an extremely important role in development of plans to settle the province.

By the 1840s, when the violence of the Cabanagem was history and the provincial government was again able to focus on other matters, several changes in the makeup of the elite class had taken place. The colonial governor general and his staff, oriented toward Portugal, were gone, replaced by a provincial president appointed by the court in Rio de Janeiro. Many of the Portuguese-born merchants who had profited greatly from the colonial trade had either left Belem or died there during the revolt. The owners of the sugar fazendas had suffered serious losses in the Cabanagem, and only a few could restore their previous influential status. Cattle ranchers on Marajó, another part of the old traditional elite, had suffered loss of herds and labor and were in equally precarious financial straits. In short, the socioeconomic makeup of the ruling class was changing.

Nevertheless, the change was a matter of degree, as a definite continuity in regional elite composition between colonial and national periods remained, a continuity which would also be readily apparent in the transition from empire to republic in 1889. The makeup of the provincial assembly was typical of such legislative bodies in the rest of nineteenth-century Brazil. Popular participation in government was severely limited by restriction of suffrage. According to the imperial law of August 19, 1846, the only people qualified to vote were males aged twenty-five years or older with an annual income of no less than 100$000 reis. Restricting the electorate even further, only qualified voters with annual incomes of over 200$000 could serve as electors and thus really participate in the electoral process. Indirect election was practiced until the reforms via royal decree in 1881, but even instituting direct elections did not measurably enlarge the voting population. The situation in Pará paralleled that in the other provinces, particularly in the northeast.[9]

Even though not required by law, only the literate property owners held office. Until the 1880s, the legislature was dominated by the most powerful landholders in the province: the surviving sugar mill owners (senhores de engenho) holding large and fertile sugar and rice lands operated by slave labor until 1888, the cattle ranchers (fazendeiros) from Marajó with vast holdings on which cattle ran wild, and to a lesser extent the powerful merchants in Belem, most involved in the rubber trade.[10] Men from these groups dominated Belem society and held the economic reins of power. They were essentially rural aristocracy in the paternalistic tradition of slave ownership in the preabolition days. Little of the paternalism was lost after abolition, due to strongly cemented traditions of loyalty and respect of their workers.

Prior to the 1880s the sugar mill owners were probably the most powerful men in politics; they were certainly the ones with the greatest economic power. Between 1840 and 1888 the slave-holding plantation owners enjoyed a heyday, while the cattle ranchers had to battle with serious problems of rustling and general lawlessness that had developed during the Cabanagem and continued to plague ranchers well into the twentieth century. They also had to face severe floods and occasional droughts that depleted herds, rampant disease in cattle and horses, and tremendous problems in getting beef to market. Cattle ranching on the Amazonian floodplain was a risky venture at best, and a bad year could leave a fazendeiro with nothing but empty land. The disease problem in the nineteenth century was primarily anthrax, Texas tick fever, and hoof-and-mouth disease in cattle, and equine trypanosomiasis (quebrabunda), which virtually destroyed the Marajó horse herds.[11] The cattle ranchers were either unable or unwilling to divert legislative attention and funding to solving those problems. For all the verbiage heard in the legislature and press about the shortage of beef in Belem, nobody appeared to be interested in financing drainage projects, law enforcement, or agronomic research. Typical was this comment of provincial president Tristão de Alencar Araripe in 1886, decrying the problem but offering no potential solutions:

This city is still without an adequate supply of good fresh meat. There are no roads to connect this region with cattle ranching provinces, by which cattle could come to market under favorable conditions. Even when there are enough cattle for slaughter coming by boat, as is currently the case, we do not have sufficient public pasture for the cattle to recuperate from the mistreatment of the voyage. We will not have as much fresh meat as is needed by a population which is growing so fast, and in such need of healthy food because of the climate, as that of this capital.[12]

The abolition of slavery dealt a severe blow to the economic power of the plantation owners, since many of the freed slaves moved to Belem or went to collect rubber, and there was no large pool of local labor to replace them. Many of those mills operating on the fringes of the sugar lands did not continue to function. The whole region of the Lower Tocantins and estuary, including parts of Marajó where sugar had been grown, went into steady decline after 1890.

While the fortunes of the plantation owners were rising and falling, and the cattle ranchers limped along with their problems, the Belem merchants rose steadily in economic power. By the time the rubber boom was in full swing, merchants who had survived the Cabanagem, plus new Portuguese and islanders who began to arrive after 1850, had begun to regain their commercial power. Because of the problems of lack of industry and the insufficient food production for Belem, it was necessary to import a great many goods from elsewhere in Brazil and from Europe and the United States, financed by the export of rubber. The merchant houses in Belem handled that lucrative trade involving everything from Danish butter and American salt and wheat to Italian marble and continental furniture and fashions, not to mention more prosaic items, such as beans and manioc flour from northeastern Brazil.

During the heyday of the rubber boom, another major component of the elite was the *aviador*. The term defies simple translation, but most commonly it refers to a supplier of goods, often as a traveling merchant representing a major commercial establishment headquartered in Belem. The aviadores were the ones who sold goods to the rubber tappers (*seringueiros*) and smallholders in upriver locations either on credit or in exchange for the rubber collected by the tappers. The term also applied to the merchants in Belem who supplied these middlemen. The system operated on a patronage system, to the very great benefit of the *aviamento* businesses. In some cases, an aviador actually owned the land where rubber was being tapped, in others he functioned as an itinerant trader.[13]

The dominant economic group of rubber-stand owners (*seringalistas*) and aviadores remained relatively distinct from the regional elite. Most of the men holding political power during both the empire and the republic came from the traditional landowning elite, not from those involved directly in the rubber trade. There was some degree of antipathy toward the rubber industry as deleterious to the overall economy of Pará. Such antagonism was usually voiced in moderate terms, since taxes on rubber provided a large share of the state's revenues.

One final point must be made in connection with the discussion of the policymakers. These men were resident in Belem, many of them supported from rural holdings they rarely saw. They were not required by law to be residents of the districts they represented. The legislature included a few men from as far away as Cametá, Vigia, and Bragança, but it appeared that the local elites of towns in the Lower Amazon and elsewhere were not clearly represented in either the membership or decisions of the legislature. In order to encourage colonization near towns such as Óbidos, Monte Alegre, Alenquer, Faro, and Santarem, town councils sent petitions and public announcements to the legislature in an effort to promote such projects.[14] Members of those councils, elected from the local population, had little connection to, or influence with, legislators in Belem. Their petitions were generally ignored, and very few agricultural colonies were created to help provision nearby towns.

The shift of power from Lisbon to Rio de Janeiro did not cause any noticeable increase in interest in settlement of the Amazon from outside the region. Whereas the colonization officials in Rio de Janeiro were responsible for overall policy, in reality most of the colonization plans were handled at the provincial level. Although local control was eminently successful in southern provinces such as Rio Grande do Sul, Santa Catarina, and later São Paulo, it was not effective in northern Brazil. Part of the problem, surprisingly enough, considering the wealth created in the rubber boom, was financial. Although tax revenues from rubber rose dramatically in the last decade of the empire, that money went to the central government, leaving Pará with insufficient funding for massive projects like immigration and colonization. Even when revenues remained in the state during the republic, the costs of the programs proved burdensome to the state coffers.

Another reason for the comparative failure of government subsidized settlement was the speed and arbitrary nature of many of the plans. Administrators, legislators, and colonization officials in Pará were pursuing a program of constant experimentation that was based on erroneous perceptions of the environment, and experiments were rarely allowed to mature before they were discarded in favor of new ones. They were dealing with an extremely large and supposedly empty region, and they had many problems to surmount that never arose in southern Brazil. The lack of continuity of planning was also due in part to the turnover of presidential appointees named by the imperial government. Those men, who were essentially governors appointed by the Crown, rarely served a four-year term, some of them staying in office for only a few months.

The effect of the composition and location of the ruling class that sat in government and made up the group responsible for colonization plans was predictable. Since they lived in Belem and identified themselves with that city, not unexpectedly they created projects that were concerned with colonies near the capital, not upriver. Had there been no outside pressures from the central government to develop some upriver colonies, colonization schemes might well have been confined solely to that area most useful from the vantage point of Belem. Colonization was primarily designed to benefit the capital city, particularly those residents who could control the flood of goods in and out of the neighboring region known as the Bragantina.[15] Except in the case of interest by the central government in securing more effective occupation of the Brazilian Guiana, especially during the friction over parts of the Amapá-French Guiana border around 1900, which put pressure on the state legislature to establish colonies in isolated spots, almost all colonies were put where they would be most advantageous to the capital.

The Issue of Food

The principal reason for the elite's interest in colonization after 1850 was the inadequate food supply for Belem's population. As early as 1860, before rubber dominated the region's economy, politicians remarked on its detrimental effect. In his report that year, president Amaral noted shortages of labor, particularly in the agricultural sector, and remarked that people must be lured away from the rubber stands and sent back to the farm.[16] Nearly every provincial president during the 1860s said much the same words. President Albuquerque noted in 1860 that products such as coffee, sugar, cravo, and vanilla had all but disappeared from the marketplace because of the migration of labor to collect rubber. He considered a higher tax on rubber to make it less lucrative and attractive to labor but was afraid that would shake an already fragile regional economy.[17] The concern for agriculture was a theme repeated over and over again. In 1874 Vice President Cruz remarked on the sad nature of agriculture, blaming it on a lack of labor, which had gone to the rubber fields.[18] His successor, President Azevedo was quite blunt in his remarks: "Free labor had begun in the last ten years to migrate to the rubber stands of Amazonas [province], and this migration now nearly has the proportions of an exodus." His solution to the problem was to encourage immigration.[19] Azevedo noted further that the manufacture of farinha had been particularly hard hit by the rubber boom, as well as coffee, sugar, cotton, rice, and even meat.[20]

President Mello Filho commented in his 1877 report that rubber collection was ruining agriculture, and he specifically noted the near disappearance of coffee, cotton, and indigo, and a serious reduction in quantities of cacao, rice, corn, and farinha.[21] In 1885, despite the attempts to bring foreigners to Pará, Vice President Souza stated that attempts to develop both agriculture and industry were failing because local inhabitants were too involved in collecting rubber.[22] Even as late as 1899, the problem had not been resolved, as Gov. Paes de Carvalho remarked that agriculture was suffering greatly for lack of labor, which had gone to the rubber fields. In what may have been a slight exaggeration, he said that "large estates have nearly disappeared."[23]

If contemporary accounts such as presidential reports are to be accepted at face value, virtually every symptom of the ailing agricultural economy was directly or indirectly attributable to the rush to the rubber fields and to the export enclave created by rubber. The actual situation was far more complex. In applying statistical analysis to several bodies of data on production of various goods in the nineteenth century, no simple cause-effect relationship could be found between increased rubber production and amounts of food production.[24] Rubber did have a dampening effect on a few products going through the Belem markets. As rubber production increased, there was a decided drop in the volume of cowhides, cotton, and Brazil nuts, all destined for export to elsewhere in Brazil and to Europe. Cacao, another valuable export crop, was not affected by rubber production at all, a statistical fact confirmed by Gov. Lauro Sodré in his 1897 report to the legislature, in which he stated that cacao was the only crop not in a state of ruin.[25] Statistically, the variation in rubber production could explain 81 percent of changes in hide production, 72 percent of cotton production changes, and 59 percent of Brazil nut production. These goods had nothing to do with actual food production for Belem, but they were the only products showing a significant relationship to rubber production.[26] The statistical relationship of rubber to foodstuffs such as sugar, rice, corn, or farinha was too small to be significant. Rubber could explain only 29 percent of the change in sugar production, 13 percent for corn, 7 percent for rice, and only 3 percent for farinha. The case of farinha is particularly important because it was the basic foodstuff of the great majority of the urban population. In fact, the changes in volume of farinha shipped to Belem were more clearly explained by the changes in production of rice. The data strongly indicates that variation within the agricultural sector affected the overall production of food far more than did the interaction of extractive goods, such as rubber, cacao, and Brazil nuts, and agricultural commodities.

The food shortages experienced in Belem during the rubber boom can be attributed to several less obvious reasons. There was an overall steady increase in permanent urban population due to both normal demographic trends and the arrival of many people involved in the export enclave. Even more of a demographic aberration, Belem endured massive short-term periodic increases in urban population due to the migrations of refugees from the droughts of the northeast. In short, there was a tremendous increase in demand for food, which was not met with a corresponding substantial increase in the supply available locally. With more people who have more money chasing fewer goods, substantial price increases were inevitable, putting some food out of reach for any but the wealthy.

At the same time, agriculture experienced serious limiting factors at precisely the time it needed encouragement. There were labor shortages, due to flight to the rubber fields, and only minimal increases in the number of small freeholders. Further, there were shortages of credit and capital needed to improve farming production, upgrade herds, and produce a more cost-efficient product. Even when surpluses were available to sell, they could not be gotten from farm to market because of the lack of transportation facilities. Finally there was a lack of anything but lip service by the government in their minimal efforts to help existing farmers.

If, as the data indicate, agricultural production remained roughly constant, or even rose, the shortages recounted were more likely due to increased demand rather then decreased supply. The capital city and surrounding municipio showed a dramatic rise in population with a tremendous jump from 35,989 in 1856 to 61,997 in 1872, and again between 96,560 in 1900 and 259,751 in 1907. The official censuses were notoriously inaccurate, although probably less so for metropolitan Belem than for the interior municipios. Further, they did not necessarily document major short-term demographic shifts. The key case in point was the repeated migrations of the northeasterners who remained in the city or municipio of Belem for relatively short periods of time before returning to the Northeast. They came in years between censuses and were largely gone by the next official headcount, and since few statistics were kept on the numbers of refugees, their numbers can only be estimated. Yet their impact was considerable as the hordes of hungry people strained the city's marketing facilities beyond capacity. It was not only a question of who would pay the bills for the food, but a far more basic problem of where the food would come from and how it would be distributed. Nor was it a problem lasting a few weeks or months, but rather several years at irregular intervals. Pará agriculturists were clearly pressed beyond their abilities to feed a rapidly and irregularly expanding urban population.

Under such conditions there would undoubtedly have been shortages for all urban dwellers, thus accounting for the outcry over lack of farinha, rice, beans, meat, and even fish. Typical of such observations was president Henriques's comment in 1886: "What food that is produced in the province is insufficient, so much so that we import large amounts of dried meat from the southern provinces and dried fish from Amazonas province."[27]

During the critical first few months of the drought migrations, food was sent from other provinces and from the imperial government. Such crisis aid was not designed as long-term relief, and when such shipments ended, local agriculture was expected to assume the burden of supplying Belem, which it could not do. Thus, Belem had to absorb a normal demographic increase, an influx of merchants and other newcomers associated with a booming economy, a certain amount of ebb and flow from the colonies, and periodic numbers of poverty-stricken and hungry refugees. At the same time there was little concomitant rise in the farming population, which could have potentially supplied the additional food.

The shortages in Belem that were denounced in newspaper and presidential report alike were not due to a quantitative drop in agricultural production caused by labor being drawn off to the rubber fields as claimed. They were the result of farmers' inability to respond quickly to a constantly and rapidly fluctuating demand for foodstuffs. When president Couto de Magalhães remarked in 1864, "the small farmer in Pará works in the extractive industry for six months of the year and is idle the rest of the time," he was certainly not seeing the larger picture, particularly since his comments were not based on personal observation.[28] Prior to the rubber boom, agriculture, which had suffered great damage during the Cabanagem, had not been oriented toward a large domestic market. An agricultural export-oriented economy had existed since colonial times, specializing in cacao, coffee, and sugar, all products whose cultivation had been greatly advanced in other parts of Brazil. Production of foodstuffs in an almost entirely rural province with widely scattered population was most commonly through subsistence farming, with occasional small surpluses being marketed in the nearest communities. Such production had to be completely reorganized and reoriented toward providing large surpluses that could be sent to the expanding urban area. Subsistence farmers could not enlarge their surpluses easily. The result was a need for foodstuffs but not enough agricultural units to provide them efficiently.

Chief among the complaints about food shortages were the problems of supplying adequate beef and manioc. These two items pose an interesting point-counterpoint; the first was confined to consumption by the relatively wealthy, while the latter provided the staple diet of the poor. A report in O Liberal do Pará in June 1871 remarked that "meat has always been so expensive that the poor cannot afford it, but now there is simply none available at all."[29] Because of the difficulties in getting beef from Marajó to Belem consumers, supplies were irregular and the meat of extremely poor quality. The shortages of farinha posed a far more pressing problem for the government, particularly after 1889, when the Republicans took over state government. Legislators could not afford to ignore the demands for solution to the food supply problem. The story of the Cabanagem had shown that the workers and the poor could and would rise against the propertied classes if they got desperate enough. Secondly, much of the political support for the Republicans came from the newly enfranchised petite bourgeoisie in Belem. These people were vocal in their demands for solutions that would provide plentiful and cheap food.

Thirdly, the aviadores purchased stock items, such as manioc in bulk, to be sold at inflated prices to rubber tappers upriver, and those purchases were generally made in Belem. Thus supply shortages drove up the prices they had to pay, when they could even fill their orders, and the increase could not always be passed on to the tappers. When the aviadores' price of manioc rose too high, tappers would adulterate their rubber to make it weigh more or would spend more time hunting and less time tapping. Either response lowered production and profit to the aviador.[30] Indeed, the significant amounts of basic commodities, such as farinha, that went into the aviamento system meant that much less food available to the urban population.

Therefore, the need to supply more food to Belem was a matter of political and commercial exigency as well as simply food on the tables of the elite. Virtually all economic interests represented in the state legislature recognized the need for greater food production, and immigration and colonization programs were deemed the best means to that end. By transforming the neighboring Bragantina region into a veritable garden, filled with prosperous communities of industrious Europeans happily supplying the food needs of the capital, all the problems would be solved. Unfortunately the truth was rather less idyllic.

The government's interest in promoting immigration and colonization was thus the official response to these problems of food supply. The dreams of the planners did not reflect reality, largely due to their inability to perceive and understand the problem they faced. It appears that the men responsible for establishing colonies and promoting settlement in the Bragantina could neither correctly diagnose the economic problems that precipitated the need for greater agricultural productivity, nor solve the problems that continually plagued the policies they pursued.

It is important to recognize another motivating factor in the governors' decisions to encourage European immigration during the republic. As far back as the early 1860s there was a genuine feeling that Europeans could provide new role models for Pará's farmers. As contracts were let to bring foreigners to Pará, politicians repeatedly made the same observations as President Graça in his 1871 report to the legislature. He remarked that foreign immigration was absolutely necessary to supply labor and demonstrate new work habits to local residents, especially in agriculture, which was nearly moribund.[31] Bringing new crops and new techniques of agriculture, they were to encourage the spread of new interest in producing food for an urban market, as well as help populate the hinterland. Such expectations were idealistic and unrealistic, given the problems of the environment and the fact that many Europeans who did come were not farmers. Nevertheless, plans to renovate the rural agricultural scene were often envisioned in the rosy light of the small freeholder producing goods for an urban market.

Under the circumstances, merchants dealing with foodstuffs had two possible alternatives. They could either import food from other provinces or they could turn attention to stimulating production within Pará. Official sources, such as presidential reports and remarks in the *Diario Oficial*, the organ of the government, offer little clue to the outcome of that collective decision. It appears that some of the export-import houses already involved in trade in foreign foodstuffs expanded their stocks, primarily of rice and wheat flour. Import-export houses were importing quantities of food from abroad, as demonstrated by published cargo lists of ships arriving from England and the United States. However, most of those foods were luxury items such as canned butter, cheeses, wheat flour, spices, etc., and were not basic foodstuffs. Random sample cargo lists from ships arriving from Liverpool, New York, and Lisbon in the late 1880s and 1890s showed most cargo to be cloth, metal goods, beer and wines, kerosene, salt, medicines, and other such items not available locally. The ships were also carrying quantities of rice, wheat flour, and durable vegetables such as onions.[32] Cargo lists from ships with home ports in Brazil were infrequently noted, but they did show some evidence of importation of basic foods in the same period.

It would therefore seem logical to assume that some merchant houses continued and expanded importation of food for both luxury and everyday consumption. However, the evidence does not indicate that increased importation was the only solution. If that were the case, there would have been more basic foodstuffs in the cargo lists, and undoubtedly there would have been some mention by the provincial presidents of the fact that heavy importation was occurring. Neither phenomenon occurred.

Merchants who were represented in the provincial government also put their support behind government policy to create new areas of agricultural production. There was no strongly voiced spirit of opposition to government sponsorship of colonies in principle, although there were constant debates over the details of such policy. Large import-exporters did not feel threatened by a policy of encouragement of local agriculture, since such policy would not have affected much of their trade. Other entrepreneurs could presumably see the potential profit in transportation, warehousing, and marketing of bulky agricultural goods for the local markets. Hopefully they could expect lower private capital investment in infrastructure, since the costs of building a railroad and establishing colonies along it would be absorbed by the provincial government, largely from tax revenues. They could also hope for lower overhead in their enterprise because of less risk involved in short-haul land transportation as opposed to more risky coastal shipping. Therefore, the idea of establishing agricultural colonies in the Bragantina, designed to provide food for the Belem markets, was acceptable to all economic interests represented in the legislature. The rubber owners and cattle ranchers who lived in Belem wanted cheaper food, and merchant interests hoped for a higher profit with less risk involved in supplying food to Belem and to the aviamento system.

After 1850, when the elites held much of the decision-making power in Belem, the overall goals of settlement policy changed noticeably from those of the eighteenth century. The goal behind the Directorate system had been to claim ownership of the basin by settling riverside populations along the major access routes. The secondary goal had been to regulate labor supply and make it available to the government and private individuals. Neither of those rationales for settlement of new areas interested the nineteenth-century legislators. Their often heated debates recorded in the *Diario Oficial* and the regular comments of the provincial presidents in their annual reports focused on the need to develop a productive agricultural zone around the city of Belem for the express purpose of feeding the urban population. Content analysis of the different annual presidential reports between 1848 and 1913, as well as the *Provincia do Pará* and *Folha do Norte* newspapers reveals virtually no interest in founding colonies to create an effective presence in unpopulated upriver areas. The only exception was the concern with elimination of the runaway slave camps, or *quilombos*, found near the Guiana border. Analysis does show a consistent run of comments about development of the agricultural zone around Belem, and such observations appear in virtually every report. Food and its availability and profitability completely replaced the eighteenth-century concerns of foreign encroachment and extraction of forest and river products.

Colonists as Policy Recipients

The above discussion of decision making and assignment of profit resulting from colonization policy has concentrated on the elites in Pará society. Since the individual settlers were an essential element of colonization schemes, their role in policy formulation must be analyzed as well.

Colonists in the national period had some measure of control over their situation, although their voice in policy was still severely limited. When colonists arrived in Belem, they were housed for a short time at government expense, then transported to their new homes, with rarely any say in their choice of destination. There was strong sentiment among colonization officials against allowing such a choice, to prevent immigrants from simply remaining in Belem, either living on public charity or going into commerce, and to keep established colonies from becoming too large, as happened in Benevides in 1879. A cogent argument against allowing colonists to choose their destinations, although not stated categorically, was that newcomers to the Amazon did not know enough about the area to make such a decision wisely. Few groups of colonists had the determination to refuse the assignments made for them. Since the various forms of aid and subvention funding did not begin until people were situated on their plots of land in the colonies, most of them were anxious to establish themselves. Furthermore, land covered with dense virgin forest looked fertile to the ignorant newcomers to the Amazon.

Once in the colonies and established on the plots of land given them in provisional title, the colonists were generally on their own. They would attract official attention only when they petitioned for help during epidemics or they spoke out against some specific grievance. The former was frequent, the latter somewhat more rare.

The case of the rebellion in Benevides in 1879 illustrates the point. This colony, twenty-nine kilometers from Belem by rail, had been used to house many of the refugees from the Great Drought of 1877–79 in Ceará, in addition to a few French and other Europeans who had settled there earlier. The population swelled from 118 in 1877 to nearly 9,000 in 1879. For a time, men from the colony were employed in road and railroad construction, medical facilities were established in the colony, and large amounts of public funds were spent on relief programs. However, by May 1879 money was becoming scarce, and even though the refugees continued to pour into Benevides, public funding was slashed, public works curtailed, and aid restricted to food, clothing, and medicine only.[33] Insubordination and general unrest began in May, and when all aid to Benevides was stopped in July, the estimated 2,000 refugees then unemployed began to agitate openly.[34]

The newspapers reported daily on the intense concern over the "rebellion" and circulated estimates of numbers of men and guns that could be raised should actual fighting break out.[35] Police troops were sent into the colony, and by the end of July the "revolt" was over.[36] The main grievances concerned the high prices of food brought to the colony, the low prices paid for goods leaving there, and the insufficient number of people to supervise and administer programs in the colony, as well as the cutting of jobs and funds. President Abreu felt that the disturbance was also in large part due to malcontents who were simply stirring up trouble, but the newspaper accounts from May through July 1879 indicate that the people demanding change were doing so because of the gross mismanagement of the colony by officials in Belem.[37] Promises of greater employment on the roads and railroad satisfied the colonists' demands, thus avoiding violence. At the same time, news came that rain had returned to Ceará, and about 1,500 refugees left Benevides for their home province, taking some of the pressure off the facilities.[38]

There were few such incidents, and the speedy decline of many colonies indicates that many would-be colonists did in fact simply move when their circumstances seemed hopeless. However, the Benevides incident demonstrated that colonists could and would become vocal and even potentially violent if the situation became intolerable. Unfortunately the lesson was imperfectly learned, and conditions in the colonies frequently reached near-intolerable levels.

Another incident that sparked considerable attention concerned the peopling of a new colony called Apeú, founded in 1883, but which did not receive any colonists until 1886. The twenty-one Azorean families who arrived there in June 1886 took one look at their future homes and refused to disembark from the train, demanding that they be returned to Belem.[39] The description of the site given by the Barão de Igarapé Mirim in the *Relatorio da Sociedade Paraense de Imigração*, demonstrated the reason for their decision. "The tiny houses belonging to the demarcated lots are not completed, and are barely covered; the shed (*galpão*) [is] in an incomplete state; the extensive area intended for rural use and the houses is unconnected, weakened and covered with the trunks of trees cut down, and from there the area is turning into scrub growth (*caapoeira*), and therefore the area is repugnant."[40] The Apeú colony never enjoyed real success; even with the arrival of the railroad, and despite an influx of northeasterners, it never became a town or municipio seat, but remained a *povoação*, a very small village. Again it must be stated that such incidents were very infrequent; most colonists went peacefully to their new homes and tried to make the best of a difficult situation.

Even as individual settlers had virtually no legitimate or positive avenues of input into policy directly affecting them, neither did the men who directed on-site colonization activities. The colonial director in the nineteenth century bore no resemblance to his eighteenth-century counterpart. Neither had much official input, but the eighteenth-century director did have much greater autonomy and power. The directors of state-sponsored colonies in the nineteenth century were supervised, salaried state employees with no real voice in policy, no real power, and no autonomy. While the colonial directors were characterized by their abuses of the system, the men in charge of government colonies from 1850 to 1911 did little to attract any official attention. Little was ever said about them in legislative debates or public press, favorable or otherwise, and they seemed to become anonymous civil servants.

Colonists were not allowed much participation in the policymaking process. The only response of colonists to policies, essentially action outside of normal procedures, was resistance either by flight or rebellion. Despite the colonists' ability to respond to intolerable conditions, however, planners persisted in a policy of not allowing colonists a voice in decisions affecting their own future. In that respect, colonists in the national period had really gained very little over the Indians before them. The colonists were not policymakers; they were the recipients of policy made for them, often with little regard for their needs and wants.

4

Basic Decisions in Colonization

Regardless of their origins and specific agendas, nearly all of the elites in government positions agreed on the need to bring immigrants to Pará to provide labor and food production to the Belem area. However, aside from the basic premise, they rarely agreed on the solutions to certain basic logistical questions. Decisions affecting overall colonization policy can be classified in three categories, and many details in each were hotly debated. First, an area had to be selected for settlement that would provide the greatest return on the financial and human investment: the question of "where to settle." Next, a group of people had to be chosen as ideal settlers in terms of ethnic and national origins and skills: the question of "whom to settle." Finally the structural framework had to be defined in terms of the types of colonies to be used and the politico-economic network within which they would function: the question of "how to settle."

A major difference between the colonial and national periods was the frequency with which new experimental schemes were devised. Policy between 1758 and 1798 changed little, since once established, the Directorate existed in basically the same form for forty years. The detrimental aspect of a colonization policy that remains unchanged for forty years is that little else remains static during that time, and a policy that was sound in the beginning may not respond adequately to changed conditions after a few years. The beneficial aspect, at least in the case of the Directorate in Pará, was that after forty years under a stable system of local government, the towns were firmly established. People governed by Directorate regulations had not had to face the constant turmoil of new plans before old ones could be properly assessed.

In comparison to the calm continuity of the Directorate policy, colonization between 1850 and 1911 was a hodgepodge of schemes, programs, plans, projects, and designs. Particularly during the period 1885–1910, new ideas were metamorphosed at an astonishing rate into the "latest and greatest" solution to the problem of settling empty lands. On the positive side, it must be acknowledged that colonization was a popular issue, and the best minds in the province were focusing their attention on it in a heady mixture of trial-by-error philosophy and a bulging treasury. The situation was anything but static, and new and innovative ideas were constantly encouraged. Pará proved to be a dynamic laboratory for experimentation in settlement of the humid tropics. However, the negative side of the issue outweighed the positive.

Part of the problem, and perhaps the most serious in the long run, was the irreparable damage done to the upland environment as colonies were carved out of virgin forest. Another serious problem was the constant turnover of plans, often simply because of a change in administration that occurred as often as four times in one year. The attitude that seemed to characterize the national period was that current plans were the only ones that mattered. Colonization plans were for the short duration only. They tended to offer short-term solutions to specific problems, with little concern about the future once the immediate aims were met.

A change in administration marked the time for examining the former executive's colonization policy and strongly criticizing the errors committed during his tenure, while simultaneously offering the new candidate's "definitive" solution to the problem, both within the context of partisan politicking. The debate got quite heated during the 1901 campaign for governor as José Paes de Carvalho, a firm advocate of colonization, was succeeded by the conservative Augusto Montenegro. Montenegro's election marked an effective end in interest in colonization projects until late in the twentieth century.[1] Once in office, a new president or governor could then initiate measures to set up colonies or related projects along his guidelines while ignoring those colonies established by his predecessor. Such studied neglect of a struggling colony was nearly equivalent to a death sentence for the settlement, since continuous aid and supervision were needed to nurse it through its early life. The high rate of decline and disappearance of colonies was as much due to the erratic governmental attention paid to them as to the destruction of the land on which they were situated.

Where to Settle?

After 1850, settlement patterns that had traditionally been beside rivers shifted substantially, away from previously settled lowlands and into the sparsely inhabited uplands. By 1850, much of the várzea land, particularly in a large radius around former Directorate towns, had been alienated in legal title or by illegal squatting. Such land was owned, if not effectively settled, thus forcing a search for new, unowned land to be used for colonization.

Penetration of the interior was reflected in the establishment of military colonies in isolated locations, the settlement of a new area, the *Zona Bragantina*, and the creation of a few agricultural colonies, such as Itauajury near Alenquer and Bom Gosto near Santarem.[2] Along the Tocantins River, an abortive attempt to re-create the apparent success of railroad and government-sponsored colonization of the Bragantina centered around the Alcobaça Railroad.

The decision to colonize the uplands was a conscious choice dependent on new methods of transportation, the perception of the environment, and the need to supply Belem with foodstuffs. Within those criteria, a number of possible areas could be considered. The Tocantins estuary was close, easily accessible, and fertile, but the best land was already held in plantation agriculture. The Rio Guamá met most of the conditions except that land closest to the mouth of the river was owned. However, its cause was not championed until some brief interest in the late 1880s, by which time the principal area was already being settled.[3] The shoreline area of Marajó facing Belem was not seriously considered because of several inhibiting factors, including lawlessness, dangerous transportation routes, floods, and the domination of most of the area by large landholdings.

The area finally chosen as appropriate for new agricultural colonies was the *Zona Bragantina*, an area of roughly 11,600 square kilometers of upland between Belem and the coast at Bragança. The land was not privately owned, except for a few relatively small areas.[4] Its soils were assumed to be fertile, due to the massive and luxuriant vegetation, a fallacy which would take decades to disprove. Vice President Guimarães set the tone for many future government officials in his remarks in 1869: "The fertility of the soil, as we all know, is astonishing, and if production does not correspond to that fertility, it is due to the lack of workers . . . which is truly the greatest obstacle appearing in the development of agriculture."[5] The area was close to Belem, and the building of a railway was expected to provide easy transportation of produce to market. Finally, it was not an area of lucrative extractive industry, producing less than 10 percent of rubber export in any given year, an important factor during the rubber boom, since it meant that land could be cleared without destroying valuable rubber stands. Further, there was no immediate lure to collect rubber, as colonists were too busy establishing themselves and growing food.

The move into the Bragantina, which resulted in the creation of five colonies during the empire and twenty-two colonies during the First Republic, began in the mid-1870s, continued unabated until the turn of the century, and sporadically thereafter. As a result, the Bragantina and neighboring Salgado are the regions with the highest population densities in the state outside of metropolitan Belem. The Bragantina-Salgado was the only area of the province that experienced such a continual attempt at colonization and development. Other attempts at colonization elsewhere in the province were isolated instances, both in time and space, and did not develop into regional poles of attraction for colonists.

Outside of the Bragantina, there was no large area of intense colonization in Pará. The North American settlement of Bom Gosto near Santarem, the Colonia Santo Antonio near Monte Alegre, and the Colonia Itauajury outside of Alenquer enjoyed modest development at best. The military colonies that were established by the national government in strategic locations had a mixed record of development. Colonia Dom Pedro II, established in 1840 in a frontier area of Amapá, was intended as an outpost to protect against French encroachment. It never prospered, and the new colony of Ferreira Gomes established nearby in 1890 faced the same problems and shared the same ultimate failure.

The Colonia São João do Araguaia (1850) on the Tocantins River near its junction with the Araguaia, and the Colonia Militiar de Óbidos (1854) near the fort and town of Óbidos, the narrowest place on the Amazon River, were designed to keep those rivers open for navigation and communication. The Óbidos military colony was dismantled because it was too close to the town and nobody wanted to stay in the colony. Only the Colonia São João do Araguaia managed to survive, a result of trade routes to Goiás and exploitation of the Brazil nut stands just downriver around Marabá.

Elsewhere in the province individual colonies grew around a few of the larger towns in the Lower Amazon region, but their impact on the economic and demographic patterns was strictly local. None of them developed into separate and individual towns. The Bragantina was the only part of the province where a network of colonies joined by roads and railroads resulted in relatively dense settlement.

Whom to Settle?

The issue of whom to settle became more complex after 1850 than it had ever been in the colonial period. Opinion and official policy oscillated rapidly, resulting in severe discontinuity of programs. Several important questions were involved in the decision of whom to choose as settlers. The two most basic and serious ones centered around the origins and skills of the colonists. The other essential questions were concerned with the mechanics of bringing foreign immigrants to Pará.

The constant debate over the origins of colonists and the frequent changes in policy attitude were the key to understanding the confusing welter of plans. The debate was essentially over using Europeans, representing the "ideal" colonists, or Brazilians, representing the fait accompli of the drought migrations from the Northeast. In general, overall policy was oriented toward the European colonist, interrupted frequently by the onslaught of masses of drought refugees.

The origins of the Europeans were also considered. Some of the immigration planners evidently held hopes that northern Europeans would colonize Pará: Poles, Germans, Russians, and Scots.[6] Nevertheless, the overwhelming majority of the Europeans who did come to Pará were from southern Europe: Spanish, French, Italian, and of course Portuguese. The issue of Asian immigration was shunted aside in a racist and highly derogatory fashion until later in the twentieth century.

Some people had serious reservations about immigration. In his *Relatorio dos negocios da provincia do Pará* (1864), José Vieira Couto de Magalhães voiced what appears in historical perspective to have been some astute observations. "Foreign colonization in Pará is a Utopia," he declared, going on to point out that Pará had no tradition of small family farms, as in southern Brazil, where Europeans had successfully settled. Further, he said that most food not imported was raised by fazendeiros, whereas the smaller farmers worked half the year extracting forest products and produced only a little surplus for market. Their minimal agricultural activity, he was quick to point out, was not due to laziness but to lack of capital and instruction, and he suggested that remedying that situation would be far more profitable to the province than simply importing new settlers.[7] Although he became a well-known and respected figure in matters pertaining to immigration and colonization, Couto de Magalhães's advice in this instance was ignored.

In view of Brazil's tremendous interest in European immigration, it is not surprising that the Pará legislators and executives were committed to the idea of populating their empty state with Europeans. The major problem was, very few Europeans cared to migrate to Pará. The majority of the Europeans, using the term loosely, who came were Portuguese, Azoreans, and Madeirenses, all from a Portuguese-language background, and those from the Azores and Madeira were familiar with a warm, damp climate like the Amazon. In 1892, governor Lauro Sodré voiced the opinion, somewhat bitterly, that all the "good" colonists were being drawn away from Pará for southern Brazil, and Pará was getting only the rejects.[8]

Along with the predilection for European colonists, there was an interest in bringing in North Americans and settling them in the Lower Amazon. Following the end of the Civil War in the United States, a group of unreconstructed Confederates migrated to Brazil, drawn by grand promises of the imperial government, coupled with their unwillingness to adapt to the conditions of Reconstruction. Most of the Americans settled in São Paulo, but a group also came to the Colonia Bom Gosto near Santarem under the contract granted to Lansford Hastings, a man responsible for a variety of wild schemes. Hailed as the ideal solution for the settlement of Pará, the plans to build the Bom Gosto colony in 1866 were an unmitigated disaster. Few colonists migrated and few of these were agricuturalists. None came with sufficient capital to sustain themselves while adjusting to a new land and culture, nor did the Brazilians in charge of the colony provide anything except land. The colonists were not accustomed to the physical environment or the local agricultural techniques. A few families stayed and were absorbed into the local population, but nearly all of the Americans abandoned the colony, most returning to the United States.[9]

After the Pará legislature realized that North Americans were not a simple panacea, they again included Europeans in their recruitment plans. However, neither Europeans nor "Yankees" proved to be ideal colonists simply by virtue of their continent of origin. Both were sought, but the debate over their skills, or lack of them, was hotly contested until the 1920s, involving primarily the question of agricultural aptitudes and training. In part because of constantly changing opinion over the emphasis to be placed on agriculturists, and in part because of faulty selection procedures, many of the colonists were not farmers and were considered practically useless by the local people. According to a report of the Belem city council, those people chosen by Hastings were not suited for agricultural work and preferred to live in Belem without any visible means of support. That description seems substantiated by the crime reports in the newspapers of Americans arrested, generally for assault and for being drunk and disorderly.[10] Similar police reports were published sporadically from 1890 to 1892 about other immigrants, under the headline "Os nossos bons immigrantes." A bitter and scathing article in the Liberal do Pará in 1874 probably described Americans: "With the pompous title of colonists, twice the government sent us some seventy foreigners, among whom some, true ragamuffins, walk among the houses begging and insulting those who refuse them. We need colonists, and greatly so, but vagrants, prisoners of the police, as it appears are some of those sent, we can easily do without, because they only serve to scandalize our people with the irregularity of their conduct. We commend to the police these vagabonds who have already made so much trouble."[11]

In general, the question of agricultural aptitude was settled in favor of the agriculturists, and immigration of those with other skills was rarely actively encouraged. Even when nonagricultural people were promised immediate employment in their various professions, they were forced to become farmers by being assigned to colonies where their professional skills could not be used.

In Brazil as a whole, one of the major issues in immigration dealt with the suitability of the European colonist as a plantation worker as opposed to a simple freeholder. Hotly debated in southern Brazil, where workers were needed in the coffee fields after the end of the slave trade, the issue rarely was raised in Pará. Occasional reference was made to the use of Brazilian migrants to work on the plantations, but there was no mention of using Europeans as plantation labor. Probably so few Europeans came to Pará that they could not fill the need for labor to replace the slaves, whereas the periodic migrations from the Northeast were large enough that some men and their families could be enticed onto the plantations. There was no particular reason to assume that the European colonists would wish to serve as slave replacements in Pará. The overwhelming desire of provincial authorities was to create a class of independent farmers whose produce would supply the Belem market.

In 1877, the situation changed dramatically, as the Pará legislators and administrators were faced with a new set of circumstances requiring new decisions and relatively little precedent on which to base them. The Great Drought of 1877–79 in northeastern Brazil forced planners in Pará to forget about the Europeans and do something about the flood of refugees from the northeastern provinces of Ceará, Piauí, Rio Grande do Norte, Pernambuco, and Bahia.

By far the largest portion of new settlers in Pará were native Brazilians, the refugees who came to escape the droughts that periodically devastated the interior of the Northeast, killing most of the animal and vegetable life in the arid sertão.[12] In a land too poor under normal conditions to provide surplus agricultural goods, the people of the sertão could usually survive one year without rain, but a second dry winter usually meant move or starve. Move they did, first to locations where water and plants survived longer than the sertão itself due to better drainage and seepage. In bad years, people would have to move farther, generally to the coastal areas, and vast numbers of refugees flooded into Fortaleza.

From there shiploads of Northeasterners embarked for Belem and Mauaus as they simply had to flee the overcrowded and pestilential slums of Fortaleza in order to survive. The Amazon was made attractive by the agents of the rubber owners who described in glowing terms the road to quick riches from collecting latex. There was also a good deal of official correspondence and encouragement from the Pará presidents to encourage Northeasterners to settle in the colonies of the Bragantina and elsewhere. The Northeasterners responded positively and migrated en masse to the wet, green banks of the Amazon.

The progression of types of aid offered to refugees in 1877–79 proved to be the model for refugee relief during subsequent droughts. At first, a number of public and private fund-raising campaigns were held in Belem and in larger towns in the interior. When the first refugees arrived in August, they were welcomed warmly and treated well. Some settled in the colony of Benevides, while others continued upriver to the province of Amazonas. However, as refugees began to pour into Pará, within a few months there were complaints of lack of shelter, food, and medicine in such colonies as Benevides, Santa Isabel, Tentugal, and Almoço.[13] The administrative machinery put together to handle the problem proved to be inadequate in the face of the thousands of refugees who came to Pará.

In an effort to improve care for refugees while they were in Belem waiting to move to other locations, the provincial government tried to set up better facilities. President Carmo ordered a large shedlike barracks to be set up in the Belem fort to house the refugees temporarily, and another in Benevides to provide shelter. He also established the inevitable commission to handle the problems at a local level and issued a number of directives on how to handle incoming refugees.[14] It was also necessary to build an infirmary, since most of the new arrivals were sick. Roughly half of the recorded deaths in Belem in 1878 were refugees, most of whom died from fevers and dysentery. The refugees also brought smallpox with them and contaminated every area they visited. Severe smallpox epidemics occurred throughout the province during 1878–80.[15]

Benevides was the first colony to which the refugees were sent, and its population expanded from less than two hundred to nearly seven hundred by July 1878. By 1879 it had become too large, with a population estimated at some nine thousand, and new colonies between Benevides and Vigia were established.[16] The Northeasterners in all these colonies received public aid and the men were employed in public works, most notably road and railroad construction. When aid was reduced in 1879, there was considerable unrest. The potential for violence among the discontented alarmed government officials, who managed to satisfy and compromise the demands of the refugees.

By June 1879, the demographic flow had become two-way, much to the chagrin of the Pará officials. By May, the newspapers reported rain in the Northeast, and on June 26, 1879, a boat arriving with a few refugees from Ceará returned to that province with twenty-three people ready to return to their sertão. The departure of that boat began the migration back to the Northeast.

The smaller colonies such as Tentugal, Almoço, and Santa Isabel suffered greatly from the exodus of Northeasterners. Benevides managed to prosper because of its size and the fact that it was already fairly well established with a group of permanent settlers who could encourage others to remain.[17] Evidently a number of Northeasterners did remain there, as Chief Judge Barradas pointed out in 1886 that "There is a large quantity of colonists from Ceará there [in Benevides] who cultivate the soil or dedicate themselves to small industries."[18]

Droughts occurred in the Northeast at irregular intervals, which meant that government officials in Pará could never be sure when the next one would come. Such a lack of regularity meant that planning had to be done on an ad hoc basis when refugees arrived. Droughts were severe enough to spark significant migrations in 1888–89, 1898, 1900, and 1904. When the refugees arrived in Belem at those times, programs for aid had to be started immediately. Usually such action followed the general outline discussed above.

There was little evidence to indicate that planners learned from past mistakes and improved their programs in subsequent years. In 1889, a group of former residents of Ceará who had settled in Belem were so incensed at treatment of their compatriots that they threatened action. "The cearense colony resident in this capital resolved to telegraph the President of Ceará with an end toward asking him to use all means in his power to impede the embarkation of emigrants for this province, in view of the inhumane and cruel manner in which they have been received here, owing to the negligence of the provincial government. The same colony deliberated also sending a telegram to the Minister of Empire, making known the miserable and saddening state to which these unfortunates have been reduced."[19] The outcry seemed to have had little effect during that migration or subsequent ones. There was, however, a growing reluctance on the part of the Ceará government to allow mass migration to the Amazon after 1889.[20]

Official discouragement did not appear to have a strong negative effect on the migrations. At least 27,000 people left Ceará for the Amazon in 1898. Between 1900 and 1916, migrations were smaller, less than 10,000 each, probably because the droughts were not as severe or widespread as earlier.[21] Those who chose to remain in Pará were housed at government expense for a short time, then loaded onto trains and deposited in various colonies in the Bragantina. In the colonies they suffered considerable hardship due to the scarcity of housing, food, and medicine. For a period of about three months during the 1915–16 drought migration as many as fifty people died daily in the colonies.[22]

Once the people were sent to the various colonies, the government interest in their welfare seemed to diminish greatly, so that plans were not carried out, food and medicines were not sent, and subsidies were not paid. The situation seemed to be a little more grim every time there was a new drought, partly because the Bragantina could not support dense sustained settlement, and partly because of government inaction. A very likely reason for the inaction before 1911, when funds were available, is that the legislators who authorized expenditures realized that many of the refugees would leave Pará within a short time, and officials would have been understandably reluctant to spend large sums on such a fruitless endeavor. After 1911, it was almost impossible to find any money to aid refugees. While legislators were unhappy, it was the colonists who starved.

Initially, the drought victims had been welcomed with open arms, as planners felt strongly that the "grand solution" had been found to problems of empty lands and a small labor pool. Time and experience proved the problems inherent in their solution. Lack of adequate preparation, poor treatment of the refugees, and refusal to recognize and admit planning mistakes, plus the poor physical condition of the refugees and their unfamiliarity with a new humid environment, meant that the refugee flood was not the answer to the planners' dreams.

In 1880 there was a sober reevaluation of the situation to date, after which the pendulum swung back to the European colonist, until the next drought. It was obvious by 1880 that colonization was not going to be easy. No plan had been a great success. The North Americans had gone home, few Europeans had elected to come, and the Northeasterners had returned to their sertão. Such apparent rejection of Pará's goodwill was blamed by the planners on everyone but themselves. The hapless colonists absorbed all the blame for the government's failure to establish stable colonies.

In 1885, the Pará Immigration Society (Sociedade Paraense de Imigração) was founded to encourage immigration from Europe. The goals and functions of the S.P.I. were patterned after the Sociedade Central de Imigração, which operated out of the imperial government to attract Europeans to southern Brazil. A semiofficial organization composed of leading members of the civil and religious community in Belem, its activities were to include sending agents to Europe, propagandizing there in favor of Pará, offering a workable package of benefits to prospective immigrants, receiving and assisting new arrivals, and administering the programs in general.[23] About the most interesting effect of the Society's propaganda was the publication in 1886 of the *Dados estatísticos e informações para os emigrantes.* The little book contained considerable information, and misinformation, on agriculture, population, slavery, general economic and geographical information, plus a great deal of rhetoric about the glories of the province, all of it designed to bring foreigners flocking to Pará. Interesting as it was, it did not appear to have encouraged any great flood of immigrants.

As the planners returned to consideration of the Europeans in the 1880s, two methodological debates were opened. The first, which was sparked by the fiasco at Apeú when colonists refused to settle in their assigned colony, raised the question of the advertising of Pará as a site for European colonization and the inducements that could and should be offered. There was considerable discussion in legislature and press in late 1886 about the desirability of telling prospective immigrants only the good aspects of Pará, or telling them everything in an effort to prevent subsequent disillusionment and bad publicity. The issue was not resolved definitively at that time.[24] The entire Apeú incident was blown out of all proportion, as it became a cause célèbre in the heated political exchanges between liberals and conservatives. The issue did little but to provide considerable bad publicity for the province.

Earlier, the question of inducements to settle had not been of particular interest, but the founding of the Sociedade Paraense de Imigração put new emphasis on the value of advertising in European recruitment. José de Santa Anna Nery, the Pará representative in Portugal, made several suggestions to improve recruitment, transportation, and location of European immigrants, but very few of his proposals were accepted.[25]

The propaganda issue reappeared again in the mid-1890s with increased interest in European colonists after the drought migration in 1888–89. Federal guidelines were established by a law passed in June 1894, which guaranteed some measure of uniformity in promises made to prospective colonists by various state governments.[26] The new regulations also apparently recognized the growing awareness that greater inducements were required to persuade people to come to a less hospitable area. This fact actually placed a heavier burden on Pará than other states trying to attract immigrants, because the state had to use more money in advertisements and other inducements to convince Europeans to choose Pará over the temperate south.

The other policy debate occurring in the waning years of the empire was over mixed colonies. The question was, should the European colonists be settled in colonies by themselves, or be integrated with Brazilian farmers? Proponents of the former position argued that newcomers should be allowed to remain isolated in order to preserve some of their culture, thereby reducing the difficulties of acculturation and the desire for repatriation, and to prevent their "contamination" by local agricultural practices such as slash-and-burn methods. Further, the refugees from the Northeast, who would be the Brazilian contingent in mixed colonies, were frequently characterized as poor colonists and agriculturists who would neither understand nor accept foreign ways.

The proponents of mixed colonies of Europeans and Brazilians argued that the Brazilians could show the new arrivals how to clear and cultivate their land, thus making the transition somewhat easier, and would also facilitate learning the Portuguese language. Integration would prevent the colony from becoming an isolated piece of foreign soil that would not fit well into the overall scheme of settlement.

One of the verbalized reasons for the encouragement of European immigration into the new agricultural colonies was the desire to demonstrate better agricultural and husbandry methods to local inhabitants. Unfortunately the ideal was never realized. Use of rudimentary tools such as a plow was rare enough to be remarked upon as an oddity. Early in the experience with immigrant colonists, it had been hoped that they might use plow agriculture and demonstrate its efficacy. Instead, most colonists adapted to local agricultural techniques. There was usually not enough room to use a plow in slash-and-burn fields, though it might have been useful in already cleared fields such as cane fields.

There was rarely any mention of the idea of introducing any new crops such as cereals, potatoes, or vegetables along with the new settlers, but rather an intensification and diversification of planting crops already known to thrive in the warm, humid environment. The available export data from new areas of colonization in the nineteenth century confirms that the Europeans did not try new crops but cultivated the usual rice, beans, manioc, corn, sugar, cotton, tobacco, and fruits.[27] For example, the 1895–97 export from Alenquer, where the Colonia Itauajury was flourishing, listed increasing quantities of farinha, beans, corn, tobacco, and some extractive products such as rubber and Brazil nuts.[28]

The key issue of mixed colonies was at the heart of colonization policy; the men proposing the idea showed considerable desire for new independent freeholders who would teach new agricultural methods to Pará farmers, thus improving agriculture and diversifying the economy. Such an idealistic aim had little chance of success because it was based on the assumption of fertile land that would respond to improved and intensive agricultural techniques, a myth thoroughly believed by the planners. The debate was somewhat academic, since most colonies were mixed as a result of the periodic influx of the refugees, but spirited nevertheless, dividing legislators, executives, and planners alike.

The changes in details of policy continued during the First Republic. Nevertheless, the pattern of encouraging European colonists except in drought times remained substantially unaltered until 1900, when overall concern for colonization policy began to wane. The earlier debates over origins of colonists began to take on strongly racist overtones. One report in 1897 characterized the Spanish colonists as lazy and inept, closing with the sweeping statement that the Spaniards had shown themselves to be poor agriculturists the world over, Pará being no exception.[29]

One final methodological debate was launched in the 1890s over the value and feasibility of private contracting to bring in European colonists. In 1894, three contracts were written with companies to bring in a total of 35,000 Italian, Spanish, or Portuguese, 80 percent of them farmers, by December 1900.[30] One contract was canceled for lack of any action, and only 13,036 colonists were brought to Pará under the orders before they were declared in default.[31]

Gov. Paes de Carvalho, despite his commitment to immigration, was determined to end private contracting. Because of poor selection, only half of the colonists had been farmers, and attrition rates from the colonies were staggering. Further, many colonists had gone into debt with the contractors in order to leave their home countries. Paes found such a situation inexcusable and declared that private contractors were making it very difficult for societies and companies involved in promoting immigration to work in Europe, as their lack of scruples made foreign governments very cautious about allowing emigration. In short, he thought the state government could handle the work much better.[32] While there was much to justify the governor's attitude, it must be pointed out that contractors Cepeda and Martins had been the most successful at bringing the much-vaunted and greatly desired European colonists to Pará. No plan before or after would approximate the numbers of immigrants they had attracted. Gov. Paes de Carvalho managed to abolish one of the few functional schemes to attract colonists, and private contracting of colonists remained a dead issue until the 1990s.

How to Settle?

The last of the three major policy decisions dealt with the question of how to settle. Like the issue of whom to settle, it was managed in the colonial period with continuity of policy, while in the national period it became a study in rapidity of change and discontinuity. Ultimately, resolution of the problem defied definitive solution in the national period. The budding spirit of trial by error during the empire gave way during the First Republic to unbridled experimentation, which prevented any real degree of policy continuity.

During the empire, three types of colonies were attempted. The imperial government established three military colonies in Pará between 1840 and 1854. Designed as military outposts to protect frontiers and trading routes, they did not develop into dynamic and independent towns.[33] Private colonies were encouraged but did not succeed. The government-sponsored and administered colonies (*núcleos coloniais*) created primarily to house drought victims proved to have the greatest stability and longevity. Benevides and Santa Isabel managed to survive the vicissitudes of fortune to become full-fledged towns and eventually *municipio* seats.

These types of colonies proliferated after 1889 with the great rush to develop colonization to new levels. Military colonization was discontinued. The private colony took a new administrative form called the *burgo agrícola*, privately owned and managed, with only minimal state involvement or financial commitment. Much of the risk involved in starting a colony was in private hands, and should the colony manage to survive the first three years, part of the cost borne by the individual would be reimbursed by the state. While innovative, the burgo agrícola was not popular, due to the expense and risk involved for private capital.

Other models were tried. The *núcleo suburbano*, established in 1898 and administered by municipal intendencies rather than the state was somewhat more common than the burgo agrícola. These settlements were located close to large towns, generally outside the Bragantina, and tended to be small and loosely organized.[34] The most common, and ultimately most functional type of colony was the *núcleo colonial:* state-run and state-financed agricultural settlements primarily but not exclusively established along the Bragantina railway. There was also some interest in creating penal colonies based on the Australian model that would serve to settle the Brazilian Guiana. An orphan asylum to prepare orphans, abandoned children, and Indian offspring to become useful citizens while simultaneously attracting settlers to the area was also proposed.[35] Neither the penal colonies nor the orphan asylum accomplished their stated aims. The state-financed "model colony" established near Belem in 1898 met a similar fate.

The brief span of time between the Revolution of 1889 and the turn of the century proved to be the peak period of activity and interest in colonization in Pará. The combination of nationwide commitment to immigration and the flow of tax revenues from the export of rubber into the state treasury provided an impetus that would never be repeated. Programs began and ended, debates were decided first one way then another, colonists came and went—all so rapidly that there was no continuity of policy except the general feeling that the area must somehow be filled with people. Colonists literally could not be sure from one day to the next about the status of their community, whether they would receive their promised aid or if it would be advantageous or even possible to try to move their produce to market. That any of the colonies survived the difficulties was in itself remarkable and could be attributed not to the planners in their mansions in Belem but to the tenacity of the lonely colonists, stuck in conditions of utter poverty and isolation in the midst of a countryside that few of them understood.

After 1900, the twilight years of colonization began, beginning with an early period of declining interest, curtailment of funds, and retrenchment of policy, and followed by a later total collapse of state support. The period 1900–1911 was marked by the end of all private contracting in immigration and colonization projects and cancellation of existing projects. Contracts for burgos agrícolas and privately owned but government-subsidized mills in the colonies were canceled.[36] The colonies under government administration in 1900 were "emancipated," thus canceling all government subsidy and aid to more than eleven thousand colonists.

The term *emancipation* in reference to colonies meant something rather different from the usage regarding slaves. Emancipated colonies lost all government subsidy, the reasoning being that the colonies had been subsidized through the crucial years of getting started and were now considered capable of managing their own economic, social, and political affairs. In fact, few of those colonies were yet capable of making a successful transition from dependent colony to independent municipality. Once the remaining colonies had been emancipated and were no longer of any financial concern to the state, no attempt was made to renew any form of subsidy.

The years 1907–11 were ones of increasingly serious financial problems for the state, first with the temporary economic slump of 1907 and then the final tumultuous crash of the entire rubber-supported economy in 1911. With finances becoming increasingly unstable after 1907, programs of all kinds were cut back; health, education, land surveys, and other such programs suffered. In such a situation, when colonization was a low priority in any case, it received little attention whatsoever.

In the final analysis, all of the decisions made to resolve the basic problems of colonization had had only limited success at best. Because of the difficulty of the physical environment with which the planners were dealing, it would have been unreasonable to expect overwhelming positive response to the projects. Given the entire situation, the failure of colonization projects was virtually assured.

Colonization was oriented toward economic development for the benefit of the elites. The situation of the colonists was not radically better than that of the Directorate Indians in terms of their ability to influence decisions made concerning their future. Mismanagement of funds, constant bungling in planning, ineptitude, unrestrained environmental destruction, and the inability to construct a realistic infrastructure for colonization all characterized planning in the national period. All the problems culminated in unrealistic goals, "super solutions," and rapidity of change in policy that did not create a network of prosperous and productive colonies in Pará. As a final indignity, the failure of the colonists to develop their struggling settlements into dynamic new towns was blamed on precisely those same people, who were only the recipients of faulty policy decisions.

5

Policy and Living Conditions

Once the first decisions were made about where, whom, and how to settle Pará, policy tended to be directed at specific problems within the context of settlement programs. Land tenure and ownership, health and education, and transportation were among the problems that received the most attention.

Land and Its Possession

Land ownership for both former Directorate villages and royal grants was chaotic between independence and 1850. There was no coherent policy and virtually no record keeping, resulting in great uncertainty over land title. The physical destruction of the Cabanagem revolt added to the confusion because of the loss of documents relating to land ownership. The only landholders who were relatively unaffected through that period were the squatters *(posseiros)*, who did not depend on legal title.

The Land Law of 1850 was designed to alleviate the confusion by legitimizing all existing titles and by setting up a policy of legal sale of public lands. Sesmarias had to be revalidated and posses legitimized, although neither action required an expensive survey, a feature of an earlier version of the law. Crown lands could be alienated only by sale, theoretically ending the illegal posse. Proceedings were so slow that it was possible to increase holdings while in the act of legitimizing them. The imperial government preferred sale in public auction after the land had been surveyed and marked into lots.[1]

The 1850 law was interpreted throughout the empire as a statute to benefit local large landholders who used its rules to acquire new land. The whole issue of the validation and legitimization of land grants was so flagrantly abused and ignored that illegal occupation continued to be relatively easy. The Law of 1850 offered very little to clarify the land ownership situation for the smallholders, such as those who owned land formerly part of Directorate holdings.

The Land Law of 1850 was as critical to the issue of colonization as it was to that of land title.[2] The land used for colonies in Pará was granted to the province by the emperor, and the provincial government was then responsible for surveying and marking it into lots. As early as 1830, because of the confusing land ownership and title throughout Brazil, local and provincial governments, ministers of empire, and even the emperor had requested a law for the distribution of uncultivated lands in order to encourage immigration. Much of the discussion over the implementation and regulation of the Law of 1850, in both the national Chamber of Deputies and Senate, involved mention of the need to provide land in clear title in order to encourage foreigners to settle in Brazil.

The Law of 1850 guaranteed colonists secure title, which was absolutely essential if people were to settle permanently on their assigned land and make improvements on it. In most cases, land for the colonies was given to individuals or colonization companies by the provincial government, as in the case of the Hastings/Love contract for the Confederate settlers in Santarem. However, the land given in the Bragantina was ceded to the province or to the company building the railway. The original contract for the railroad in 1874 stated explicitly that "with a purpose of [establishing] colonization centers, the *president of the province* is authorized to concede to said enterprise or company ten square leagues of land, *from that [land] possessed by the province* along the Bragança road, without any cost to that enterprise" (emphases added).[3]

There was relatively little concern vocalized in government circles in Pará over the problem of land ownership and validation during the empire. One of the earliest mentions of public lands in a presidential report occurred in 1872, when the provincial president, the Barão da Vila da Barra, stated that although there had been several petitions for purchase, no titles had yet been given. He also voiced the opinion that national lands should not be given in large pieces to single individuals but should be used for small farmers and those who could not afford to buy the land.[4] Since public land could be alienated only through sale, he would presumably have had to set a very low price ceiling on such transactions.

Ten years later, a total of fifty-two lots had been bought from public lands in fifteen municipios, most of them in Prainha on the Lower Amazon and in the municipio of Belem.[5] In 1878 it was mentioned that judgeships *(juizes comissarios)* had been set up in fourteen municipios scattered throughout the province for the purpose of registering claims and entering petitions, and in 1886 such activities had been established in twenty-nine municipios. It was also announced in 1886 that demarcation of lands had stopped for lack of personnel.[6]

It appears that the Law of 1850 did little to change landholding patterns in Pará. The isolation of the province made it possible to ignore the regulations with impunity, and the tremendous difficulties involved in surveying and marking lands would have made compliance most difficult in any case. Finally, neglect of the law under such circumstances was the most logical choice of a provincial legislature dominated by rural elites far from central government control in Rio de Janeiro.

No action regarding land ownership was taken during the first few months of the First Republic, but noticeable administrative change did come in 1891. Responsibility for administering the registration of lands and sale of public lands was given to the individual states in Article 64 of the federal constitution. That provision meant that the Pará government was solely responsible for creating a method of regularizing land ownership and sale based on conditions as they were perceived.[7] Theoretically it was a sensible decision, because the specifics of the situation in Pará were poorly known or understood in Rio de Janeiro, and having the decision-making power closer to home should have meant local decisions for local problems. Actually, little changed.

State Decree 410 of October 8, 1891, set forth the new rules in great detail.[8] The state government set up the Bureau of Public Works, Lands, and Colonization (*Repartição de Obras Públicas, Terras, e Colonização*) and kept the right to reserve such lands as it deemed necessary to found colonies, open roads, supply wood for naval construction, and for the defense of frontiers, forts, and military installations. Public lands could be acquired only by purchase. The regulations for revalidation of sesmarias and legitimization of posses were much the same as in 1850. One purely local change was the definition of "effective cultivation," which was required before a posse could be legitimized, since it included trees and other vegetation for extractive industry and pastures with corrals. Thus, it was possible for a posse composed of rubber trees to be legitimized without any agricultural activity whatsoever on the property.

Another basic change was elimination of the requirement that all posses must be surveyed, a process that had greatly impeded the legal process. Contiguous unalienated land could be claimed once the survey was complete, though owners of rubber stand posses were not eligible for that privilege. Current occupants of unalienated property were to have first priority for buying it. Purchase of such land obligated the owner to allow free access to neighbors and removal of water not being used.

The other major shift from the 1850 law was Article 23, which stipulated that land taxes would be assessed according to the size of the holding, and the use to which it was put, smallholders being exempt. There had been a conspicuous absence of a land tax clause in the 1850 law. In Pará, as nearly everywhere else in Brazil, the land tax was evidently a dead issue, as no efforts were made to collect such taxes. Tax revenue from rubber provided most of the government income, and the legislators did not tax their own holdings as long as public revenues were adequate.

In the report of the Bureau in 1892, the first assessment was made of the new system. The director reported that in some of the interior municipios, intendants and councils in charge of land registry were assuming too much power and unduly favoring the squatters. He stated that many applications for purchase of unclaimed land had been received, and some published, but no final action had yet been taken. He also noted that surveying was at a standstill.[9]

By the time of the 1893 report, registration was evidently progressing with smoother and faster action and fewer claims of abuses. Law 82 of September 15, 1892, had lowered the cost of unclaimed land, and as a result increased numbers of petitions were being received. In the 1894 report, Director Henrique de Santa Rosa remarked that there were many petitions but few actual sales of public lands, due to the cost of surveying, which had to be borne by the would-be purchasers.[10] Again in 1895 it was noted that despite a continuing increase in the numbers of requests for purchase of public land, lack of surveying crews and slow communication with municipio governments had greatly slowed the process.[11]

The pattern that clearly emerged from the annual reports was one of excessive delay and bureaucratic red tape. Having opened the doors to individual purchase of public land, the government agency responsible for handling matters was totally incapable of coping with the flood of requests. An effort to handle the problem by extending the filing date of petitions was a failure.[12]

In his budget speech in 1898, Gov. Paes de Carvalho summed up the criticism of the land sale system. Noting that prices were so low that the state gained very little, he also criticized the length of time required to complete the process, owing to the legal and physical difficulties of surveying the land. He felt that the state should take over the surveying, and the public lands along the Belem-Bragança railroad should be divided into lots and sold in auction rather than by the more cumbersome petition method. He also reported that he was trying to establish the land tax as a way to increase state revenues, but with little success.[13]

The problem and confusion of land ownership in the Bragantina had become severe by 1900, when many of the colonies were emancipated, as provisional titles had to be revalidated and converted to definitive titles, while public land sale continued erratically. Finally in 1900, Gov. Paes de Carvalho called for complete new registry of all titles of the colonists and announced that the area was closed to further grants of public lands. In

August 1900 a new regulation to confirm the Land Laws of 1892 and April 1900 was published, but there was no change from the original 1891 law.[14] One last effort was made in 1902 to improve the chaotic situation by the law that gave definitive titles to qualified colonists in various colonies of the Bragantina. Those titles were given without payment of any kind.[15]

By 1900 the issue of land ownership had effectively died down as motivation for change had dwindled. The rationale behind the original law in 1850 had been to improve conditions so that foreign colonists would settle in Brazil, it being rightly felt by legislators and ministers at the national level that lack of clear title to the land was a major inhibiting factor. The sentiment after the Revolution of 1889 was a combination of the desire to attract immigrants and to make some order out of the anarchic situation of registry of legal title. When the state government became responsible for the handling of land laws in Pará, the revalidation of existing holdings attracted the greatest attention. The government was authorized to set land aside for colonies, but such action was done quietly and without fanfare.

Thus, official concern over the question of land ownership was centered more on the problem of posse and sesmaria legitimization than on the assigning of lands to the colonists. Once a colony was established and lots measured, the government ceased to take an active interest in tenure. The criteria by which lots were assigned was never stated in any newspaper article or official publication other than an occasional remark about how one group had received a particularly poor piece of land in a colony, as opposed to another group which had evidently been awarded all the best land. The government's concern with the registry of titles was, if anything, more trouble to the colonists than the aid it was theoretically supposed to provide, since occupants of lots were constantly having to revalidate in compliance with new laws. The problem of land tenure and legal ownership in Pará was oriented toward the large landholders, not the colonists.

The Care of the Infirm

The problem of providing adequate health care was another of the more serious obstacles affecting colonization in the nineteenth century. Medical facilities were theoretically considered a necessary accoutrement of a government-sponsored colony, even if they were rarely provided.

The problem of disease and its attempted control received considerable attention and discussion in the national period. Periodic epidemics were much more common than in the colonial period because of improved transportation and rapid travel. The most notorious epidemics were yellow fever in 1850 and bubonic plague in 1903. Every exodus of refugees from the Northeast brought serious epidemics, usually smallpox, and a host of lesser ailments. Malaria continued to be an accepted fact of life.

The actions taken to deal with disease also reflected perception of the problem. Vaccination was possible against smallpox, and more aids such as quinine for symptomatic relief of malaria were more widely available. Disease was seen as a problem that would respond to active treatment instead of simple isolation of patients and towns until they recovered or died. Finally, it was recognized that immigrants would not come to such an unhealthy port as Belem, and therefore disease must be brought under control. Thus, health became a factor for consideration in formulating colonization policy.

Smallpox remained a constant threat. There was a major outbreak in 1819, brought by slave ships, which spread through the interior and caused a reported 2,200 deaths.[16] A good portion of the deaths during the Cabanagem were due to smallpox in and around Belem. In 1840 vaccination was made obligatory, but the law was unenforceable because of the difficulties in finding public officials to give inoculations and in securing sufficient active vaccine from Europe.[17] There was also some public reaction against vaccination, as President Abreu reported in 1881 that "reluctance of the population" to take advantage of the opportunity was the reason for only 270 vaccinations for the entire year. In 1888 the campaign enlisted schoolteachers in the interior to vaccinate because of the lack of any other qualified individuals. The available statistics on vaccination in the nineteenth century show that slaves were rarely immunized, most of the vaccinations were done in Belem, and results were impossible to ascertain because many primary reactions were never reported.[18]

Despite attempts at vaccination, smallpox continued to come in waves, with major outbreaks in 1851–52, 1866–67, 1872–76, 1878–80, 1883–85, 1887–88, 1896–97, 1899–1901, and 1904–7. It was no small coincidence that the years of drought migrations were ones of serious epidemics. The Northeasterners left ports where smallpox was rampant, and when they arrived in Belem and moved onward to various colonies, they spread the disease even more effectively than the African slaves had done. Attempts to vaccinate them as they arrived were erratic and ineffective.

Yellow fever was a new disease in Pará, and one of particular interest in a study of colonization, because it was evidently a selective disease throughout Brazil. Quite simply, foreigners were most susceptible to it, so the implications for a policy of encouraging European immigrants to come to Pará were fairly obvious. The disease arrived in 1850 via two ships from Pernambuco. Nearly half of the deaths in Belem that year were attributed to yellow fever, and the epidemic lasted five years in the capital with declining mortality rates.[19] Once yellow fever had come to Pará it recurred frequently, with scattered cases in 1857, 1860, 1861, 1871, 1872, 1876, 1878, 1879, 1882, 1885, 1887, 1888, 1904–8, and 1909–12. Eradication programs were begun about 1912 along the guidelines set by Oswaldo Cruz in his campaign against the disease in Rio de Janeiro.[20] Significantly, after 1912 yellow fever in Pará nearly vanished, despite repeated arrivals of victims from other fever ports.

It was discovered in the original 1850 outbreak that yellow fever was far more dangerous to foreigners than to Brazilians. Since it was precisely after 1850 that interest in immigration and colonization was developing, such a discovery was an unhappy one. Because of its affinity for nonimmune, newly arrived immigrants, mortality among foreigners who came to settle was higher than among the established local population. As long as the foreigners did not remain in Belem but moved quickly to the colonies, their likelihood of contracting the disease was not great. However, because of the constant movement of immigrants between capital and colonies, and since many of the immigrants preferred to return to Belem rather than remain in the colonies, yellow fever found numerous victims.

Cholera morbus was a frequent visitor to Pará despite attempts at rigorous control, although it reached epidemic proportion only once. It first arrived on the heels of the yellow fever epidemic in 1854, brought by colonists and spread quickly in virulent form throughout almost the entire province. The rapid and extensive spread had been due largely to the panic flight that ensued when it was known that cholera was present. Cametá was hardest hit, with ninety to a hundred cases reported a day for several months, out of a population of less than seven thousand. Provincial president Angelo Custodio went on a personal inspection tour there and died of the disease contracted on the trip.

The situation became critical in Belem due to food shortages, since people who normally supplied the city refused to come near the pesthole. The provincial government that had sent blankets, food, money, and medical teams into the interior had to beg for similar aid from other provinces. Amazonas, Maranhão, Ceará, Pernambuco, and the imperial government sent food, livestock, and medicine.[21] Luckily the 1854–56 outbreak was the only serious one, although cases were reported in 1866–69, 1874, 1885, and 1888. Cholera, spread through contaminated water, was a potentially devastating disease in an area such as Pará, where adequate sewage systems and sanitation were exceedingly rare. The principal method of control was quarantine and embargo of vessels from infected ports, these measures being fairly effective.

The most feared epidemic disease was bubonic plague, *peste negra*, but prompt and thorough action on the part of the Department of Sanitation prevented it from being a menace in Belem. Plague first arrived in Brazil from Portugal in 1899, and its progress along the coast from Santos to Rio de Janeiro, Salvador, Recife, Fortaleza, and São Luiz brought it to Belem in November 1903. Its arrival was expected, and vaccination and rat eradication programs were ready to be put into effect quickly. The outbreak was over by 1907, and there were only occasional cases reported subsequently.

Fevers, labeled "febres," "febres intermetentes," and "febres palustres," most of which were malarial, were so common as to be accepted as normal. The presidential reports mentioned fevers only when they were particularly severe or widespread, and there was scarcely a year when some part of the province was not struck severely. Instead of simply noting the common presence of malaria, however, attempts were made to remove the conditions that facilitated its presence, generally a matter of draining stagnant water. Municipal councils were responsible for seeing that no stagnant water was left near towns, and President Barros noted in 1856 that where the work had been done the incidence of malaria dropped remarkably.[22] The same observation was made in 1863 in reference to Gurupá, an area notorious for malaria. Malaria has remained a serious problem to the present, however. Despite drainage and mosquito programs and the availability of antimalarial drugs, it is still endemic.

There were many other diseases mentioned in the annual reports. Many were the so-called childhood diseases now easily preventable by immunization, but killers in the nineteenth and early twentieth centuries. Measles, mumps, whooping cough, scarlet fever, and croup were all responsible for numerous deaths each year. Occasional outbreaks of typhoid, diphtheria, and beriberi completed the epidemiological scene, along with the omnipresent tuberculosis and leprosy. Pará was simply not a healthy place to live.

One of the worst problems in the control of disease was the lack of medical personnel. Few towns outside of Belem had resident physicians, and even temporary resident doctors were rare enough to be an object of comment. Teams of medical and paramedical personnel were sent out as needed in times of emergency, but usually that was the most that could be done. According to the 1872 census, out of thirty-three municipios, only twelve, including Belem, had any members of the medical profession, either physicians, surgeons, pharmacists, or midwives. There were only 167 such people in the entire province, and 95 of them, over half, were in metropolitan Belem. Excluding the city of Belem, there were 1,857 people for every member of the profession. When considering also the difficulties involved in reaching medical help, it is surprising that epidemic disease was not a more serious problem.[23]

There was little mention of epidemic disease in the programs designed to attract colonists to Pará. Colonization agents in Europe probably deliberately downplayed the problem, claiming that stories of pestilence in Pará were part of the general slander of the North. The immigrant guide published in 1886 blamed the problem of malaria on the living habits of local people, also mentioning the reputed longevity of the local population, especially those involved in agriculture. According to the guide, "All foreigners who live in Pará are in a perfect state of health," a statement that can only be regarded as total prevarication.[24] The discovery that disease was both endemic and epidemic was undoubtedly one of the disillusionments that caused immigrants to leave the colonies.

The Teaching of Children

The subject of education was frequently discussed during the empire and early in the First Republic, although rarely in connection with colonization. In an area as large as Pará, with a relatively small and widely scattered population, the problems of providing the required primary education were nearly insurmountable. The number of primary schools and matriculations rose very slowly from 35 schools in 1848 to 241 schools in 1893.

By the 1870s almost every municipio had at least one primary school, usually in the largest town, but educational facilities in the interior were inadequate or absent. The main problems were scarcity of even remotely qualified teachers, low to nonexistent salaries, the total isolation of interior posts, and the unstable size of populations. The number of schools and students were deceptive, because at any given time up to a quarter of the schools might be closed for lack of teachers, students, or money, and the attendance rarely exceeded half of the matriculation. Children might attend for only a few weeks or months until they were needed at home, or the families migrated in search of rubber.

From 1900 to 1911 relatively little legislative and executive interest was shown in promoting education in Pará. Gov. Lauro Sodré, in keeping with his positivist philosophy, did try to improve education in the interest of modernization. He established a normal school and a vocational-technical institute in Belem, and he tried to develop a rural educational network involving most towns. In fact, however, education rarely touched the lives of most of the scattered rural population. It certainly was no inducement for immigrants to come to Pará.

When Augusto Montenegro took over the governorship in 1902, his policy retrenchment in colonization was extended to education, and most of the laws related to education that were passed in 1902–3 were designed to reduce the number of schools and teachers. The economic difficulties culminating in the 1911 crash made it necessary to cut the education budget once again, and after 1911 education joined every other service provided by the government in being virtually eliminated.

Education was rarely mentioned in specific reference to colonization, either in terms of benefits to be granted to colonists or in the propaganda to get them to settle in Pará. There was no deliberate misrepresentation, as in the case of health; education was simply not mentioned. With the exception of contracts for the burgos agrícolas and such private ventures, reference to the need to build schools in the colonies was notably absent.

Concern in providing educational facilities for new settlements was extremely limited. Education consistently had a relatively low priority, well below the more important economic and commercial aims of colonization policy. During both colonial and national periods there were laws stating that children were to be educated, but such laws were either ignored or only marginally observed, due to the excessive difficulties of providing schools and teachers. Education was not perceived as an essential service to provide to colonists.

Transportation

Land and water transportation received considerable attention in the national period, partially because of the need to reach far-flung areas and partly because of advanced technology. The change in navigation services was largely due to two factors: the opening of the Amazon Basin to foreign shipping by Imperial Decree 3749 of December 7, 1866, and the use of steam power for river travel.

The Companhia de Navegação e Comercio do Amazonas (usually referred to as the Companhia do Amazonas) was founded in 1852 under ownership of the future Barão de Mauá. The route of the company was to be from Belem to Nauta, Peru, and there were clauses calling for establishment of sixty settlements of Indians or Europeans along the route on lands to be granted by the imperial government.[25] In fact no such settlements were constructed. Although some smaller companies did exist, the Companhia do Amazonas, or Amazon Steam Navigation Company, as it was called after purchase by British interests, dominated river navigation.[26] It did well financially until 1911, when it lost its principal cargo, rubber, and went into financial decline.

Alongside the development of steam navigation on the Amazon itself, there was a concerted effort to expand the transportation network away from the rivers. At first the emphasis was on road construction, attention later being focused on railroads in the 1870s with the beginning of the Belem-Bragança railroad. The Bragança railroad and the less-well-known Alcobaça railroad on the Tocantins River were complementary to water transportation and did not compete with river travel.

There are several explanations of the Pará government's determination to have a railroad in the Bragantina. Railroads attracted worldwide interest in the 1870s, with track being laid in North and South America, Western Europe, and Russia. Brazil joined the railroad craze and began building railroads in the south. Thus, there was a considerable degree of "demonstration effect" that encouraged the Pará planners that they too could partake of modern inventions. Further, the Pará leadership at that time was becoming more development minded, and a strong feeling grew in the government that railroads would do a great deal to improve agriculture, commerce, and eventually industry in the Bragantina. There may have been a good deal of British salesmanship involved also, since all the rolling stock was British, and a British company took over construction of the tracks in 1883.[27] Finally, there was undoubtedly a good deal of private interest involved, and a large portion of the money spent on construction probably went in graft.

The Bragança railroad was a constant issue in the legislature during the construction period. The *Diario Oficial,* which reported the daily workings of the state government, often contained debates and heated discussions over the vast sums of money spent and the choice of personnel to administer the railroad. The repeated charges of mismanagement, nepotism, and political favoritism indicated that the railroad suffered considerably from internal problems. An editorial in 1886 roundly criticized the construction company: "We are absolutely against the railroad between this capital and the city of Bragança. One who has a desert to conquer in the center of the country in order to gain productive settlements, is not going to consume rivers of money in search of the littoral already navigated and served by steam navigation, especially when in the whole central zone of this littoral, there is no agriculture, there is no commerce, that could correspond to the enormous expenses of the railroads."[28] President Henriques voiced much the same opinion, saying that the railroad, which traveled through desolate, uninhabited land, was not fulfilling the purposes for which it was built: to supply Belem with cattle and fish from the area, nor would it ever do so. "The railroad appears to me to be a work without a future, and an extremely onerous one for the province," he concluded.[29]

The Bragança railroad was never a profitable enterprise. Construction was costly, and additional funding was constantly requested until completion of the tracks in 1908. Between 1886 and 1890, when the track was not quite halfway to Bragança, the railroad that served colonies from Apeú to Belem operated at a constant deficit, with expenses nearly doubling receipts. In 1894 an article in *Provincia do Pará* listed the income and expenses of six railroads in Brazil; the Belem-Bragança Railroad was the only one operating at a loss. In 1899, a survey of income and expense for the Belem-Bragança Railroad since 1874 showed a deficit every year, with expenses sometimes as much as two and a half times the income.[30]

Despite the state financial commitment to the railroad until 1911, there was still outcry that rolling stock was outdated and insufficient, and that salaries and personnel were excessive. Complaints came from the private as well as public sectors. The colonists claimed that the railroad functioned as a monopoly, leaving them no alternative routes for shipping their produce to market and forcing them to pay prices they considered extreme. Whereas their complaints about high freight rates could be countered by the profitability of their agricultural produce in the Belem market, the competition of cheaper goods from the coast and Guajará would have limited their ability to compete successfully.

On the other hand, the charge of monopolistic practices was solid. The Bragança railroad opened an upland area away from navigable rivers, so that water transportation was not a possible alternative. There was no road parallel to the railroad that could have been used for carting; rather, paths seldom interconnected, and there is little evidence that farmers in the colonies had enough oxen and horses to move goods in bulk. The railroad was the only means by which farmers in the Bragantina could move their produce to market. The claims of high freight rates were supported by President Araripe in his 1885 report in which he stated that the railway was not encouraging agriculture because of the high charges to move agricultural produce.[31]

Despite complaints over charges, people obviously did use the railroad. Traffic in passengers and their baggage increased substantially between 1885 and 1912. The railroad carried 9,300 passengers and 1.6 million kilos of merchandise in 1885, which rose to 202,738 passengers and 17.4 million kilos of merchandise in 1912.[32]

Since the railroad was used, even as it ran at a loss, it is worth some conjecture on its impact on the process of colonization. The colonies alongside the tracks or connected by short paths had to depend on the railroad for their link to the outside world. Colonists arrived by train, bought their food and construction materials from stores supplied by train, sent their mail by train, and shipped their produce to Belem by train. If freight rates had been lowered through greater government subsidization, the colonies might have developed a more efficient agriculture in response to an urban market willing to pay their prices.

Unfortunately the Bragança railroad was finished too late, only three years before the collapse of the rubber economy brought financial ruin to the entire area. After 1911 there was no government subsidy to buy new rolling stock, repair track and bridges, or help lower freight rates. The railroad fell into decline along with every other government program after 1911, and by the time of partial economic recovery in the 1940s and 1950s, roads had been built offering competition the railroad could not bear. The Bragança railroad never really had a chance to prove its merit.

The only other publicly funded railroad, the Alcobaça, or Tocantins, Railway, was even less successful and more of a political football than the Bragança railroad. It was planned in the 1880s to bypass dangerous rapids on the Tocantins River. Partisan squabbles, fully covered in the press, characterized the plans for its construction, and work did not begin until the national government took control of the railroad in 1891.[33] Eventually, two hundred kilometers of track were laid from Tucuruí (Alcobaça) to a point across the river from the village of Jacundá. The stretch was the full extent of the Alcobaça Railroad. The general feeling was that the railroad served little if any purpose except to consume federal funds that could have been more profitably spent elsewhere.[34]

No other railroads were built, although several were projected. One would have connected Santarem with Cuiabá, capital of Mato Grosso; a less ambitious plan was to build a short railroad to bypass rapids on the Tapajos.[35] None of these projects got beyond the feasibility study phase.

Railroads were popular and fashionable, but roads were cheaper, and so increasing attention was paid to road building as a means of opening up the interior. The *Diario Oficial* from 1892 to 1911 published many laws calling for the contracting and building of various long and short roads, including Óbidos-Guianas, Rio Capim-Maranhão, Santarem-Curuá, Cintra-Marapanim, Santa Izabel-Vigia, Igarapé Mirim-Abaeté, and many others. Most of the shorter roads, such as the Santarem-Curuá, which passed through an area of attempted colonization, and the Santa Izabel-Vigia roads were built, although with time extensions.[36] The longer roads, such as the Acará-Maranhão road to connect Belem with São Luiz, remained fantasies, and it was impossible to reach São Luiz directly from Belem by land until 1974.[37]

The vast improvement in transportation technology, which made the extensive road building and the two railroads possible, was both a boon and a curse. Improved technology made the Bragantina the most attractive choice for development and settlement in the nineteenth century. Had it not been for the railroad, it is highly unlikely that the government would have chosen any upland area for settlement.

However, the underlying assumptions about the environment with which the developers were dealing were incorrect, so that technical advances in transportation made possible the unrestricted exploitation of an area incapable of sustaining large populations with the agricultural technology then available. It was assumed that nature would provide bountiful harvests once land was cleared of its luxuriant forest and planted. The assumed correlation between rich vegetation and fertile soil was derived from experience in temperate climates where nutrients are stored in the soil. In the humid tropics, nutrient cycling takes place above ground, and nutrients are stored in the branches, stems, leaves, and roots. Thus, when the trees themselves are destroyed, so also are the available sources of nutrients for the vegetation grown there.[38] An area of poor soils and fragile environment was exposed to the most destructive exploitation possible through intensive small-plot garden crops in populous colonies. Within a few years of such cropping, the signs of environmental destruction became obvious. Land formerly cultivated was soon abandoned, colonists produced crops for only two or three years, and areas of older settlement declined in economic importance.

Such signs of imminent economic collapse were not attributed to inadequate agricultural techniques but were simply blamed on the colonists for their inability to make obviously fertile land flower. The colonization planners of the nineteenth century cannot be censured for their lack of knowledge based on what we know today, for they acted in line with then-accepted theories of the fertility of the soils. Rather, they can be criticized for their inability to recognize their error within a few years, before destruction had spread too far.

Perhaps the lack of a concept of land scarcity contributed to a lack of concern over the effect of sustained yield agriculture on the environment. Certainly there was an apparent abundance of land, but land near the center of colonies was quickly exhausted, thus requiring either moving the colony or rejuvenating the land. Rather than plan specifically for either alternative, there was simply a series of recriminations against the colonists. Regardless of who was to blame, it must be argued that the penetration of the Bragantina made possible by the building of a railroad left a legacy of severe environmental destruction. The problem of need for improved transportation could not be solved without some detrimental results.

The routes of trade were controlled from the capital by means of the Companhia do Amazonas and its successors in the case of water transportation, and the Belem-Bragança Railroad in the case of the land-based transportation in and out of the Bragantina. The boats of the transportation companies moved from Belem to ports where the lucrative rubber and other products could be loaded for subsequent shipment to Belem and ultimately abroad. The decisions on routing were made in Belem in the merchant houses and transportation companies and had little to do with economic interests of individuals in interior towns.

For that reason, the transportation network assumed the simple, unintegrated trunk-line form, with nearly all movement being directly between major interior points and Belem. There were few if any small companies plying the waters between the municipio seats to supply the looms of Porto de Moz with cotton from Santarem, or beans from Monte Alegre for the pots in Faro. The intermunicipio trade did not become established during the nineteenth century, when transportation was opening upriver frontiers. In all probability, had intermunicipio trade developed freely, centers of local industry and a more diversified agricultural economy could have developed, resulting in a definite challenge to Belem's economic control. Such was not the case, however, and the flow of wealth remained from the interior into Belem.

Trade in the Bragantina municipios followed much the same pattern as in the upriver municipios. Instead of water transportation, the Bragança railway provided the trunk line from the colonies and ultimately from Bragança to the capital. Several short branch lines were built as colonies were established at longer distances from the main tracks. By far the greatest volume of traffic on the railroad traveled between the municipios and Belem, with very little short-haul intermunicipio trade taking place. The agricultural goods being produced in the entire zone did not vary radically from one municipio to another, so that the exchange of goods rarely occurred, whereas most of the foodstuffs, particularly those items that had to be processed, such as corn, sugar, and rice, were shipped directly to the capital. In view of the reports of hunger and food shortages fairly frequently encountered in the newspapers and presidential reports, many of the municipios could not provide sufficient food for the local residents, who then had to purchase food from Belem markets, thus exerting a further strain on food supply. Shortages of basic food staples was yet another burden placed on the struggling colonists in the nineteenth century.

The people who came to Pará to settle thus had to deal with some serious and longstanding problems. Land titles were hopelessly tangled in bureaucratic red tape. Medical facilities were virtually nonexistent at a time when epidemic disease was common. Education remained unimportant to the government. Transportation opened new areas to exploitative farming methods and environmental destruction. All in all, the struggling colonists had a plethora of problems with which to cope just to survive.

6

Migration and Demographic Change

In any scheme of colonization, the single most important element is the human one. The mode of behavior of colonists in Pará had a lasting impact on the environment itself, on the policies devised to administer settlement, and on the economic and demographic situation that developed. In spite of the many difficulties and hardships faced, people did move to Pará and stayed to raise families. Although population increase has historically been slow, it has occurred, and for that reason alone, colonization must be considered to have been in some measure successful.

Demographic Change and Growth

Pará has never been a populous region, and in fact has always had one of the lowest population densities in Brazil. At any given time, only Amazonas and the other states and territories of northern Brazil have had fewer people per square kilometer. Population growth between 1758 and 1911 was significant but sporadic. The statistical sources, although prone to inaccuracy, do show that the population of 55,318 in 1773 had increased substantially to 796,679 in 1911. The colonial period was one of slow growth, while the pre–rubber boom period showed a considerable gain in population compared to the late eighteenth century, going from 156,775 in 1848 to 215,923 in 1862. The increase would probably be even more impressive if figures were available for the 1836–48 period, since the casualties of the Cabanagem revolt (1835–36) meant a definite population reduction. Conservative estimates of mortality as a result of the fighting, famine, and epidemics of the Cabanagem years were about 30,000 dead out of a population of approximately 100,000.[1] The years from 1848 to 1862 was an interim period between the Cabanagem and the rubber boom, before immigration from Ceará and abroad, when population was slowly but not markedly increasing. The third stage, 1862–1911, the years of rubber and immigrants, shows a rapid climb, from 215,923 people in 1862, to 796,679 in 1911, with the most notable rise coming toward the end of the period, when Northeasterners were settling with greater permanence and foreign immigrants were coming in larger numbers.

Migrants and Settlers

In the national period, the constraints on potential colonists were much less severe than during the Directorate. There was always a serious problem of attrition in the colonies, particularly among the foreign immigrants, who evidently found it exceedingly difficult to cope with the unfamiliar situation. However, their mobility was much greater than that of the Directorate Indians, and they could not be forced to remain in the colonies.

The principal constraint on new settlers arriving in the agricultural colonies was financial, since the incentives offered to foreign immigrants to settle in Pará were not free. Passage to Pará, the cost of land, house, tools, seeds, and the food or cash subsidy were almost always billed to the immigrant families as a loan, usually repayable in a ten- to twenty-year period. Theoretically, until the debt was repaid, those immigrants who came under such contracts, as most did, were legally obligated to remain in the colony, producing crops. Their produce was normally sold to a contractor who set aside a percentage of the sale price for payment on the loan. In fact, however, it was difficult to force people to stay in the settlements, and once they moved out, the debts proved almost impossible to collect.

It is not easy to document such departures from the government-run colonies of the Bragantina, but the privately managed colony of Nossa Senhora do Ó, located on an island in the bay facing Belem, did maintain records. The semimonthly newspaper, O Colono de Nossa Senhora do Ó, published frequent announcements of colonists who had left the colony before their debts were paid. Within a few days of the arrival of the first families in 1855, over half of the colonists had left without paying their debts.[2] Both the owners of the colony and the provincial legislators considered the situation deplorable, but the fact that the colonists left because of the cholera sweeping the area was not considered a mitigating circumstance. A notice several months later stated that one colonist had fled the colony without passport, official papers, or permission, and the writer called for stricter police supervision of travel to prevent future occurrences. Later that year it was reported that settler families had abandoned their plots in search of wealth as rubber gatherers.[3]

The founding of Apeú in 1883, discussed in chapter 3, provided another instance of public discussion about the debts of the colonists. Before they left the islands, the Azorean immigrants had signed a contract with officials from Pará, the terms of which were explicit. Their passage was to be paid to Pará and was free, providing they remained in the colony of

Benevides, where they were assigned. Upon arrival, they were reassigned to Apeú, then uninhabited forest, and they refused to remain there. The government therefore demanded that the immigrants repay the cost of passage; the immigrants refused, saying that the provincial government had broken the contract.[4] A copy of the contract was reprinted in the newspaper, as well as in the report of President Barradas that year. The Barradas reprint left out the clause about Benevides, thus making it appear that the breach of contract was made by the colonists. The matter went into litigation for several years and dropped quietly from public view. Although it was never specifically announced, the immigrants were released from their obligations, and most resettled in Belem.

Brazilian colonists, specifically the refugees from the droughts in the Northeast, were not subject to the financial restrictions of the foreign immigrants. They did not commit themselves legally to settle in the agricultural colonies in Pará. They did not sign contracts as colonists, and their only financial commitment was to pay for the definitive title to their land in the colonies. If they left the colony without paying for the title, the land reverted to the state, but there was no assessable debt. The Northeasterners who went to the Bragantina colonies did so because there were no facilities for them in Belem, and the promise of food, medical care, and land in the colonies was a powerful attraction.

One of the most difficult problems for colonization planners was the outward flow of Northeasterners from the colonies. At first it had been expected that they would remain in Pará permanently, increasing the labor pool and helping to settle and develop vast, and assumedly fertile, lands. Such a situation did not materialize. In every instance of drought migration to Pará between 1877 and 1911, the great majority of the refugees went back to the Northeast as soon as the rains had begun again there. During nondrought years, a large number of Northeasterners did migrate to Amazonia, but the majority of them moved upriver to the rubber fields. Relatively few remained in Pará, but those that did generally took up permanent residence in the agricultural colonies.

The first major return, in 1879 and 1880, was regarded calmly as a normal action. President Abreu pointed out that "if not in totality, at least a great part of the cearense refugees consider . . . their stay here to be only a temporary one, and have firm intentions of returning to their province as soon as circumstances improve, and this is a very natural sentiment."[5] By the time of the 1889 return, President Braga took an even more pragmatic position, saying that he had hoped that the Northeasterners would replace the recently emancipated slaves, but since the migrants did not want to work, they should be sent back to Ceará.[6]

There was also a certain measure of bitterness against the ephemeral nature of the migrations. The provincial government spent a good deal of money to provide the migrants with homes, land, food, and medicine. Some of the funds came from the imperial government, but provincial money was also used, and administration of all funds was handled at the provincial level. Local money was regarded as an investment in the future, a way of bringing more people to settle an admittedly underpopulated area. Theoretically, the economic growth that would result from such a population increase would far outweigh the initial investment. It was therefore understandable that after several migrations had come and gone, the planners were reluctant to continue to allocate money for colonies of Northeasterners. By the time of the 1904 drought there was a distinct coolness in the reception given refugees, and once they began to leave, the government quickly closed the colonies.[7] After 1910, little money was spent for refugee aid because of the poverty of state coffers, but even without the economic disaster of 1911, it was probably inevitable that refugees would receive little assistance.

The Cearense migrations had a definite impact on Pará. Although the majority of the refugees returned to the Northeast, perhaps a third of them did remain permanently in Pará, bringing an influence on language, food, and the economy as they were absorbed into the local population. The majority headed upriver to tap rubber, but those who chose to stay in the Belem area settled in the towns of the Bragantina and in Belem itself, where they have dominated much of the commercial sector. Even though their numbers were not as large as originally hoped, the government's involvement in their settlement was amply repaid.

Colonization in the national period was not confined to foreign immigrants and drought refugees. Undoubtedly, the greatest official attention was focused on settling newcomers to Pará, but the fact was also recognized that local people were also moving into the colonies. At first the shift of local populations was not encouraged, as the colonization officials felt that the sheltered and assisted existence in the colonies should be reserved for newcomers as they adapted to a new environment and assimilated into a new culture. That view began to change by the early 1880s, when it was decided to allow local people to move into the colonies to help in the adaptation and assimilation. Probably, a part of the reasoning was also to fill empty houses of those colonists who had refused to remain in the colonies.

The people from Pará in the colonies rarely merited attention, and there are few clues to their origins. Those moving into the small colonies near the various towns scattered throughout the basin undoubtedly came from the surrounding area, perhaps close to the towns themselves. In the Bragantina, the picture is more complicated, since there were simply no towns in the area until the coming of the railroad and establishment of the first colonies, such as Benevides and Apeú. Probably the local paraenses had lived near Belem or may have come from the fringe areas of the fertile lands in the Lower Tocantins, peripheral to the sugar and rice plantations. Paraenses worked on the construction crews of the Bragança railroad and resided in the colonies along the route. In any case, by virtue of their numbers and their knowledge of local conditions, despite little official attention, they were an important force in building the colonies into stable towns.

The Men of Ceará

The drought migrations from the Northeast in the nineteenth century provided some of the largest numbers of immigrants coming to Amazonia and to Pará in particular. However, within the overall context of Amazonia, different groups of cearenses, as they were collectively called, apparently went to different areas of the basin. In the case of the upriver province/state of Amazonas, the census figures indicate that substantially more men than women came to the rubber fields to become tappers. In Pará, on the other hand, the cearenses apparently came largely as entire families, some to tap rubber and a great many more to settle in the colonies established by the local government.

Official reports support this statement. In 1889, the Ministry of the Empire report stated that 4,923 families had left Ceará for other provinces between September 1888 and April 1889, during which time the area was suffering severe drought, of which 777 families had gone to Pará, a total of 6,266 people.[8] In Ceará, the 1872 census showed that for every 1,000 males there were 975 females. In the 1890 census, after two large-scale migrations, the ratio rose to 1,041 females to every 1,000 males. Apparently more men than women were leaving the province, but the change in ratios is not large enough to suggest that only men were involved in the migration, probably because so many immigrants came with their families to settle in Pará.

Several inferences about the gender distribution of the population may also be drawn from the census materials from 1773 to 1900, as shown in table 6.1. The colonial censuses do not show an equal gender distribution among all racial groups, although the total figures do show a roughly similar division for 1773 and 1783. Using the complete censuses of 1773, 1783, and 1707, which counted Europeans, Indians, and African slaves, the data show a fairly equal distribution by gender among the whites, a

Table 6.1. Male and Female Percentages of Total Population, Pará, 1773–1900

Year	% Male	% Female
1773	50.66	49.34
1783	49.95	50.05
1797	48.23	51.77
1848	49.69	50.31
1853	47.68	52.32
1856	49.60	50.40
1872	51.77	48.23
1890	50.65	49.35
1900	48.70	51.30

Source: Statistical programs PARA6N, 7N, and 8N. My calculations.

noticeable predominance of females among the Indians, and a very marked male predominance among slaves. The latter situation is to be expected, since male slaves were preferred, and the available data on colonial slave importations to Pará show a preponderance of males.

The figures for the Indian populations may have been biased somewhat by the absence of men away on fishing and collecting expeditions. Such a bias would depend largely on the month that the censuses were taken, since such expeditions were usually seasonal. In an effort to test the reliability of those censuses, other population counts that covered the whole region between 1770 and 1797 but included only Indians, were used. Taken at various times of the year, they showed remarkably little variation in the male-female distribution. As a final test, data from individual villages throughout the 1758–98 period were used, with the same results. Thus, it seems fairly certain that Indian women held a 4 to 5 percent numerical advantage over Indian men, a division that did not change appreciably by decade or region. The colonial demographic data indicate that throughout Pará, women in the Directorate villages outnumbered men.

Between 1848, the date of the first systematic census in Pará after independence, and 1872, the first national level census, the percentage of males in the population did increase significantly. The rise was most noticeable between 1856 and 1872, when it jumped by over two percentage points. However, those figures do not necessarily indicate an in-migration skewed by gender. The rubber boom was not in full swing as early as 1872 and therefore cannot really be considered an important causal factor in attracting men to Pará to gather latex. In one of the rare references to rubber gathering before 1880, Provincial Secretary Domingos Soares Ferreira Penna, who traveled extensively in the interior, remarked that whole families moved to the rubber stands from other parts of the province during the summer, returning home when the rains came.[9] Furthermore, the first major immigration as a result of the droughts began in 1877, five years after the census. Censuses covering the periods of large migrations add further information. Between 1872 and 1890, during which there were two large migrations, the percentage of males actually dropped. It rose again by 1900, though not as high as before the migrations in 1872, and by 1920 it had declined a little. Thus, it appears that, as a general rule, intact families fled the droughts together rather than being split up, with women and children remaining in Ceará while heads of households sought their fortunes in the Amazon.

Newspaper reports substantiate this assumption, as nearly every mention of the incoming Northeasterners referred to families. The 1877–79 drought provides one of the best-documented examples, with the first cearenses reported arriving in Pará being families coming in June, July, and August 1877. In April 1878 the Public Aid Commission in Santarem notified the provincial government that they were assigning land to cearenses, using size of family and abilities of family members as criteria for size of land grant. In Benevides that same year, a report on the miserable conditions there specifically mentioned that many cearense families had four to eight children and simply could not feed them on the government subsidy. In November 1878 an asylum for widows and orphans, the Asilo Cearense, was established in Belem for those migrant women and children who had lost husbands and fathers. In 1879, a report from Bragança mentioned that the cearenses there were well fed and every Northeasterner family had its own house.[10]

The 1877–79 drought migration was not unique in this respect. People fleeing from the droughts came as family groups, probably for several reasons. It would have been a far more compassionate act for a husband to bring his family with him to an uncertain future in Pará than to abandon them to certain death from disease and starvation in Ceará. Finances would not have been an issue, since passage was supplied by the Pará government. After arriving in Belem, many of the single men who did come went on to the rubber fields upriver, but those with families more frequently chose to remain in Pará and move into the agricultural colonies of the Bragantina. Although many such migrants subsequently chose to return to Ceará when the rains began again, most probably came to Pará with the expectation of making a new home there. Certainly one factor that encourages permanent settlement of a population new to the area is the presence of family units, couples with their children to work the land together. The prospect of raising a family in new and unfamiliar surroundings was undoubtedly more attractive when seen in the context of farming their own land than when considering making a living tapping rubber in the vast forests. Although many did return to the Northeast, the population counts of those who remained behind in the colonies and elsewhere demonstrate that almost all of those who remained were in family groups.

The discussion of migration and demographic growth indicates one basic fact about population in Pará. Whether voluntary or involuntary, Brazilian or foreign, nearly all of the people responsible for filling the towns in Pará between 1758 and 1911 were migrants or offspring of migrants. The growth of population in Pará during that period was due to the forced migration of Indians downriver into established settlements in the colonial period, foreign immigration in both colonial and national periods, and semivoluntary internal migrations within Brazil that focused on Pará and the Amazon Basin in the national period. Immigration of large numbers of people to areas of new settlement was the only way that the region could be rapidly and expeditiously populated.

CONCLUSION

The terms *success* and *failure* are subjective and relative, particularly when considering the outcome of nearly two centuries of effort to colonize the Lower Amazon Basin. In some respects, those efforts were successful: new towns were established, old ones were made permanent settlements, and people came to live there and stayed. In other respects, however, settlement policy failed. In absolute terms, there were more towns and more people, but in subjective terms, the quality of life in those settlements was somewhat less than ideal. Planners of colonization did not devote their energies out of any humanitarian interest, but the quality-of-life argument becomes critical in persuading people to remain in the embryonic towns. Because of the difficulty in living in the isolated towns, and the attraction of Belem, many would-be inhabitants chose to leave. Without those people the towns would die and the overall goal of settling empty lands would be defeated.

Thus, some elements of colonization were successful, while others ultimately failed. To the extent that planned settlement of Pará has succeeded, a set pattern of development has generally occurred. Despite the different circumstances and socioeconomic backgrounds of towns founded in the colonial and national periods in Pará, the stages of development have remained remarkably unchanged for the entire 1758 to 1911 period.

The first stage was a potentially critical situation, involving the actual establishment of the colony, bringing the settlers to the site and getting them established on their lands. In the colonial period, such relocation was done largely by force, real or threatened, to bring the Indians in descimentos to the Directorate towns. The establishment and settlement of Mazagão also fit this first stage. All of the provincial and state governments' attempts after 1850 to establish the various types of colonies also represent the critical first state. The potential for failure was very real, as exemplified by the early attempt to set up a colony at Apeú in 1883. In the colonial period, attempted settlements that never got off the ground included Vila Viçosa de Madre de Deus and Rebordelo.

The second stage was one of subsidization, supervision, and dependence of the settlement, during which time its physical development began to take shape. The whole forty years of the Directorate belong to this stage, as Indian villages were governed by outsiders with minimal association with local tribal authorities. All decision-making powers rested in the hands of men who were not culturally members of those communities. The Indians' labor subsidized the villages through the *negocio do sertão*, but that income was shuttled from the village to the government, and then back again some time later. Had the Directorate ended at virtually any point throughout most of that period, the Indians would have abandoned the towns and the forest would have reigned again.

During the national period, this stage was most visible in the first five years in the life of the colonies set up by the provincial presidents and state governors. Fields were cleared, crops planted, houses built, the urban nucleus created, some public services provided, and a marketing system begun. Control was still directed from authority external to the community, and inhabitants had very little decision-making power. It was a dynamic period with considerable visible development subsidized by the income from collecting and agriculture in the colonial period and by public revenues from taxes on rubber in the case of the national period. Any interference with the flow of public revenues into the settlements in the national period was disastrous at this stage, since there were few crop surpluses or nongovernment financial resources and little economic independence. In the colonial period, disaster was more apt to strike because of disease, crop failure, Indian attack, flood, or other occurrence with which the colonial officials could not deal effectively. During both periods, any degree of financial disruption tended to cause severe repercussions in the development of the towns, due to the tremendous dependence of the settlements on outside authority, resources, and money.

The third stage marked the beginning of another potential crisis. In 1798, the Directorate came to an abrupt close, and the villages were left alone to fend for themselves for a half century or more. Those that survived could claim some economic or geographical reason for existence and enough of a nascent power structure to survive as a community. For example, Santarem could control traffic on the Tapajós River because it was located at the mouth of the river where it met the Amazon. Obidos, on the main channel, could monitor activity on the Amazon because it sat at the narrowest point of the entire river. After a relatively short period of subsidization of government-sponsored colonies during the national period, support was withdrawn through emancipation of the settlements, making them into villages or towns with the same privileges and responsibilities as other such units. Ending the subsidization represented the cutting of the financial umbilicus, after which the former colony was nominally independent, with no more claims on government monies. Such a critical period of withdrawal of organizational and financial support was characterized by a large percentage of new towns falling into serious economic difficulties.

The operational model of the third stage was "survival of the fittest." Towns such as Esposende and Fragoso in the colonial period, and Ferreira Gomes and Nossa Senhora do O' in the national period, whose existence had never moved above the marginal level, died out completely. Those towns that failed to survive the critical third stage generally had not developed the economic base, demographic increase, and power infrastructure to create a new community. As in nature, only the most fit survived this stage, a necessary one in the process of selecting those towns most apt to continue as viable urban units.

The fourth stage provided the resolution of the crisis period, as the new towns struggled to adjust and continue to develop a strong and stable economic base. Many former colonies did not survive readjustment, either becoming tiny population clusters or disappearing entirely. In the waning years of the colonial period, the third stage occurred with the 1798 abolition of the Directorate, and the fourth stage covered the years 1798 to 1850, during which time little attention was paid to encouraging new settlement or bolstering development of existing towns. In the national period, most government-sponsored colonies experienced the readjustment phase after emancipation around 1900. Regardless of their origins, all towns had to face drastic fiscal readjustment when the rubber boom ended.

Those former colonies that managed to survive the readjustment period, which lasted five to ten years in the national period and a great deal longer in the colonial period, then entered into a more positive final stage. With varying degrees of rapidity, people of such towns began to achieve certain goals, the summation of which could be called the "criteria of success." These goals provide an estimate of the degree of success enjoyed by a town in terms of its inhabitants and the political-economic framework within which it exists. The achievements included the provision of a full spectrum of services for the inhabitants, either by local personnel or as part of a statewide network, as in the case of education and health care; development of local agriculture developed to a point of potential self-sufficiency, along with simultaneously encouraged intermunicipio trade; eventual diversification of the economy with the beginning of light industry and nonagricultural employment; and local policy decisions effectively made at the local level through a town council and through local participation in municipio-level decisions, rather than having such decisions handed down from state officials in Belem, where local situations might not be fully understood. Also included in the criteria were the eventual political maturity, which would involve inhabitants of those communities in the state and regional political power network, and a stable, growing population characterized by demographic patterns not widely disparate from state-level averages, and by few signs of significant exodus to larger urban centers.

Some of those goals have been achieved, significant others have not. There must be some degree of diversification of the economy, primarily in the secondary sector, which can provide employment for an urban nonagriculturist population. Throughout much of the Bragantina, that diversification has not taken place. The few towns where it has occurred have seen substantial growth and development into regional centers of employment, but most towns have remained economically backward. Further, there must be a considerable degree of involvement by all economically active groups in the overall economic network of the region through export of goods and surplus production in return for other items not produced locally. Economic self-sufficiency was no mark of success if it developed into economic isolation. In addition to commerce itself, such involvement in the regional economy included establishing new businesses of all types, generating new jobs, and circulating money. Again, those towns participating in a diversified economy are part of an interregional network as well. Those that have remained primarily involved in subsistence agriculture and gathering of forest products have continued in their marginal status.

In short, the social and cultural needs of the population must be met, a sense of community must develop, the local political power structure must be responsive to local problems and capable of dealing with them, and the community must develop an economic situation that transcends the primary sector and integrates the community into a larger economic system to the benefit of both community and system. It would be rash indeed to say that any colony that accomplished all of these aims is *ipso facto* a success, but the chances are good that any town with most of those objectives already attained is permanent, stable, and unlikely to be destroyed except by extraordinary events.

Many of the former colonies of the late colonial and early national period have not yet achieved these goals. An examination of colonies since 1850 in terms of their economic growth, political power, and social development shows that no more than 10 of the 137 towns under observation have yet reached that stage. Perhaps a third of those towns have not yet completed the full roster of achievements but are well on the way to attaining the goals. Many more await a more uncertain future. A rough measurement of success can be ascertained by looking at former colonies in 1970 in terms of their administrative status, indicating the regional importance of many of these towns. Of the towns founded and administered by the Directorate between 1758 and 1798, 46 percent were municipio seats in 1970, 33 percent were small towns, and 21 percent had vanished. Of towns founded as colonies between 1840 and 1911, 21 percent were municipio seats, 60 percent were small towns, and 19 percent no longer existed.[1]

As would be expected, these figures indicate that towns founded earlier have become more firmly established as municipio seats, and some of them as heads of larger political divisions, than those founded in the national period. The comparative percentages of complete failures were roughly similar. The small-town category is significantly larger for towns founded in the national period than for those founded in the colonial years. Such a pattern probably illustrates the fact that the same process is operational in both cases, but more advanced for towns established in the eighteenth century. The former colonies listed as small towns may become municipio seats in the future. Quite possibly, the reason for so many nonmunicipio-seat towns, which are largely in the Bragantina, is the relative abundance of towns vis-à-vis land area and the proximity of such towns to the metropolis of Belem, the shadow effect thus inhibiting independent development of those towns.

Whatever criticism can be leveled against government efforts to settle Pará between 1758 and 1911, it must be recognized that large areas were settled effectively. Waterside settlement along major rivers increased dramatically between 1758 and 1911, and the increase is attributable both to population growth and policies of settlement. The Directorate system provided an ethnocentric and exploitative means of acculturation and settlement, but the system also included a forty-year-long policy that firmly established almost half of its towns as permanent urban nuclei. Those Directorate villages, based on earlier mission settlements, developed from hamlets in the late eighteenth century into municipio seats in the nineteenth century.

During the national period, colonization efforts were not nearly as uniform or widespread, as only the Bragantina area was being developed consistently. Colonies developed in the national period had both advantages and disadvantages in comparison with those of the colonial period.

Transportation and communication were much easier with the advent of steam navigation and the railroad. Disease was a treatable phenomenon. Individual colonists had a greater measure of political and economic freedom of choice. On the other hand, improved agricultural and transportation technology made it possible to exploit a fragile environment much more efficiently and rapidly, leading to ecological damage, which in turn has caused the agricultural economy of the Bragantina to suffer. Land tenure was uncertain, lacking clearly stated and efficiently administered land laws for smallholders. The single product export of rubber provided large amounts of public revenues not always wisely or sparingly spent. Changes in policy in terms of basic issues of who, where, and how to settle were made so rapidly that lack of policy continuity was a definite problem.

In examining the pattern of colonization in Pará between 1758 and 1911, one fact becomes crystal clear. The degree of success of colonization that can be attributed to Pará is the result more of the efforts of the settlers themselves than the efforts of the governors, legislators, and planners. The colonization projects set in motion by such officials received little attention after being put into force. The people who settled in the towns, whether through coercion or free will, managed to keep their communities alive and functioning in most cases. Credit for the continued existence of those towns must accrue to those who lived in them, and only to a lesser degree to those who operated the administrative machinery. Colonization programs resulted in a network of towns that, while not comparable to similar programs elsewhere in Brazil, still represent a massive effort to settle people in previously underpopulated sections of the humid tropics.

Perhaps therein lies the lesson of past experience for colonization efforts in the Lower Amazon. Programs, plans, and projects will come and go. Super solutions will continue to appear to offer the definitive answer to all the problems. Different political ideologies in different administrations will focus on different priorities. But ultimately, the success or failure of towns founded under government direction will depend on the people who choose to remain there. When they identify themselves as members of that community and are then willing to work at making that settlement into a viable unit, then the successful colonization of that area will be assured.

The patterns of growth and stagnation of settlement in the century and a half covered in this study amply demonstrate the problems in colonizing the humid tropics. Yet the problems of colonization and settlement are just as real today as ever. The stages of development of communities are being lived out today, but no lessons have been learned from the past.[2] The efforts to find the ideal settler put in the perfect spot under the best possible administration have not produced widespread settlement and economic development of the region.[3] Under the circumstances, there is little reason to suppose that current efforts will be the definitive solution. The fact remains that what was difficult in the past will continue to be difficult in the future.

EPILOGUE

Lessons Unlearned, Attitudes Unchanged

The Amazon today is under the assault of new attempts to develop and exploit the region. Over the past decade, the international press has carried many stories about the widespread burning and destruction of huge areas of previously undisturbed forest, the relocation and encroachment on indigenous reserves, and many other stories of destruction. The plight of the Indians and other local people and the environment in which they live has been increasingly publicized, but the destruction continues.

Much of what is written would lead the reader to believe that this destruction is a recent phenomenon. In fact, it is an extension of an exploitative mentality that is centuries old. When the Portuguese first committed to ownership of the basin and began trying to use its local people to produce wealth, the extractive mindset was born. It was clearly manifested in the social and economic policies of the Directorate and the reports on diminishing availability of certain products. It was again apparent in the nineteenth-century economy, based almost exclusively on rubber tapping. It is equally obvious today.

A good deal has been said in this book about the Indians and their treatment by the Portuguese government. A brief glance at these people today shows that their situation has only worsened. The number of people classified as indigenous by the Brazilian government, estimated in 1996 as approximately 320,000, has steadily fallen as they are increasingly subjected to contact and manipulation in the name of development.[1] The survivors have been relocated onto reserves in areas where the Brazilians until recently have had little interest. However, today virtually no area of Amazonia is hidden from the developers, and the Indian reserves have been systematically violated.[2] Large sections have been eliminated from reserves to open land for mining, logging, and settlement. Even within the reserves, miners, rubber tappers, ranchers, and lumbermen have entered illegally to strip resources. Roads are built through reserves, and airstrips accompany military posts, particularly in the protected lands under control of the Calha Norte Project. The Calha Norte, or "Northern

Border," highway will open huge areas to deforestation and displace some of the last intact tribes of Amazonia, such as the Yanomami.[3]

The federal government has been exceedingly ambivalent on the Indian issue. On one hand, they have forced miners from Indian reserves; on the other hand, in 1966 they issued Decree 1775. This decree allows commercial interests to protest the demarcation of Indian lands and appeal inclusion of land in the reserves. In the first four months after the decree was promulgated, 531 claims from miners, loggers, ranchers, and government officials had been filed, targeting eighty-three different Indian areas.[4] Some claims were rejected immediately, but others have gone successfully through the entire appeals process, such as the loss of a piece of land the size of Rhode Island from the Macuxi reserve in December 1996.[5] Ultimately, all claims were denied, after having caused a wave of open conflicts in which one tribe promised a fight to the death or collective suicide if they were evicted.[6] The Indians may have dodged the bullet for the moment, but Decree 1775 remains on the books.

Loss of their ancestral territory is nothing new for the Amazonian Indians. They were forcibly relocated by the Directorate and often fled before the advances of the rubber tappers and settlers in the nineteenth century. Throughout history, the conquering Luso-Brazilian culture has held that far too few Indians controlled far too much land. The attendant implicit assumption has been that Europeans can do a far better job of using the land for the benefit of a great many more people. As the indigenous population has steadily declined, there has also been a government consensus that large parts of the rain forest are "empty" and thus available for numerous forms of exploitation.

Part of the problem may well be the basic regard for land itself. Europeans have a long history of regarding land as an object to be owned, simply a factor of agricultural production. Most indigenous people do not regard land in terms of ownership per se, but as an environmental "given," much like air, to be used as needed but not privately owned. Such an attitude, in conflict with a dominant culture, has always been and will continue to be ignored and passed over as nonmodern and unacceptable. "Land hunger," the desire for land ownership, is one of the most basic motives behind European frontier movements on every continent, in every century.

Since the end of the military regime in 1985, and because of increasing international attention to the Indians' situation, the Brazilian government has made some changes in policy. New and larger reserves have been set aside, laws now prohibit encroachment by settlers and miners on Indian lands, and the tribes are now legally recognized by the constitution of 1988 as having the right to maintain their own cultures.[7] Yet, these laws are passed in Brasilia, and local conditions certainly indicate that the letter of the law is only superficially enforced. Basic attitudes toward the Indians remain unchanged, and they are still perceived as an obstacle to progress.

Yet, the indigenous people have a great deal of knowledge that could be useful in sustainable development of Amazonia. Studies of the Kayapó in particular have demonstrated a wealth of information about successful forest management without degradation of the ecology.[8] They have lived successfully within the constraints of the environment for centuries by specific planting and harvesting techniques that farmers would do well to imitate. Further, anthropologists and other researchers are constantly publishing findings concerning indigenous biomedical knowledge.[9] Because of native peoples' intimate knowledge of the forest and its fauna and flora, they hold a vast amount of information about many remedies. Further, because of the endemicity of organisms in the rain forest, different tribes have vastly different knowledge of local species variations not found in other areas, even relatively close ones. The extinction of tribal groups, even their relocation on reserves, means the loss of a tremendous body of knowledge of incalculable value to the biomedical and pharmaceutical industries.

Laws protecting Indian land and peoples are acknowledged and enforced only when it is politically expedient to do so. When foreign investors offer major sums to exploit some region such as the Carajás iron mines, the land is taken from the local tribes and the people are relocated.[10] When gold is discovered on Indian lands, the government is nearly powerless to stop the rush of miners, as has happened in Roraima and southern Pará.[11] While reserves are demarcated for Indian use, neighboring landowners may stake legal claim to large portions of the land by invoking Decree 1775, resulting in many years of court proceedings and lack of clear title to the land. Whenever local authorities or the military, which still controls a great deal of Amazonian affairs in the name of national security, claim the necessity of a road or railway through Indian lands, the projects are approved. In short, the indigenous peoples are watching their territories shrink to a tiny fraction of what their ancestors claimed.

A few of the tribes have become politically active since Brazil's return to democracy. There are a few organizations, such as the Union of Indigenous Nations, which have brought a number of groups together to fight politically for their rights.[12] Also emerging are grassroots movements involving the Indians with other local groups previously unfriendly to them, such as miners, rubber tappers, and small farmers. Together, they have publicized their cause with marches, protests, and other public appearances, as well as working through the legal system to secure title to their lands. They have also been increasingly active on the international scene, working with various nongovernment organizations. The national print media has also taken up their cause on occasion. The indigenous movement is generally regarded as the group most able to slow or stop some of the more destructive development schemes, witness the Kayapó resistance to the proposed dams on the Xingú River.[13]

Another major topic in this work has been the emphasis on transportation and its role in the attempt to settle people in portions of Amazonia. During the eighteenth century, the problem of transportation was relatively simple and was tied to the problem of labor. Goods could be brought from the backlands to Belem by only one means, canoe transport using Indian rowers. It was constantly difficult because of the increasing scarcity of able-bodied men as the native populations shrank. But it caused virtually no environmental damage. In the nineteenth century, with the advent of the railroad era, transportation took on a new dimension. The limited use of railroads in the Bragantina had a double impact on the forest and human ecology of the region: heretofore inaccessible areas were opened to nonindigenous settlement and degradation, and the forest was cleared to supply railroad ties, fuel, and agriculture. A pattern began that tied transportation to the opening of new lands for settlement and exploitation and to the growth of towns and cities.

It was a pattern that in the twentieth century has reached monstrous proportions. Just as proponents of the Belem-Bragança railroad gleefully announced the coming of European-style agriculture and settlement to the environs of the capital city, so too the government promised a great new world for Amazonia as it entered the modern national picture with the construction of the Belem-Brasilia highway in 1960. Within a decade, the TransAmazon highway was an environmental fact, followed by the Santarem-Cuiabá road. Then began an explosion of road building, crisscrossing Amazonia in all directions, opening new land for colonization, exposing new mineral resources, dislocating indigenous populations, and devastating the ecosystems for many miles on either side of the roads.[14] Existing towns exploded in population; new towns, villages, and hamlets sprang up everywhere. Some were population centers designed as part of the government colonization scheme, the elaborate plan of *agrópolis* and *agrovila* typical along the TransAmazon. Others were spontaneous clusters of people devoted to supplying and practicing a specific activity such as *garimpagem* (gold mining). Still others were associated with specific projects, such as Daniel Ludwig's ill-fated Jarí Project or the enormous iron mines of the Carajás Project.

Within the towns and cities, social divisions became far more noticeable than ever before. The large landowners, ranchers, and owners of rubber groves and Brazil nut stands remain as the entrenched elite. However, their traditional control of political and economic structures is now effectively challenged by an emerging urban middle class.[15] Relatively new to the basin except in Belem and Manaus, they have been enormously successful at accumulating capital as middlemen in sale of extracted resources and in transportation of goods along the highways. They are also the group acquiring large sections of cleared land and degraded forest, buying land at speculative prices as a hedge against ruinous inflation.

There is much discussion today about the relative responsibilities of three levels of government in creating sustainable development in the Amazon. The international bodies, primarily financial and environmental, appear most efficient at providing expertise, technical knowledge, and to a lesser degree, debt financing. The World Bank in particular has poured enormous amounts of money into Amazonian megaprojects, most of them turning out to be some of the most socially and ecologically destructive projects ever seen in the tropics. The Polonoroeste project to open up the area of Rondonia was a gigantic failure and was followed by the Planaflora project, which was the supersolution to its predecessor's disaster. After expending huge sums of money without any positive outcome, the World Bank has now investigated the entire scheme.[16] The federal government, which in this century has assumed most interest and responsibility for development of northern Brazil, has experienced great difficulty in managing regional programs from Brasilia. Until very recently, local government has had virtually no voice in policy formulation, enactment, and enforcement.

The new trend appears to seek to turn increasing control over to the states and reduce both federal and international hands-on management. Lack of local people's involvement was one of the major reasons for the failure of the US$229 million Planaflora project, according to the World Bank report.[17] However, such plans overlook a well-documented change in Amazonian society, the growth and entrenchment of the nonagricultural middle class. These people, who would obviously benefit from a nonmoving frontier based on sustainable development, may have another agenda. This is precisely the group that has been buying land for its speculative value, creating a new "hollow frontier" and encouraging further deforestation.[18] Measures giving greater local control may well be seen as new opportunities for becoming wealthy. Such aspirations combined with new status as large landowners may therefore put the middle class square in the camp of established elites, particularly the cattle ranchers, and thus prevent new programs from benefiting the local people for whom the programs were created.

In at least some discussions, local control is considered to be at the level of the people actually trying to eke out a living in the forest. The key to local control lies specifically with those people and the extent to which they can collectively have an impact on local and regional government actions. If it is left to state governments without such input, the power and influence of traditional elites, such as cattle ranchers and other large landowners, the newly emergent middle class, and the multinational corporations will effectively block any attempts at sustainable settlement.

For sheer numbers, the social group most responsible for the urban growth has been the poor. Cities like Marabá, which dates back to the mid-nineteenth century, and Altamira, largely a product of TransAmazon growth, have mushroomed in size as people seek a better way of life than they can find along the roads. Many are colonists who have failed to establish themselves on land granted them in government colonization projects. As land values soared due to speculation, they have sold their lots for sums far in excess of the agricultural potential and moved to urban settings.[19] Others living in the sprawling slums came as labor in building the roads and have remained because, difficult as their existence is in the Amazon, it is preferable to the bleak situation of the labor market in other parts of Brazil. Still others came to Amazonia, lured by the dream of riches in the gold fields, and have remained because prospects elsewhere seem dim.

Building the spiderweb of roads throughout the basin has been the key to all the other development schemes that have so drastically altered the landscape. They have been built in the same wild rush to integrate Amazonia into the rest of Brazil that the Belem-Bragança railroad was built to integrate that region into the shadow of the capital of Pará. The mind frame has not changed. The motives have not changed. Only the scope and impact have changed.

A comparison of the settlement policies of the eighteenth and nineteenth centuries and the contemporary assault on Amazonia may seem at first glance to have very little in common. In fact, there are a great many common themes in the two stories. Historical trends established with the first serious attempts by Europeans to settle and exploit the Amazon have been perpetuated in the late twentieth century. The mind set that saw

Grão Pará as a source of forest riches for the European luxury trade was virtually the same one motivating Brazil's government today to work in tandem with capitalists from southern Brazil to strip Amazonian resources for the use and pleasure of more developed parts of the nation.

Certainly there are differences in detail. The major problem facing the Directorate was the control of labor, the most precious commodity of that time. Control and manipulation of labor during the rubber boom remained of paramount interest. In the twentieth century, labor scarcity is not nearly the issue as previously, given Brazil's some 157 million population. Today the scarce commodity is usable land, a factor of production that is becoming increasingly precious as the population continues to grow. Brazil no longer needs to attract colonists from Europe, but there has been a strong incentive to colonize the Amazon in lieu of meaningful agrarian reform elsewhere in Brazil. Control of land is of the same vital interest today that control of labor was two centuries ago and has led to intense conflict, violation of human rights, and bloodshed.[20]

Other distinctions could be made. Certainly the damage done to the Amazonian ecosystem by the Portuguese and the nineteenth-century Brazilians was a tiny fraction of the devastation wrought by D8 bulldozers and million-hectare reservoirs today. But the point must be made that the differences are in detail only. The motivations and guiding interests are still the same. The attitudes toward the entire basin and its native peoples remain unchanged. The overwhelming belief that the Amazon exists for the benefit of the metropole, whatever its name may be, has suffered no mutation.

There are a number of historical trends visible in the present-day "development" of the Amazon. The geopolitical fear of foreign encroachment can be read in the earliest motivation to establish a Portuguese military presence in the Amazon. Today it takes the form of the Calha Norte Project, which establishes military posts and airstrips within native reserves on the northern borders. It was probably the most powerful single impetus behind the TransAmazon highway, which was originally conceived as a military road. It is quite visible in much of the government rhetoric and actions regarding the presence of foreign researchers and international agencies concerned with the Amazon. The Brazilians want foreign loans to develop the area, but they most certainly do not want foreign presence or foreign interference in their plans. As an illustration, monitoring the extent of deforestation is most effectively done from LandSat satellite images, but in 1992 the Brazilian government stopped funding for that analysis. They claimed that continuous analysis was not necessary and that five-year intervals were sufficient for documentation. In fact, continuous analysis was clearly disproving the government allegation that the rate of deforestation was slowing. The truth is that even taking into account regional differences, deforestation is proceeding at an increasing rate, with estimates in 1994 that 12 percent of the rain forest is now gone.[21]

Another common thread is the official attitude toward the original inhabitants. During the Directorate, a great deal of attention was paid to the Indians, primarily because of the importance of their labor. Forced relocation of populations into sites where they could be "civilized"—that is, absorbed into the dominant culture—was the means employed. The racial attitudes of the Portuguese held that, while the Indians were human and not just animals, they were perpetual children who had to be taught to speak, dress, and live like their superiors. The benevolent paternalism of the Jesuits, and to a lesser degree the Directors, has been replaced today by a "throwaway" mentality. The Indians today are regarded as an impediment to the development of the region, and the attitude has been to acculturate, relocate, or exterminate them in the name of progress.[22]

Along with a highly racist attitude toward the Indians have gone some basic assumptions about the entire environment. The Portuguese were rather daunted by the immensity of the entire highly unfamiliar area. They certainly felt a need to bring portions under agricultural production, but they also relegated most of the forest to a region of seasonal foraging for exotic items. Some of those goods were hunted into near extinction. The nineteenth-century experience saw a shift in that attitude, putting more credence in a tropical paradise of European-type farms on vast fertile soils. The majority of the forest, removed from civilization, was a source of great extractive wealth but was also considered a potential site for future agriculture. In the twentieth century there remains a mix of extractivism and agriculture, with the technology to level the forest over previously unimaginably huge areas.

The common theme is the attitude that the forest and the land it stands upon have no intrinsic value. The only value to the encroaching people lies in its productivity when the trees are gone and other plants are growing that will produce revenue.[23] Only cleared land has any value, which is one of the reasons for the vast deforestation, as people take possession of holdings, clear them, and sell them, often already planted in grass.[24] This moving frontier is not unique to Amazonia but was first reported in nineteenth-century southern Brazil. As long as there is financial reward rather than penalties for ongoing frontier deforestation and subsequent sale, the phenomenon will continue.

A historical trend of some duration relates to the search for all-encompassing solutions to the problems of development and the financial means for securing those solutions. The story of attempted colonization during the rubber boom depicts a situation where supersolutions, one after another, were attempted, using large sums of government money during a boom economy. During those years, money was rarely a major consideration in devising and implementing settlement programs. The only times that it was discussed at length was during occasional reductions in the world price of rubber or when vilifying one's political enemies.

Throughout the history of the frontier in Brazil, and in Amazonia particularly, there has been a government predilection for the "supersolution," or as it is now known, the megaproject. Grand plans are developed with elaborate organization, volumes of regulations, and enormous sums of money. The plan is put into effect, exists for a few years until the inherent flaws and mistakes are too noticeable to ignore any longer, and the whole plan is scrapped. The budget is cut or eliminated altogether; construction of roads, bridges, and railroads is halted abruptly; a great deal of highly critical verbiage appears in the press and legislature; and the settlers who had been enticed to participate are abandoned. More recent information suggests that on the dawn of the millenium, the megaprojects still threaten the forest, perhaps more than ever.[25]

Within a short period of time, sometimes a matter of weeks, a whole new scheme is announced that is touted to solve all the problems and pave the way to the future. It becomes the new supersolution and begins its own evolutionary decay. Previous mistakes are never adequately analyzed to avoid future catastrophes, as in the World Bank's attempt to rectify the Polonoroeste project by funding the Planaflora project. Support for preceding programs evaporates, and people dependent on it are left to struggle on their own. Destruction of the environment, be it river, soils, forest, fauna, or flora, is the only sign that the great solution ever even existed.

Such was definitely the picture in the nineteenth century. Certainly in today's age of instant communication and complex technology, such plans appear at a far faster rate than ever before. The speed of the master plan is matched by the speed of destruction. Yet the thinking behind the TransAmazon colonization, the Polonoroeste, the Perimetral Norte, the Jarí Project, the Calha Norte, Carajás, Planaflora, and so on is identical to the extractive mentality of the Directorate and the settlement schemes during the rubber boom. What has changed is the speed and the potential for permanent devastation. There is still a desire for the instant fix, the grand solution to a basic agenda—exploit and extract from the environment the maximum possible in the shortest period of time, with public, private, and human capital.[26] What has changed still remains the same.

It is no accident that the recent heyday of megaprojects of settlement and transportation in the Amazon occurred during the "economic miracle" growth years of the 1960s and 1970s. There was a great deal of government money available to subsidize such development and an enormous amount of private capital to match it. In many ways, the collapse of the miracle may have been the salvation of yet-untouched areas of the basin.

Once again, those in charge of conforming Amazonia to human settlement and profit are debating the relative advantages and pitfalls of public versus private funding of colonization.[27] It is not a new debate, although present figures appear to feel they are treading new ground. There is much rhetoric about having discovered and learned from past mistakes. Yet, the observer must stand back and look at what is meant by "the past." It is essential to define that past, not in terms of failed projects of the 1970s and 1980s but in terms of the larger historical past. In the heyday of the rubber boom, when public money was thrown at the problem of colonization, the solution chosen was publicly funded colonies. Those projects continued until the money ran out, whereupon privately funded colonies were attempted. In the hyperinflated economy of the 1960s and 1970s, the same approach was resurrected in the TransAmazon program and others. However, the inevitable collapse of the "Brazilian Miracle" in the 1980s and 1990s has brought about a rethinking of the public expenditures involved and the return on those investments. As a result, there is now a strong movement toward private funding, local control of programs, and the new buzzword, "sustainable" development.[28]

Another attitude that appears to have remained historically constant is the tendency to blame the victims for their failure to succeed in the projects devised for them. The directors' reports were full of references to their charges' inability or unwillingness to complete the plethora of tasks assigned them, their refusal to respond to wage and profit incentives, or their inconvenient habit of dying of imported diseases or fleeing into the forest. The officials in charge of running the government-sponsored colonies in the nineteenth-century Bragantina often mentioned that settlers, particularly the Europeans, would not produce enough agricultural commodities to become successful farmers or, more importantly, to supply the market in Belem. Settlers who arrived from the drought-stricken Northeast without any resources whatsoever, malnourished and often sick, were constantly blamed for not becoming instant successes on their holdings. When colonists occasionally protested the intolerable conditions in the settlements and the failure of the government to deliver on its promises, they were labeled as troublemakers and criminals. When prospective colonists refused to disembark at their destination, where promised roads, houses, and cleared land were absent, the press described them as ingrates.

Little has changed in recent years. Settlers brought to the Trans-Amazon projects from the arid Northeast or from southern Brazil were not instant successes. Many abandoned their infertile land after only a few years, often moving to nearby towns and cities in search of work. Others sold their holdings when offered sums inflated by the land's speculative value. Still others continued to eke out an existence on their plots, usually deeply and perennially in debt.[29]

All such people were blamed for their apparent failures. Reports described them as lazy, stupid, or ignorant, stubborn in maintaining their style of agriculture. The fact that credit was rarely available as promised, extension services were nonexistent or at best severely overworked, soils were generally infertile, and transport of goods to market hard to find and impossibly expensive was quietly overlooked. The overall problem that people new to the region had no experience in managing a humid tropical forest ecosystem and were not given the agronomic assistance they needed was rarely mentioned. Thus, once again the families who came in response to recruitment for colonization projects were categorized as the reasons for the eventual failure and collapse of those schemes.[30]

Beneath the common themes lies a more enduring way of thinking that has pervaded all of the plans for using Amazonia since the first European set foot in the region. The Amazon Basin has been and remains a colony of the more developed parts of the world. In the minds of developers ever since the seventeenth century, the sole purpose of any attention to this enormous tropical forest and river system has been to extract its riches. In strict mercantilist fashion, its purpose is to profit the mother country, whether that is Portugal or other parts of Brazil. If extraction of profits accidentally benefits the Amazonian people and ecosystem, that benefit is distinctly peripheral to the priority of profiting other people in other places. On the other hand, if extraction of profits destroys the environment and impoverishes its people, such losses are considered an acceptable price for development.

One example well illustrates this point. As Brazil becomes an increasingly industrial nation, there is a tremendous demand for new sources of energy. Since Brazil has few oil reserves, other sources of energy have been sought, and the most obvious one has been the hydroelectric potential of Brazil's rivers. It was only a matter of time until the idea of damming the rivers within the Amazon system became extremely attractive. In 1987, the government released the 2010 Plan for damming tributaries of the Amazon, primarily the Xingú and Tocantins-Araguaia Rivers. Seventy-nine dams are planned, with a potential generating capacity of 72,822 megawatts. In addition, two dams already under construction near Manaus and the iron deposits at Carajás in Pará have come on line.[31]

Impact studies dealing with the environment and the local populations have been difficult to complete since they are financed by the same agencies responsible for building the dams. Even so, those studies that have been completed point to a serious number of concerns. Deforestation in and around the reservoirs will cause erosion and silt buildup behind the dams that will render them useless. Rotting vegetation in flooded areas will result in pollution and algae proliferation that will destroy fishing resources. There will be a serious rise in incidences of waterborne diseases, such as schistosomiasis and onchocerciasis, as well as malaria. Existing populations will have to be relocated, including some 35,000 Indians along the Xingú and numbers of settlers along the TransAmazon highway, who were settled there by the government. Relocations will cause social upheaval, exposure to diseases, loss of self-support, and dependence on government assistance. Filling the reservoirs will disrupt food supply, drinking water availability, sanitation, and transportation. A flourishing trade between the Xingú and Belem will be eliminated by the dams. Vast timber resources will be wasted by flooding. Above all, a great many species of fauna and flora will become extinct with destruction of their habitat. The list goes on and on.[32]

In spite of such negative impact, the government intends to complete these projects in order to supply electricity to industrialized parts of Brazil. The devastation is an acceptable price to pay for increased energy potential. The thousands of megawatts that will supposedly be generated will supply a demand expected to quadruple 1987 levels by 2010. However, less than 10 percent of that increased demand is expected to come from Amazonia, while 45 percent of the electricity generated will come from that region.[33]

Resistance has been strong against the Xingú projects, but it may be able to do little more than delay the inevitable. Opposition from indigenous alliances has proved the most powerful; in addition, alliances have formed between Indians, small farmers, rubber tappers, and local miners.[34] Whether political action by local populations can stop one more example of extraction of Amazonian resources for the good of other places remains to be seen.

Deforestation is probably the single greatest danger facing Amazonia today. The World Wildlife Federation issued a report in 1997 finding that Brazil is number one in the world in deforestation.[35] Over centuries, slash-and-burn agriculture has been practiced with relatively little environmental impact until the last thirty years. Today the forest is being destroyed at a frightening rate by the use of modern equipment. The federal government has been extremely reticent to admit the devastation, but now states that one-eighth of the rain forest has been destroyed by farmers and loggers in the last twenty years. An environmental bill passed in February 1998 that would have imposed strict penalties for ecological crimes was weakened considerably by presidential veto after heavy lobbying by logging interests.[36] In addition to the "routine" cutting and burning, in 1998 the fires in the Amazon promise to make 1998 the worst year in history for devastation, outstripping the five million acres burned in 1997. Partially due to the El Niño–caused drought, fires started by farmers and loggers have raged out of control, burning some 1.5 million acres of savanna and 3.5 million acres of forest in March 1998.[37] The fires have destroyed entire habitats, wiped out a third of the crops in Roraima, and killed an estimated twelve thousand head of cattle, but the most serious threat was the incursion of unchecked wildfires into the Yanomami Indian Reserve. Fire-fighting efforts have been minimal, and only seasonal rains would stop the onslaught.[38]

Any number of additional examples of disaster could be cited. Indiscriminate logging of hardwoods, particularly mahogany, for the world market has nearly eliminated those trees; a government two-year ban on mahogany logging came too late for most stands.[39] Further, because of the manner in which such logging takes place, a great many other trees are also destroyed. Informal gold mining, or garimpagem, has literally carved holes in the forest, destroying forest and water habitats and severely polluting rivers with mercury, to supply the world gold market.[40] Gold mining, even though primarily done by small-scale prospectors, is big business in Brazil. The Ministry of Foreign Relations estimated 162 tons of gold were mined between 1990 and 1993; that is the amount officially counted and does not count illegal prospecting and mining.[41] Larger mines, Serra Pelada in Pará being the most horrific example, have had an even larger impact on local ecosystems. The iron mines at Carajás are carving up an entire mountain of iron ore, destroying part of an Indian reserve, and the pig iron factories associated with Carajás are responsible for huge deforestation for charcoal. A great deal of the land that has been cleared and burned has been turned into mediocre pastures for beef to satisfy urban markets in the rest of Brazil. Fisheries have been polluted by mercury, destroyed by floodplain logging, or severely depleted to provide fish for national and international markets.[42] The list goes on and on. Yet in no case does the income generated by these extractive activities remain in or return to Amazonia, the identical pattern of Portuguese settlement in the eighteenth century. The Amazon remains just as much a colony as it was three hundred years ago.

An oft-quoted truism is that "those who do not know history are doomed to repeat it." Yet, looking at the past 250 years of attempts to settle and exploit Amazonia, one has to wonder if there is not a good deal of truth to that statement. Curupira would not be pleased.

APPENDIX A: MAPS

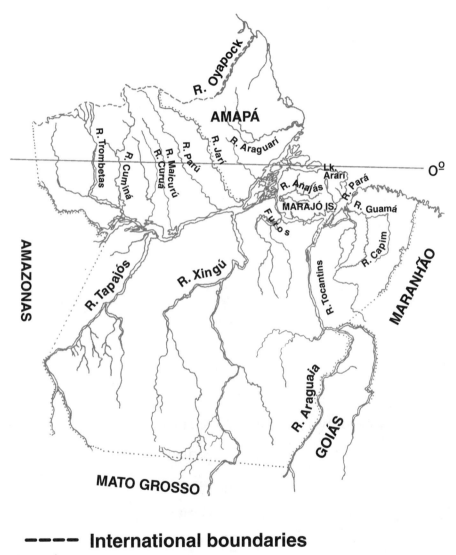

```
---- International boundaries
........ State boundaries
```

Map A: Geography of Pará

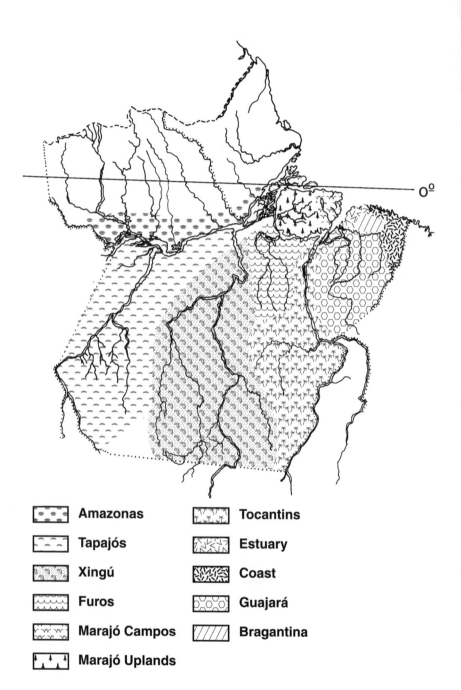

	Amazonas		Tocantins
	Tapajós		Estuary
	Xingú		Coast
	Furos		Guajará
	Marajó Campos		Bragantina
	Marajó Uplands		

Map B: Geographic Regions, Pará

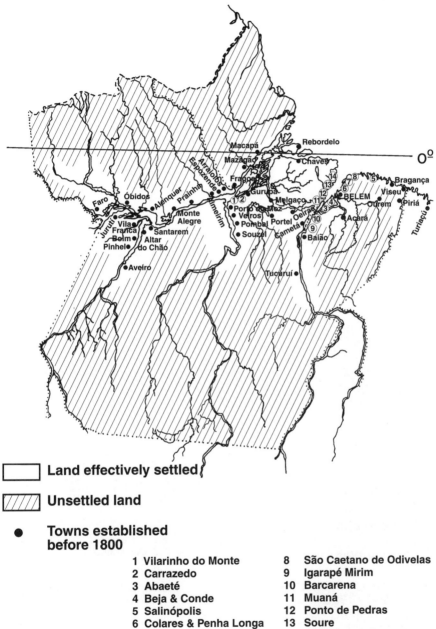

Land effectively settled

Unsettled land

● Towns established before 1800

1 Vilarinho do Monte	8 São Caetano de Odivelas
2 Carrazedo	9 Igarapé Mirim
3 Abaeté	10 Barcarena
4 Beja & Conde	11 Muaná
5 Salinópolis	12 Ponto de Pedras
6 Colares & Penha Longa	13 Soure
7 Vigia	14 Salvaterra & Condeixa, Monsarás, Mondim

Map C: Settlement in 1800, Pará

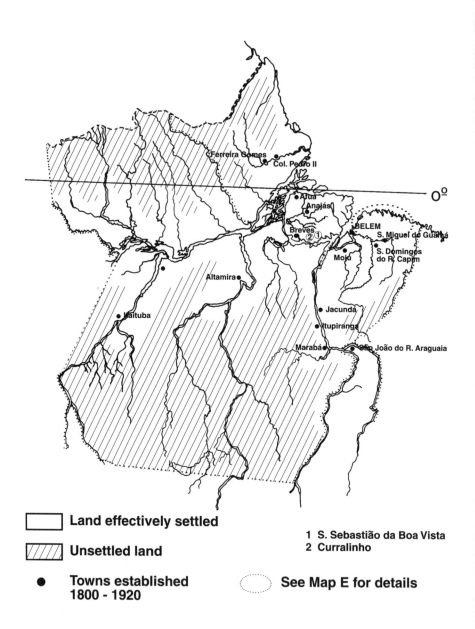

Land effectively settled

Unsettled land

● Towns established
1800 - 1920

1 S. Sebastião da Boa Vista
2 Curralinho

See Map E for details

Map D: Settlement in 1920, Pará

Map E

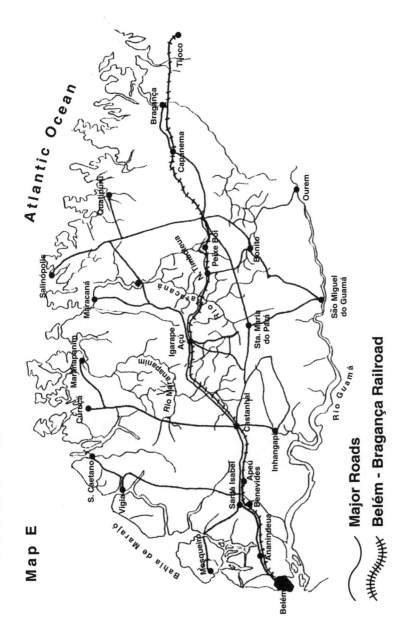

∿ **Major Roads**

⊣⊢⊣⊢⊣⊢ **Belém - Bragança Railroad**

Map E: Zona Bragantina, Pará

APPENDIX B: DATA COLLECTION, RESEARCH DESIGN, AND STATISTICAL ANALYSIS

Behind the statements about economics and demography in this monograph lies a good deal of computer analysis. Bearing in mind Disraeli's observation about lies—"there are three kinds of lies: lies, damned lies, and statistics"—a discussion of data collection, constraints on the data, and the research design itself is in order.

Data-Processing Programs

The statistical data in this study were drawn from four separate groups of sources and were processed in four separate programs. Two programs are based on colonial period data: PARA6N, which deals with population, tithing, and exports from Directorate villages, and PARA8N, which included only exports from Belem to Lisbon. The national period data on population and exports to Belem by municipio are treated in PARA7N, while two series of data, one representing total annual imports into Belem from the interior, and the other concerning exports from Belem to other ports in Brazil and abroad, are included in PARA5N. The various types of sources consulted are discussed below according to the program in which they were used.

PARA6N

The sources for the PARA6N program include a massive set of data from individual Directorate towns, scattered throughout the collections in the Biblioteca e Arquivo Público do Pará (BAPP) in Belem. The bulk of the data for the entire Directorate period is derived from the 565-volume collection entitled "Correspondencia de diversos com o governo," which contains all extant correspondence between directors and other local officials and the governor general in Belem. The collection is arranged by year, and the first four hundred volumes contain most of the colonial material. Documents are unorganized within the bound volumes. Because various lists of population, men in service, tithes assessed and paid, and goods sent downriver are encountered throughout the series, it is infeasible to list individual documents, so the series is cited as a whole. One six-volume series entitled Estatística da população, BAPP 954–59, contains Directorate period documents concerning village population. Again, because each volume contains as many as two hundred individual documents, the series is referenced as a whole. Other references used in this program are composite tables called *mapas* or *mapas gerais* for the whole captaincy. Some originals and additional copies of material in the Conselho Ultramarino archives were eventually returned to Brazil and are now housed in the National Archives and other repositories in Rio de Janeiro.

PARA8N

The documents used for the PARA8N programs are almost all copies of the originals in Lisbon. Very little of the composite information from these lists came from sources in Belem. It appears that general export manifests were sent yearly to Lisbon, as well as some general censuses taken in random years were also sent. When the court moved to Brazil in 1808, the most recent manuscripts on the demography and economy of Pará were brought along. These and copies of earlier manuscripts put together by Brazilian scholars late in the nineteenth century are housed in the Arquivo Nacional, in the Conselho Ultramarino collection of the Instituto Histórico e Geográfico Brasileiro, and in the Biblioteca National do Rio de Janeiro. A total of twenty-two export lists were used in PARA8N.

PARA7N

The municipio-level reports for the national period have proved to be the most difficult to collate. Economic data for this program were drawn partially from ledgers of the Recebedoria de Rendas do Estado do Pará. However, due to the condition of nineteenth-century materials in the BAPP, only three manuscript ledgers were usable, and only one of those, the 1893 list, fit the time period of this study. Therefore, the bulk of the economic data used in this program were obtained from such published sources as annual presidential reports, the *Diario Oficial*, *Provincia do Pará*, and *Folha do Norte* newspapers, which reproduced statistics from manuscript ledgers no longer available.

These data account for substantially all goods brought into Belem from outlying municipios for local consumption or for export. Posts of the Recebedoria de Rendas at each market were required to register all incoming goods and collect proper fees. Prior to the opening of the railroad between Benevides and Belem in 1883, all such goods passed through the Ver-o-Peso market and branch market at the Reduto, both part of the port. After 1883, a second market in São Braz was used for goods coming into Belem by land transportation, while the Ver-o-Peso continued to handle all goods arriving by water. Because of the specific circumstances of the routes into Belem, confined primarily to those ending at the Ver-o-Peso and the São Braz markets, the potential for transportation coming in through other routes is low. Belem was not served from the hinterland by a network of roads, so those people living in the agricultural zones were rather effectively restrained from using alternative routes and thereby avoiding the inspection and payment of duties.

The demographic material in this program is taken almost entirely from published censuses. Before 1872, these censuses were conducted by the provincial government and were admittedly inaccurate to some degree. No attempt is made to acclaim their accuracy; the figures are presented and used as the perceived size of population of any given municipio, based on actual head count and educated guess. They are not perfect, but as a time series they show a fairly strong internal consistency and leave no notable outriders in the range. These figures represent those available to government planners, who used them as sources of general information. They are utilized in this monograph in the same spirit.

Problems with Data Collection

There are numerous potential problems in collection of socioeconomic data, particularly in the humid tropics, some serious, others simply time consuming. However, all of them have a solution, provided the researcher is willing to be ingenious in approach and ruthless in culling data.

Miscopying

One of the most common problems encountered in data collection is that of miscopying. It can be very difficult to ascertain if a manuscript is the original or a contemporary copy. Sometimes an error may occur due to a 1 read as a 7, or a 0 as a 6. An error can often be traced to a simple mistake in arithmetic. At other times digits are accidentally repeated. Printing of official reports did not necessarily improve the situation, due to proliferation of materials and the potential for printing error.

How can miscopying be controlled in data collection? The ideal solution is to collect only from primary sources, but this solution is certainly not always possible. Another, rather tedious, solution is to copy all records of the data found. The perpetuation of error through repeated copying is well known; but when, for example, a document in Belem and a composite sent to Portugal agree, in opposition to another copy in Rio de Janeiro, the researcher has at least an idea of which document may have the greatest chance of relative accuracy. Numbers that show up as distant outriders to the rest of the values for that variable are suspect, but if the rest of the data is well grouped around a regression line, those outrider values can be eliminated. Numbers that appear to have too many digits may be handled in the same way. Recomputing totals taken from the cited sources is a worthwhile endeavor. In short, the problem of miscopying is potentially serious, but definitely surmountable.

Margins of Error

A related problem is that of margin of error. In countries such as England and France where there has been a long tradition of collection of material such as demographic data and export-import trade information, the margin of error can often be held at 10 percent or less. However, in using statistics from the underdeveloped countries, particularly from regions such as the Amazon, where the original collection and compilation of material is extremely difficult, an error margin of 10 percent is unrealistic. As a general rule of thumb, the data was handled with a toleration level of 15 to 20 percent, depending on time of record and type of data. The margin is rather high, but anything lower would mean virtually no data. Since scientific laboratory experimental data often involves a margin of error of plus or minus 10, the figure of 20 percent is not unreasonable.

Bias

There are also some errors in primary sources due to bias in the original recording of the information. Bias was usually potentially definable in either positive or negative form. The national period economic data provide an ideal example. According to the provincial laws, all produce arriving in Belem, whether for local consumption or for subsequent export, had to be logged into the record books of the Recebedoria de Rendas. As pointed out earlier, the tax-collection posts at the waterfront market and the end of the railroad can be expected to have recorded most of the traffic coming into Belem by those two routes. The provincial, and later state, Recebedoria de Rendas posts were staffed with inspectors, scribes, and guards whose function was to make sure that all goods were noted on the books and the proper taxes, levies, and fees were paid. The whole process was supposed to be carefully regulated and apparently was. To encourage the personnel of the posts to do their job efficiently, they were supposed to receive a 1 percent commission in addition to salary.

The two-way bias thus becomes evident. In the first place, there may well have been a false inflation of noted products in the interest of a higher commission, though such practice would have been held in check somewhat by the record of the total taxes collected. There was, on the other hand, a very likely possibility that merchants would pay individual inspectors a personal fee to overlook the importation of undutied goods. Corruption was probably more of a problem for export goods like rubber, which was taxed at a rate as much as 50 percent of market value, than for foodstuffs for local consumption, on which the fees and market duties were much lower.

Another factor to be taken into consideration is the possible importance of smuggling and illegal trade. On a small scale, farinha, beans, and rice, and probably meat and fish also were probably brought into the city by a few small farmers living nearby, who would sell door to door or set up illegal stalls in the markets. Obviously, official statistics on the importation of foodstuffs to Belem would not reflect the amount of food coming in illegally.

There are two definitive answers to this potential bias. First of all, the literature, or "soft data," does not indicate public notice of smuggling. There is little if any mention in press, presidential report, or legislative debate about the need to curb smuggling. The lack of verbal recognition is significant. If smuggling had been a major problem, the merchants who made up a good portion of the politicians could have been expected to decry the deplorable practice, since it was not favorable to their business. It is theoretically true that a merchant might have been involved in both smuggling and legal food trade, but if that were the case, mention might be expected of the impossibility of control of smuggling, or some such tone of moderation. Instead, there is no mention at all. It could also be argued that smuggling escaped attention because it was such a commonly accepted practice. In the first place, that situation seems unlikely, since smuggling is recognized as an illegal practice. Second, none of the foreign travelers' accounts from the period mention widespread smuggling. Some of those travelers were highly critical of practices and customs of the local populations in Brazil, and there is no reason to believe that such critics would have failed to report blatant smuggling. Further, the foreign travelers were generally interested in local customs, and selling door to door might well have been the sort of practice they would have noted, yet there is little such mention in the accounts.

Standard Measurements

One of the smaller, but somewhat time-consuming, problems with economic data from the early national period and the colonial period is the
lack of standardization of measure. The metric system of weights and
measures was not officially adopted in Brazil until 1872, but beginning in
the 1840s there were occasional attempts to try the new system when reporting economic production in Pará.

Colonial data was standardized in some cases, using the arroba for
weight and the alqueire for volume, but in a far greater number of reports
from Directorate villages, the production was listed in terms of baskets,
pots, straws, and hands. Hides and skins were sometimes listed by weight
and sometimes by unit. The lack of standardization taxes the researcher's
ingenuity, since only a few weights and measures, such as pots and baskets, had official conversion equivalents. Further, Amazonian terms were
not necessarily the same in meaning as elsewhere in Brazil. For the hands,
pots, and baskets, the solution lies in the colonial documents themselves,
because directors would often quote the measure in terms of baskets or
pots weighing a certain amount, and by accumulating a large number of
reports, a workable mean can be established. Conversion of arrobas and
alqueires to kilograms and hectoliters can be done by reference to contemporary accounts that indicated appropriate conversions. Conversion of
kilograms or arrobas to hectoliters is a tedious job because it involves the
weighing of samples and subsequent conversion of weight to volume.
Rice, beans, corn, and manioc flour often had to be converted in this manner. The conversion of hides and skins was done by asking merchants
about representative weights, thus converting cowhides, alligator skins,
lizard and snake skins, and pelts of spotted cat, deer, and anteater to unit
measure rather than kilograms. Precise accuracy is impossible, but the
measures are probably very close to the actual amount. Table B.1 shows
conversions based on this research.

Demographic Statistics

Demographic statistics present their own set of problems, but again, the
resolution of those problems is not impossible. Probably the most important problem to consider in demographic statistics is the isolation and
dispersal of population, the two ways in which such statistics are commonly biased. Censuses were conducted by traveling census takers assisted by local inhabitants, usually priests, and often paid on a per-capita
scale according to the numbers of people they counted. Therefore, it is
logical and correct to assume a potential bias toward overreporting in

Table B.1. Table of Conversions of Sample Weights and Measures

COMMON MEASURES

1 arroba (arb.)	15 kilograms (kg.)
1 alqueire (alq.)	13.8 liters (lt.)
1 pote	15.7 lt.

LIQUID MEASURE (Usually for aguardente)

1 frasco	2 lt.
1 canada	7 lt.
1 barril	20 lt.
1 frasqueira	24.7 lt.
1 almude	32 lt.
1 pipa	560 lt.

SPECIFIC MEASURES

1 basket dried fish	6–8 arb.
1 basket salt fish	9–11 arb.
1 basket mullet	200–300 fish
1 basket crabs	3 cofos, about 50 crabs
1 basket manatee meat	7 arb.
1 ball rubber	10 kg.
1 basket Brazil nuts	3.3 alq.
1 paneiro Brazil nuts	1 alq.
1 canudo salsa	0.5 arb.
1 canudo cravo fino	0.13 arb.
1 canudo cravo grosso	0.33 arb.
1 pano caulk	1 arb.
1 basket cacao	2.5 arb.
5 leaves tobacco	1 kg.
1 mão corn	1 alq.
1 paneiro farinha	1 alq.
1 basket cotton	2 arb.

order to raise the census taker's salary. On the other hand, census takers were understandably loath to travel long distances up lonely and dangerous rivers to count small population clusters. For that reason, underreporting was probably a far more serious bias than overreporting. Frequently, second- or thirdhand guesses were used as estimates of populations in relatively inaccessible locations.

The absence of reporting altogether was common. There was probably not one complete census for Pará in the sense that all municipios actually reported complete returns. However, by looking at trends over time, particularly when the data were coalesced into regional distributions, a number of valid observations can be made.

Even though there were some problems in the compilation of demographic materials, it is certainly legitimate to claim value for the existing figures. It would be academically valuable to know the actual size of the population in Pará for any given period of time, and thereby the extent to which real figures varied from official ones. Nevertheless, the official figures were the ones used by people planning colonization, education, and health service policy. The official figures, even if only approximations, were the information base for policy decisions. Perceived values under such conditions are actually more valuable than precise and accurate values ascertained a hundred years later. The official censuses were the only source of demographic information available to the government officials, and they used them with the idea that they were the best data available.

Spatial Units

One final and perplexing and sometimes frustrating problem in data collection is the changing base unit for data treatment. During the national period, economic and demographic data were normally presented in terms of political-administrative units, the municipios, at times broken down into districts or parishes. However, the municipio per se does not provide a standardized spatial unit over time. Ever since municipios were created in Pará, their boundaries have fluctuated like the membranes of a hundred amoebas. Districts were added in time for one census, deleted by the next. Boundaries changed from one side of a river to another, thereby eliminating or adding a village to the roster. Municipios changed names, and the unsuspecting researcher may discover a "new" municipio, only to find a later description of it which makes it clear that only the names have been changed. The whole affair can be complicated in the extreme.

The case of Benevides illustrates the point. The town was founded in 1875 and appeared in the 1890 census as a district of the municipio of Belem. In the 1920 census it was still in Belem. Later it was transferred to the municipio of Santa Isabel, another former district of Belem, for a few years, whereupon it then became part of the new municipio of Ananindeua in 1943. It was counted as a district of Ananindeua in the 1950 and 1960 censuses, but sometime before 1970 became a municipio in its own right. Almost every municipio in the state has had a similar sort of history.

The solution to the basic unit problem is rather straightforward. Rather than discuss specific towns or municipios in this study, I have grouped them into regions, usually based on watershed and macrogeographical features, such as upland and lowland Marajó. Analysis by region permits the researcher to ignore many of the fluctuating boundaries and is the only workable solution when dealing at a state level. If a researcher were to work on a regional or subregional level, the best alternative would be to use the parish or district as the unit of analysis and delve into a study of constant changes of jurisdictional boundaries.

Analysis

Having briefly discussed the sources used for data in these programs and the solutions of problems encountered, the next point to take under consideration in an examination of statistical analysis is the manner in which those data were used. The case was defined as a specific year for which complete figures were available, entered as numeric ordinal data, and, in the case of the large files, organized into regional subfiles. Statistical analysis was done with the Statistical Package for the Social Sciences, using first an array of preliminary statistics, including mean, median, standard deviation, standard error of the mean, range, variance, and kurtosis. If the standard deviation for any variable was too large, that data was not used for further analysis, since it indicated too great a degree of variability. Other variables were eliminated because of a large number of missing cases, which would make bivariant or multivariant analysis inaccurate.

Once the preliminary work was complete, a group of variables was selected that might possibly be interrelated according to other "soft" data sources consulted. In the colonial data a group of economic variables was used to create a Pearson correlation matrix, using zero-order Pearson correlation coefficients and including the variables in each coefficient, the coefficient itself, the number of cases, and a one-tailed test of statistical significance for the coefficient. The variables used were: salsa, Brazil nuts, cacao, tar, caulk, rice, corn, sugar, fish, turtles, turtle butter, and manatee meat. For the national period data, the choice of variables was severely limited by the number of missing values, so that only rubber, Brazil nuts, cacao, rice, sugar, and farinha were used. Such commodities as *cachaça*, corn, beans, tobacco, hides, meat, and fish were not recorded regularly enough to give consistent data runs.

The matrix of Pearson correlation coefficients demonstrated several potentially interesting relationships. In the case of the colonial data programs, there was very little correlation of relationship between any products, which seemed to indicate that no product was being systematically encouraged at the expense of other products. In the two programs of national period data, the absolute lack of correlation between rubber and various agricultural and forest products was an unexpected and thought-provoking result. The next step was to test relationships of various agricultural products with others, using rubber as a constant, by means of multivariant partial correlation coefficients. The result was an insignificant coefficient level, less than 0.6000. Similar results were found in the colonial data, and partial correlation coefficients did not prove useful because holding one variable as a constant was not consistent with other soft data. The final step in the data treatment was stepwise multiple regression analysis. In each data set, a group of variables was chosen which had the fewest missing values and the greatest internal consistency, and which might have been expected to have some relationship between them other than simple co-linearity. For example, in the national data, rubber, Brazil nuts, and cacao were chosen as export products, and rice, sugar, and farinha were chosen as agricultural products which would indicate local consumption trends. In the colonial data, salsa, Brazil nuts, cacao, turtles and turtle oil, rice, fish, and sugar were the principal items used. Once the variables were selected, regression equations were set up in series, using no more than five variables at a time. Regression analysis was then run for each equation, rotating the variables so that each one assumed the dependent role once. While the colonial data failed to produce significant coefficients of determination, the nineteenth century material suggested a picture far different from the newspaper and official reports of the time.

Rubber and the Agricultural Economy, a Statistical Analysis

The constant outcry that emphasis on rubber was ruining agriculture was evidently not altogether true. Granted, at the same time that more and more rubber was collected for export, it was also becoming increasingly difficult to obtain sufficient quantities of basic foodstuffs to feed the urban population in Pará. The two phenomena were not necessarily causally related as originally thought. If in fact increased rubber production were causing a severe decline in all other aspects of the economy, as claimed, then a strongly negative single correlation (Pearson correlation) would be expected for a large number and variety of other products. The data suggest a somewhat different situation. Table B.2 shows Pearson correlation coefficients (R) for all important agricultural, extractive, and fishing products with rubber, with the correlation considered significant at 0.6000 or above, positive or negative.[1]

Another statistical measure, called the coefficient of determination, dependent on computation of the bivariant simple correlation coefficient, can be used to clarify the significance of correlation coefficients.[2] The coefficient of determination shows that rubber production variation can potentially explain 81 percent of change in hide production, 72 percent for cotton production, and 59 percent for Brazil nut production. The agricultural products shown here were not those considered basic dietary staples

Table B.2. Pearson Correlation Coefficients for Series 6 Data

VARIABLES	R
Rubber and Hides	-0.8976
Rubber and Cotton	-0.8460
Rubber and Brazil Nuts	-0.7658

Source: Statistical Programs PARA5 and PARA6.

but were the only combinations with rubber that gave significant correlations.[3] Table B.3, series 6 shows correlations for basic foodstuffs. Even though there are some negative correlations shown, the levels are much too low, with the possible exception of sugar, to make them valid examples to illustrate the original thesis. Change in rubber production could explain only 29 percent of sugar production change, 13 percent of corn change, 7 percent of rice change, and 3 percent of farinha change. In short, rubber was not the "prime mover"; there was some other reason for the apparent decline in agricultural production.

Pearson correlation coefficients only indicate the probability that the original thesis will not prove valid. To take the analysis to a more sophisticated level, multiple regression techniques were employed. By using rubber as the key dependent variable and allowing the independent variables to enter the equation in stepwise fashion, at their chosen levels rather than being forced into a specific order, it again shows that the economic picture was considerably more complex than originally thought. Two series of data were used separately, the first (Series 6) showing goods coming into Belem from the interior of Pará, and the second (Series 5) showing export from Belem to other parts of Brazil or abroad.

Table B.3, series 3, shows the specific values for the first series.[4] Brazil nut production appears to have been affected considerably by farinha and cacao. These variables were undoubtedly acting independently, since analysis over time shows considerable yearly variation. The important point to note for this argument is that rubber appears as a very insignificant factor in the equation, causing a change in R^2 of only 0.1 percent. Cacao production was strongly affected by rice and only minimally by the other selected variables. Rubber showed a change in R^2 of only 0.4 percent, another very insignificant level. Cacao was not adversely affected by rubber during the peak boom years, a situation confirmed by contemporary accounts such as Governor Sodré's 1897 report in which he stated that cacao was the only crop not in a state of total ruin.[5]

What about basic foodstuffs? Rice and cacao showed a strong correlation, but the relationship is probably accidental, since there is no reason to

Table B.3. Coefficients from Regression Equations of Rubber and Other Products

Dependent Variable	Independent Variable	R	R^2	R^2 Change
Series 6 (Based on 114 observations)				
Brazil Nuts	Farinha	0.73583	0.54145	0.54145
	Cacao	0.82875	0.68682	0.14537
	Sugar	0.83193	0.69210	0.00528
	Rubber	0.83289	0.69371	0.00161
	Rice	0.83331	0.69441	0.00070
Cacao	Rice	0.84866	0.72022	0.72022
	Brazil Nuts	0.85593	0.73262	0.01240
	Farinha	0.87528	0.76612	0.03350
	Rubber	0.87804	0.77095	0.00483
	Sugar	0.87864	0.77200	0.00105
Rice	Cacao	0.84866	0.72022	0.72022
	Farinha	0.89150	0.79477	0.07455
	Sugar	0.90130	0.81234	0.01757
	Brazil Nuts	0.90153	0.81276	0.00042
Rubber	—	—	—	—
Farinha	Brazil Nuts	0.73583	0.54145	0.54145
	Rice	0.75364	0.56797	0.07455
	Cacao	0.78873	0.62210	0.05413
	Rubber	0.79740	0.63585	0.01375
	Sugar	0.79784	0.63655	0.00070
Sugar	Rice	0.51095	0.26107	0.26107
	Brazil Nuts	0.53307	0.28416	0.02309
	Cacao	0.53899	0.29051	0.00635
	Rubber	0.54043	0.29206	0.00155
	Farinha	0.54169	0.29342	0.00136
Series 3 (Based on 1,076 observations)				
Farinha	Rice	0.78977	0.62374	0.62374
	Rubber	0.79968	0.63948	0.01574
	Sugar	0.79993	0.63988	0.00040
	Brazil Nuts	0.79998	0.63996	0.00008
	Cacao	0.80000	0.64000	0.00004
Rice	Farinha	0.78977	0.62374	0.62374
	Rubber	0.79297	0.62881	0.00507
	Sugar	0.79589	0.63344	0.00463
	Brazil Nuts	0.79596	0.63356	0.00112
	Cacao	0.79603	0.63366	0.00010
Sugar	Rice	0.13944	0.01944	0.01944
	Farinha	0.14339	0.02056	0.00116
	Brazil Nuts	0.14356	0.02061	0.00005
	Rubber	—	—	—
	Cacao	—	—	—
Brazil Nuts	Cacao	0.05641	0.00318	0.00318
	Rice	0.05754	0.00331	0.00013
	Farinha	0.05899	0.00348	0.00017
	Rubber	0.05962	0.00355	0.00007
	Sugar	0.06005	0.00361	0.00006
Cacao	Brazil Nuts	0.05641	0.00318	0.00318
	Rice	0.05788	0.00335	0.00017

continued

Table B.3—*Continued*

Dependent Variable	Independent Variable	R	R²	R² Change
	Farinha	0.05889	0.00347	0.00012
	Rubber	—	—	—
	Sugar	—	—	—
Series 5 (Based on 15 observations)				
Cacao	Sugar	0.26003	0.06761	0.06761
	Farinha	0.26500	0.07022	0.00261
	Brazil Nuts	0.48854	0.23867	0.16845
	Rice	0.49411	0.24415	0.00548
	Rubber	0.50180	0.25180	0.00765
Brazil Nuts	Farinha	0.99299	0.98603	0.98603
	Cacao	0.99430	0.98864	0.00261
	Rubber	0.99439	0.98882	0.00018
	Rice	0.99444	0.98891	0.00009
	Sugar	—	—	—
Rice	Rubber	0.57157	0.32669	0.32669
	Farinha	0.58179	0.33848	0.01779
	Sugar	0.58943	0.34743	0.00895
	Cacao	0.59316	0.35184	0.00441
	Brazil Nuts	0.59761	0.35713	0.00529
Farinha	Brazil Nuts	0.99299	0.98608	0.98608
	Cacao	0.99437	0.98878	0.00198
	Rice	0.99444	0.98892	0.00014
	Rubber	—	—	—
	Sugar	—	—	—
Sugar	Rubber	0.42890	0.18395	0.18395
	Cacao	0.47158	0.22239	0.03844
	Rice	0.47758	0.22809	0.00570
	Farinha	0.48332	0.23359	0.00550
	Brazil Nuts	—	—	—

assume a causal relationship between rice grown primarily on plantations in the Lower Tocantins and cacao gathered or harvested from other
sections of the basin. In this particular case, rubber was eliminated from
the regression analysis because of its total lack of significant level. Farinha
production was most closely correlated with Brazil nuts and rice, but the
levels of the coefficient of determination are lower than they were for
other regressions. Presumably such lower levels may be attributed to
greater variation and to home production, which never appeared in official figures. The figures for farinha are particularly significant in relationship to rubber because farinha is the basic foodstuff in the basin. Since
rubber made a difference of .01 in the coefficient of determination, it can
only be assumed that its effect on farinha production was minimal. The
relationship of sugar to other products is somewhat suspect because of
the lower levels encountered. Very little is explained by those figures, and

the most significant fact to emerge from them is the relative positioning of rubber vis-à-vis the other factors, once again a very low degree of change. It would thus appear fairly conclusive that rubber was not the villain responsible for declining availability of agricultural goods in Belem.

Because of the controversial nature of the findings, another entirely separate data set was also examined using the identical tests. This third set dealt with intrastate commerce, listing the usual extractive, agricultural, and fishing products, according to the municipio of origin, for the years 1861, 1864, 1885, 1893, 1897, 1899, 1920, 1927, and 1928. The resulting figures did vary somewhat from the other internal commerce series of data, primarily because different years were used, but the general conclusions were the same. Rubber simply did not have the devastating effect on agriculture that was claimed. The change in farinha shipment to Belem was primarily explained in terms of rice production, with rubber a minor contributing factor. Rubber proved to be even less of an influence on rice production. Regression in the case of sugar, Brazil nuts, and cacao gave low levels of significance, undoubtedly because of the curvilinear nature of the data, but once again, in the relative ranking of the variables, rubber had too low a level of significance or influence to enter the equation. Thus, this data series further demonstrates that rubber was not the operational force at work in the agricultural economy, as claimed.

One final test was made to determine rubber's role as prime mover in the economy. Multiple regression analysis was done on sugar, farinha, and rice using parallel sets, one with rubber, one with cacao, and one with Brazil nuts. The results demonstrated that of the three possible export products, only rubber had any significant effect on farinha and rice production. Even so, for all of those "determinant" variables, the change in the coefficient of determination was exceedingly small, and there seemed to be a strong indication that variations within the agricultural sector affected the interrelationship far more than did the interaction of extractive and agricultural economies.

NOTES

Introduction: The Place, the Time, the Setting

1. Portugal, *Directorio que se deve observar nas povoações dos indios do Pará e Maranhão emquanto Sua Magestade não mandar o contrario* (Lisbon, 1757). For purposes of clarity, the term *Directorate* will be used to refer to the system as a whole, and *Directorio* to refer to the document containing the regulations. See map C, "Settlement in 1800," in appendix A.

2. See map A, "Geography of Pará," in appendix A.

3. See map B, "Regions of Pará," in appendix A.

4. Canoes of the small *igarité* and *montaria* varieties seen on the river today are nearly identical to those depicted in the watercolor plates of Alexandre Rodrigues Ferreira's *Viagem filosófica*, drawn in 1783. Plates 33–36, 38–42, and 49 of the 1970 edition.

5. João Pereira Caldas to Manoel Bernardo de Mello e Castro, April 7, 1773, and March 7, 1773. Same author to Francisco Xavier de Mendonça Furtado, June 26, 1761.

6. José de Napoles Tello de Menezes to Royal Court, June 9, 1780.

7. Marcos José Monteiro de Carvalho to André Corlino Monteiro, May 26, 1781.

Chapter 1: The Context and Structure of the Directorate

1. An excellent monograph on early Brazilian history is Bailey W. Diffie's *A History of Colonial Brazil, 1500–1792*, and the classic study is Charles Boxer, *The Golden Age of Brazil, 1695–1750*. See also Francis Dutra, *A Guide to the History of Brazil, 1500–1822*, and Leslie Bethell, ed., *Colonial Brazil*.

2. For detailed discussions of early treatment of the Indians by missionaries and others, see Mathias Kiemen, *The Indian Policy of Portugal in the Amazon Region, 1614–1693*, and John Hemming, *Red Gold: The Conquest of the Brazilian Indian, 1500–1760*. See also, David Sweet, "A Rich Realm of Nature Destroyed: The Middle Amazon Valley, 1640–1750."

3. Denevan, "Aboriginal Population of Amazonia," 234.

4. See Maxwell, "Pombal and the Nationalization of the Luso-Brazilian Economy."

5. For an excellent collection of correspondence between them, see Mendonça, *A Amazonia na era pombalina. Correspondencia inédita*.

6. See Nunes Dias, *Fomento e mercantilismo*.

7. "Regimento e leis sobre as missões do Estado do Maranhão e Pará sobre a liberdade dos indios." Unpublished manuscript. Portugal, 1686.

8. See map C, "Settlement in 1800."

9. Fernando da Costa Ataíde Teive to Royal Court, June 30, 1768.

10. *Directorio*, arts. 26, 29, 32, 44, 51, 64–67, 73, 75.

11. Mendonça, *Correspondencia inédita*, 1:385–95.

12. *Directorio*, arts. 1, 2.

13. Ibid., 7, 8.

14. Ibid., 6.

15. Ibid., 12, 74.

16. Ibid., 11.

17. Ibid., 15.

18. Ibid., 13, 14, 41. Interestingly enough, liquor was allowed for the Indians participating in expeditions into the interior. See art. 42.

19. *Directorio*, arts. 87, 88.

20. Ibid., 89, 91.

21. Ibid., 1, 2.

22. Ibid., 77.

23. Ibid., 76, 78, 79.

24. Menezes, "Condições com que são concedidos aos particulares os indios silvestres dos novos descimentos," 1792.

25. Spaulding, *Huarochirí*, 124–34.

26. MacLeod, *Spanish Central America*, 120–42.

27. *Directorio*, art. 28.

28. Ibid., 57.

29. Letters from the villages of Monte Alegre 1761, Vigía 1773, Salvaterra 1778, Boim 1790, Pinhel 1790, 1791, Chaves 1792, Cajary 1792, Obidos 1793, Cajary 1794, et al. These and other letters from directors to the governor that have survived are in the "Correspondencia de diversos com o governo" collection in the Biblioteca e Arquivo Público do Pará in Belem. The letters accompanied the annual reports and lists of goods sent downriver, and were usually simply cover letters. There are some, however, which spoke of specific problems.

30. *Directorio*, arts. 17, 46.

31. Ibid., 21, 22.

32. Ibid., 17, 18.

33. Ibid., 19, 22.

34. Ibid., 21, 22.

35. Ibid., 24.

36. Ibid., 25.

37. Letters from the villages of Pinhel 1790, Boim 1790, Portel 1791, Souzel 1792, Oeiras 1793, Altar do Chão 1795.

38. Souza Coutinho, "Plano para a civilização dos indios na Capitania do Pará," August 2, 1797, para. 9.

39. Letters from the villages of Gurupá 1761, Veiros 1764, Melgaço 1765, Boim 1765, Conde 1770, Salvaterra 1770, Boim 1770, Vila Vistosa da Madre de Deus 1771, Almeirim 1779, Chaves 1789, Salvaterra 1792, Altar do Chão 1797. In their cover letters to the governor each year, the directors mentioned problems they had solved, but rarely asked for advice on a particular difficulty.

40. Letter from the village of Soure 1773.

41. "Mapa dos escravos e libertos e os rendimentos anuais," "Relação do gado vacuum."

42. *Directorio*, arts. 81–86.

43. Ibid., 80–86.

44. Baena, *Compendio das eras*, 184. Manoel Barata, *Apontamentos*, 25.

45. Letters from the village of Mazagão 1770, 1771.

46. Fernando da Costa Ataide Teive to Royal Court, March 13, 1770. Ataide Teive to Royal Court, March 29, 1770. Manoel Bernardo de Mello e Castro to Francisco Xavier de Mendonça Furtado, April 28, 1761.

47. Letters from the village of Mazagão 1772, 1773, 1774.

48. Letters from the village of Mazagão 1772, 1797. Marcos José Monteiro de Carvalho to Martinho de Mello e Castro, February 5, 1770. Bento Vieira Gomes, Cirurgião Anatómico, December 14, 1782. Mathias José Ribeiro, Ouvidor Geral, to Martinho de Souza e Albuquerque, October 7, 1784. Martinho de Souza e Albuquerque to Royal Court, December 26, 1784.

49. Martinho de Souza e Albuquerque to Royal Court, December 26, 1784.

50. João Pereira Caldas to Manoel Bernardo de Mello e Castro, November 5, 1775.

51. "Relação dos presos."

52. "Relação dos cazais," "Relação das familias," 1764. "Relação das familias," 1766–69.

53. *Directorio*, arts. 92–95.

54. "Plano . . . dos indios," para. 36.

55. Letters from the villages of Salvaterra 1771, 1775, Mauá 1775.

56. "Plano . . . dos indios," para. 12.

57. Ibid., 14, 18.

58. Ibid., 7.

59. *Directorio*, arts. 39, 40, 43, 45, 72.

60. Ibid., 49.

61. "Plano . . . dos indios," para. 7.

62. *Directorio*, art. 50.

63. Letters from the villages of Gurupá 1763, Vilarinho do Monte 1779, Portel 1785, Santarem 1793. Manoel Bernardo Mello e Castro to Francisco Xavier de Mendonça Furtado, August 9, 1759. José de Napoles Tello de Menezes to Royal Court, June 9, 1780.

64. Von Martius, *Natureza, doenças, medicina, e remedios dos indios brasileiros.*

65. "Mapa dos escravos," for the indicated years.

66. Manoel Bernardo de Mello e Castro to Francisco Xavier de Mendonça Furtado, August 6, 1759.

67. Conde dos Arcos to Visconde da Anadia, July 26, 1804.

68. Letters from the villages of Obidos 1761, Pinhel 1770, Melgaço 1772, Vigia 1774, Pombal 1777, Ponta de Pedras 1780, Abaeté 1781, Outeiro 1793, Marajó (Fazenda Ararí) 1796.

69. "Indios mandados para trabalharem na fortaleza."

70. Letter from the village of Santana de Cajary 1794.

71. Letters from the villages of Arraiolos 1797, Veiros, Pombal, Souzel 1799.

72. Letter from the village of Mazagão 1796. Mathias José Ribeiro to Martinho de Souza e Albuquerque, October 7, 1784. Martinho de Souza e Albuquerque to Royal Court, December 26, 1784. The 1783 report was by Bento Vieira Gomes, December 14, 1782.

73. *Directorio*, art. 7.

74. "Plano . . . dos indios," para. 4.

75. João Pereira Caldas to Manoel Bernardo de Mello e Castro, April 7, 1773.

Chapter 2: The Economic Basis of Settlement in the Eighteenth Century

1. Bunker, *Underdeveloping the Amazon*, 14.

2. Hemming, *Red Gold*, chap. 9–11, 15, 18–21.

3. Sweet, "A Rich Realm of Nature Destroyed."

4. Hemming, *Red Gold*, 57.

5. *Directorio*, art. 63.

6. Ibid., art. 65.

7. Ibid., art. 58.

8. Ibid., art. 72. See also, MacLachlan, "Labor Structure," 210.

9. Souza Coutinho, "Plano . . . dos indios," para. 9.

10. Manoel Bernardo de Mello e Castro to Francisco Xavier de Mendonça Furtado, August 9, 1759.

11. Mathias Ribeiro to Martinho de Souza e Albuquerque, March 15, 1784.

12. Francisco de Souza Coutinho to Luis Pinto de Sousa, August 1, 1796.

13. *Bando*, July 2, 1796, Francisco de Souza Coutinho.

14. Letter from the village of Pombal 1772.

15. Letters from the villages of Porto de Moz 1764, Obidos 1766, Almeirim 1770, Boim 1773, Portel 1778.

16. José de Napoles Tello de Menezes to Martinho de Mello e Castro, September 5, 1781, and October 25, 1783. "Relação dos indios silvestres," Oficio of November 19, 1781.

17. Letter from the village of Portel 1771.

18. Oficio, Frei M. Bispo de Pará to Tomé Joaquim da Costa, Royal Court, July 11, 1758. João Pereira Caldas to Manoel Bernardo de Mello e Castro, April 7, 1773. Bando, May 23, 1773. José de Napoles Tello de Menezes to Martinho de Mello e Castro, May 31, 1783. Francisco de Souza Coutinho to Martinho de Mello e Castro, December 9, 1798. Oficio, Francisco de Souza Coutinho, December 7, 1797.

19. João Pereira Caldas to Manoel Bernardo de Mello e Castro, March 7, 1773.

20. Letters from the villages of Soure 1759, Obidos 1761, Melgaço 1772, Santana de Cajary 1794.

21. Letters from the villages of Macapá 1759, Melgaço 1764, Colares 1770, Pombal 1774, Outeiro 1779.

22. Letters from the villages of Portel 1785, Cintra 1785, Santarem 1796.

23. Pereira, "Negros escravos," 153–85. The term *mucambo* was a local one for refugee slave camps. Elsewhere in Brazil, the more common term was *quilombo*.

24. Oficio, Francisco de Souza Coutinho, April 20, 1798. See also Mendonça, *Correspondencia inédita*, 1:280. Letters from the villages of Gurupá 1763, Melgaço 1765, Pombal 1772, Santarem 1787, Bragança 1796. See also Baena, *Compendio das eras*, 217.

25. Coutinho, "Plano . . . dos indios," para. 14, 18.

26. Letters from the villages of Pombal 1772, Santarem 1787.

27. Manoel Bernardo de Mello e Castro to Francisco Xavier de Mendonça Furtado, November 5, 1760.

28. d'Azevedo, *Os jesuitas no Grão Pará*, 229.

29. Letters from the villages of Oeiras 1770, Pinhel 1779, Gurupá 1773, Salinas 1774, Santarem 1781.

30. Salles, *O negro*, 48. Nunes Dias, *Fomento e mercantilismo*, 1:469.

31. Ferreira, "Estado presente da agricultura do Pará," March 15, 1784. Manuel Bernardo de Mello e Castro to Francisco Xavier de Mendonça Furtado, November 7, 1760.

32. The Cabanagem is one of the lesser known of those revolts. See Robin Anderson, "The Caboclo as Revolutionary"; Boiteux, *Marinha imperial versus a Cabanagem*; Hurley, *A Cabanagem*; and the definitive Raiol, *Motins políticos*.

33. Salsa was sarsaparilla, the root of a small tree of the *Labiadas* family used to make medicinal teas and restoratives, not to be confused with the use today of the term to refer to parsley. Cravo was the aromatic bark of a tree (*Dicypellium caryophyllatum*), with a scent very similar to clove.

34. Sweet, "Rich Realm," 62–67.

35. Maxwell, "Pombal and Nationalization," 612.

36. Letter from the village of Altar do Chão 1797.

37. Manuel Bernardo de Mello e Castro to Francisco Xavier de Mendonça Furtado, April 28, 1761.

38. Analysis of the regional distribution of export products is based on the extant annual lists from each village. The surviving lists and reports are bound in the "Correspondencia de diversos com o governo" collection in the Biblioteca e Archivo Público do Pará in Belem.

39. For an excellent discussion of the annihilation of turtles, see Smith, "Destructive Exploitation of the South American River Turtle."

40. Letter from the village of Almeirim 1785.

41. Ferreira, "Memoria sobre as tartarugas," n.d.

42. Ferreira, "Memoria sobre a jurarareté," 1786. Also, Ferreira, "Memoria

sobre as variedades de tartaruga que hão no Estado do Grão Pará e do emprego que lhe dão," n.d.

43. Ferreira, "Memoria sobre a jurarareté." These figures meant that over 1.5 million eggs were destroyed in an average year. If even 10 percent had matured, the loss to the turtle population would still have been approximately 1,135,000 individuals.

44. Ferreira, "Memoria sobre a jurarareté."

45. Ferraz, "Memoria de alguns produtos espontáneos e não espontáneos."

46. Ferreira, "Relação dos peixes dos sertões do Pará," n.d. Also, Ferreira, "Descrição do peixe pirarucú," 1787. The pirarucú were frequently reported up to 3.5 meters long.

47. Baena, *Compendio da eras*, 205.

48. Francisco de Sousa Coutinho to Court, February 6, 1792.

49. Verissimo, *A pesca da Amazonia*, 13. Since the data are incomplete, the actual figures were probably at least double those given here.

50. Letter from the village of Monsarás, 1777.

51. "Cartas de data e sesmaria," vols. 842–61.

52. Francisco Xavier de Mendonça Furtado to Diogo de Mendonça at the Royal Court, January 18, 1754. "Edital," March 24, 1797. See also, Ferreira, "O estado presente da agricultura do Pará . . . ," 1784.

53. See Alden, *O significado da produção de cacau na região amazónica*, especially 52, 54, 56.

54. Barata, *Antiga produção*, 14, 17, 18–20.

55. Letter from the village of Salvaterra, 1792.

56. Barata, *Antiga produção*, 13. His statement is substantiated by village records.

57. João Pereira Caldas to Manoel Bernardo de Mello e Castro, June 18, 1777.

58. "Circular," from João Pereira Caldas, December 4, 1773. There were also reports of poor farinha production from the villages of Oeiras in 1771 and Bragança and Vila Nova d'El Rei in 1797.

59. Letter from the village of Alenquer, 1781.

60. Letters from the villages of Monte Alegre 1761, Conde 1777, Pinhel 1791, Outeiro, Pinhel, Cajary, and Arraiolos 1792, Obidos 1793, Porto do Moz 1794, and Vila Nova d'El Rei 1795.

61. Letters from the villages of Conde 1790, Vila Franca and Salvaterra 1792, Monsarás 1796, and Santarem 1797.

62. Letters from the villages of Boim 1790, Souzel and Pinhel 1792, and Altar do Chão 1793 and 1795.

63. Barata, *Antiga produção*, 21–24.

64. "Mapa dos escravos e libertos e os rendimentos anuais dos engenhos e engenhocas existentes na Ilha Grande de Joanes, termo de Monsarás," October 20, 1790.

65. Letter from the village of Marajó 1759. Also, Barata, *Antiga produção*, 43.

66. Letter from the village of Marajó 1762.

67. Ibid., 1794.

Chapter 3: The Elites and Their Role in Colonization

1. The heavy toll of economic and demographic destruction required nearly twenty years to repair, during which time provincial governors were concerned with reconstruction, not colonization. See Robin Anderson, "A Cabanagem," 22–27, and "The Caboclo as Revolutionary," 51–88.

2. Browne, "Government Immigration Policy," chap. 4.

3. Lei de 15 de dezembro de 1830, art. 4.

4. Browne, "Policy," 122.

5. Ibid., 132–33, 192–93, 283–84.

6. Weinstein, *The Amazon Rubber Boom 1850–1920*, 109.

7. Ibid., 125–29.

8. Ibid., 134.

9. Chandler, *The Feitosas and the Sertão dos Inhamuns . . .* , chap. 3. Also, Pang, *Bahia in the First Brazilian Republic.*

10. Salles, *O negro*, 115.

11. Teixeira, *O arquipélago de Marajó*. Chermont de Miranda, "Molestias que afetam os animais domésticos," 438–68.

12. *Falla . . .* Tristão de Alencar Araripe . . . March 25, 1886, 8.

13. Weinstein, *Rubber Boom*, chap. 1.

14. *Provincia do Pará*, January 28, 1890; February 6, 1890; December 17, 1890; January 31, 1891; November 10, 1892; August 20, 1895.

15. See map E in appendix A.

16. *Fala . . .* Angelo Thomaz do Amaral . . . August 15, 1860, 67.

17. *Relatorio . . .* Antonio Coelho de Sá e Albuquerque . . . May 12, 1860, 41.

18. *Relatorio . . .* Guilherme Francisco Cruz . . . January 17, 1874, 14.

19. *Relatorio . . .* Pedro Vicente de Azevedo . . . February 15, 1874, 62.

20. Ibid., 64.

21. *Falla . . .* João C. Bandeira de Mello Filho . . . February 15, 1877, 161.

22. *Relatorio . . .* João Lourenço Paes de Souza . . . September 16, 1885, 111.

23. *Mensagem . . .* José Paes de Carvalho . . . April 15, 1899, 20.

24. For a discussion of the statistical tests applied, see appendix B.

25. *Mensagem*, Lauro Sodré, February 1, 1897, 21.

26. These figures were constructed by using the coefficient of determination test. The Pearson correlation coefficients from which they were derived are in appendix B.

27. *Relatorio . . .* João Antonio d'Araujo Freitas Henriques . . . October 6, 1886, 63.

28. *Relatorio . . .* Dr. José Vieira Couto de Magalhães . . . August 15, 1864, 15.

29. *O Liberal do Pará*, June 15, 1871.

30. Weinstein, *Rubber Boom*, 21

31. *Relatorio . . .* Dr. Abel Graça . . . August 15, 1871, 37.

32. Such lists appeared in most issues of the daily newspapers from roughly 1880 to 1910. Specific examples used include reports in *Provincia do Pará*, November 29, 1884; January 23, 1891; and January 29, 1891.

33. *Provincia do Pará,* May 2, 1879; May 4, 1879; May 6, 1879; May 10, 1879; June 15, 1879; July 8, 1879; July 15, 1879.

34. Ibid., July 8, 1879.

35. Ibid., July 8 to July 13, 1879.

36. Ibid., July 25, 1879.

37. *Relatorio,* José Coelho da Gama e Abreu, 1879.

38. Ibid.

39. *Provincia do Pará,* August 26, 1886. *Fala,* Joaquim da Casta Barradas. Muniz, *A imigração e colonização do Estado do Grão Pará,* 44. Cruz, *A Estrada de Ferro de Bragança,* 19. Rocha Penteado, *Problemas de colonização,* 1:14–15.

40. Muniz, *A imigração e colonização do Estado do Grão Pará,* 44.

Chapter 4: Basic Decisions in Colonization

1. *Folha do Norte* editorials from February 13 to March 21, 1901.

2. See maps in appendix A.

3. *Provincia do Pará,* March 3, 5, 30, 1889.

4. *Liberal do Pará,* August 29, 1875; *Relatorio,* Guilherme Francisco Cruz, January 17, 1874, 15.

5. *Relatorio* . . . Miguel Antonio Pinto Guimarães . . . August 15, 1869, 9.

6. *Provincia do Pará,* editorial May 23, 1899. *Relatorio* da Repartição de Obras Públicas, Terras, e Colonização of 1897, in *Diario Oficial* (hereafter referred to as D.O.), January 18, 1898.

7. *Relatorio* . . . José Vieira Couto de Magalhães, August 15, 1864, 14–15.

8. *Mensagem* . . . Lauro Sodré . . . July 1, 1892, 17–19.

9. *Relatorio* . . . Pedro Leão Velloso . . . April 9, 1867, 19–20; *Relatorio* . . . Joaquim Raimundo Lamaré . . . August 15, 1867, 42; *Relatorio* . . . Joaquim Raimundo Lamaré . . . August 6, 1868, anexo 16; *Relatorio* . . . Abel Graça . . . August 15, 1871, 35; *Relatorio* . . . Pedro Vicente de Azevedo . . . February 15, 1874, 63; *Relatorio* . . . José Coelho da Gama e Abreu . . . June 16, 1879, 21. Herbert H. Smith, *Brazil, the Amazons and the Coast,* 141–42. Lawrence Hill, "Confederate Exiles to Brazil," 192–210. See also, Dawsey, *The Confederados.*

10. *Relatorio* . . . Francisco Maria Correia de Sá e Benevides . . . February 15, 1876, 51. *Jornal do Pará,* September 1, 1868 and January 22, 1871.

11. *Liberal do Pará,* March 13, 1874.

12. See Brooks, "Flight from Disaster," and Cunniff, "The Great Drought."

13. *Provincia do Pará,* August 1, September 22, 25, October 11, 14, 1877.

14. *Fala* . . . José Joaquim do Carmo . . . April 22, 1878, 6–7.

15. *Liberal do Pará,* July 6, 9, 24, 1878. *Provincia do Pará,* January 5, 9, 1879. *Relatorio* . . . José Coelho da Gama e Abreu . . . February 15, 1879, 3.

16. *Liberal do Pará,* July 24, 1878. *Fala* . . . José Coelho da Gama e Abreu . . . June 16, 1879, 20. *Provincia do Pará,* April 30, May 4, 14, 1879.

17. *Relatorio* . . . José Coelho da Gama e Abreu . . . February 15, 1881, 42–44.

18. *Fala* . . . Joaquim da Costa Barradas . . . November 20, 1886, 51.

19. *Provincia do Pará,* February 24, 1889.

20. Telegram from Governor Acciolly (Ceará) to Governor Paes de Carvalho (Pará), printed in *Provincia do Pará*, June 17, 1898. Also, *Provincia do Pará*, March 26, April 3, 1900.

21. *Provincia do Pará*, June 10, 1898; April 25, 1900. *Folha do Norte*, June 1, 11, 20, 22, 26, 28, July 25, August 14, September 5, 28, November 23, December 9, 1900. *Mensagem* . . . Augusto Montenegro . . . September 7, 1904, 41.

22. *Folha do Norte*, February 26, May 2, 11, 1916.

23. Founding act, in attachments to *Fala* . . . Tristão de Alencar Araripe . . . November 5, 1885. *Fala* . . . Tristão de Alencar Araripe . . . March 25, 1886, 59.

24. The debates were covered daily in the collections of *Diario Oficial*, *Provincia do Pará*, and *Folha do Norte*. See also *Provincia do Pará*, November 7, 1886.

25. *Fala* . . . Tristão de Alencar Araripe . . . March 25, 1886, 124–27.

26. Lei 223, June 30, 1894, in D.O., July 5, 1894.

27. *Provincia do Pará*, June 24, July 29, 30, 31, August 2, 31, 1898.

28. Ibid., September 4, 1898.

29. D.O., January 8, 1898.

30. Ibid., September 20, 1894, April 11, 14, 16, 18, and May 16, 1895.

31. *Relatorio*, of Repartição de Obras Públicas, Terras, e Colonização of 1897, in D.O., December 21, 1897, and subsequently December 22, 24, 25, 30, 1897, January 5, 7, 8, 13, 18, 19, 20, 1898. "Quadro demonstrativo dos imigrantes introduzidos pelos senhores Emilio Adolfo de Castro Martins e Francisco Cepeda . . . ," in *Relatorio*, José Paes de Carvalho, February 1, 1901, in D.O., February 5, 1901. *Folha do Norte*, May 29, 1900.

32. Speech to Legislative Congress on the budget, printed in *Provincia do Pará*, April 20, 1898.

33. J. V. Couto de Magalhães, *Memoria sobre as colonias militares nacionais e indígenas*, 15.

34. The núcleos suburbanos were established by Lei 581 of June 20, 1898, in D.O., June 22, 1898.

35. *Relatorio* of Repartição de Obras Públicas, Terras, e Colonização of 1897, in D.O., January 20, 1898. Lei 654 of June 12, 1889, in D.O., June 14, 1899. Lei 597 of June 27, 1898, in D.O., July 1, 1898.

36. Decreto 1125 of February 28, 1902, in D.O., March 4, 1902. Decreto 1303 of May 2, 1904, in D.O., May 5, 1904. Lei 866 of October 17, 1903, in D.O., October 21, 1903.

Chapter 5: Policy and Living Conditions

1. Dean, "Latifundia and Land Policy," 616, 618, 621.

2. Browne, "Policy," chap. 11.

3. *Liberal do Pará*, May 22, 1874.

4. *Relatorio* . . . Barão da Vila da Barra . . . November 5, 1872, 61–62.

5. *Relatorio* . . . Manuel Pinto de Souza Dantas . . . January 4, 1882, 115–16.

6. *Relatorio* . . . João Capistrano Bandeira de Mello Filho . . . March 9, 1878, 89. *Fala* . . . Tristão de Alencar Araripe . . . March 25, 1886, 36. *Relatorio* . . . Manuel Pinto de Souza Dantas . . . January 4, 1882, 115–16.

7. D.O. July 4, 14, 1891.

8. Ibid., October 10, 1891.

9. Ibid., July 8, 25, 1892.

10. Ibid., April 28, May 1, 2, 5, 6, 9, 1894.

11. Ibid., April 11, 14, 16, 19, May 7, 1895.

12. Ibid., June 2, 1895, May 26, 1898.

13. *Provincia do Pará,* April 20, 1898.

14. *Folha do Norte,* July 25, 1900. D.O., September 3, 1900.

15. D.O., October 15, 1902.

16. Vianna, *As epidemias do Pará,* 19–21.

17. Ibid., 22–23.

18. *Relatorio* . . . José Coelho da Gama e Abreu . . . February 15, 1881. *Relatorio* . . . Francisco Cardoso Junior, May 6, 1888, 7. *Relatorio* . . . Francisco Maria Correa de Sá e Benevides . . . February 15, 1876, 17. *Relatorio* . . . Manuel Pinto de Souza Dantas Filho . . . January 4, 1882, 59.

19. Vianna, *Epidemias,* 48. Also, Brito and Cardoso, *A febre amarela do Pará,* 19–20.

20. *Mensagem* . . . João Antonio Luiz Coelho . . . September 7, 1912, 42–47. See also Cooper, "Oswaldo Cruz and the Impact of Yellow Fever," 49–52.

21. *Exposição* . . . João Maria de Moraes . . . 1855, 3.

22. *Exposição* . . . Sebastião do Rego Barros . . . May 29, 1856, 9.

23. Brasil. *Recenseamento da população . . . 1872.*

24. Pará. *Dados estatísticos,* 34–35.

25. Decree of August 30, 1852, clauses 14, 15. *Relatorio* . . . Barão de Arary . . . October 1, 1866, 17. *Relatorio* . . . Joaquim Raimundo de Lamaré . . . August 6, 1868, 34.

26. *Relatorio* . . . Abel Graça . . . August 15, 1871, 17–18. *Fala* . . . João Silveira de Souza . . . April 18, 1885, 43.

27. *Provincia do Pará,* February 14, 1883, editorial. *Provincia do Pará,* December 22, 1883. *Fala* . . . Tristão de Alencar Araripe . . . March 25, 1886, 43.

28. *Provincia do Pará,* November 13, 1886.

29. *Relatorio* . . . João Antonio de Araujo Freitas Henriques . . . October 6, 1886, 135.

30. *Provincia do Pará,* May 10, 1890, May 7, 1894, July 17, 1911.

31. *Relatorio* . . . Tristão de Alencar Araripe . . . November 5, 1885, 11. *Provincia do Pará,* August 8, 1898.

32. *Fala* . . . Tristão de Alencar Araripe . . . March 25, 1886, 43. *Mensagem* . . . João Antonio Luiz Coelho . . . September 7, 1912, 145.

33. *Liberal do Pará,* May 4, 1875; *Provincia do Pará,* April 26, 1885, November 26, 1886. Also, see *Provincia do Pará,* editorials in May 27, 28, 30, 31, and June 2, 5, 7, 8, September 18, October 23, 1888, et al. See also, *Relatorio do Ministerio de Industria, Viação, e Obras Públicas,* 1892, 33–35. Also, *Provincia do Pará,* August 24, 1890, and D.O., November 1894.

34. *Folha do Norte,* May 26, 1918.

35. D.O. September 11, 1892. D.O., July 4, 1894.

36. Ibid., August 26, 1892, May 29, June 20, July 3, 4, 1894.

37. Ibid., June 20, 1894.

38. Fittkau and Klinge, "On Biomass and Trophic Structure," 2–14; Stark, "Nutrient Cycling," 24–50; and Stark, "Nutrient Cycling II," 177–201.

Chapter 6: Migration and Demographic Change

1. Raiol, *Motins políticos* . . . , 3:1001 n.

2. *O Colono de Nossa Senhora do Ó*, October 15, 1855.

3. Ibid., February 15, May 30, 1856.

4. *Provincia do Pará*, August 28, 1886. *Fala* . . . Joaquim da Costa Barradas . . . November 20, 1886, 51.

5. *Relatorio* . . . José Coelho da Gama e Abreu . . . February 15, 1880, 28.

6. *Relatorio* . . . Antonio José Ferreira Braga . . . September 18, 1889, 20.

7. *Mensagem* . . . Augusto Montenegro . . . September 7, 1904, 41.

8. *Relatorio* . . . Antonio Ferreira Vianna, anexo, 13.

9. Penna, *O Tocantins e o Anapú*, 84.

10. *Liberal do Pará*, June 12, 1877, November 5, 1878. *Provincia do Pará*, July 25, August 1, 1877, January 2, 1878, April 20, 1879. Comisão de Socorros, Santarem, *Oficio*, April 24, 1878.

Conclusion

1. Brasil, Instituto Brasileiro de Estatística, *Sinopse preliminar do censo demográfico, Pará*, 1971.

2. There are a number of excellent studies on contemporary colonization of the basin. Of particular value are the works of Emilio Moran, Nigel Smith, Marianne Schmink, Charles Wood, Susanna Hecht, Alexander Cockburn, and Anthony Anderson.

3. A great deal of research in all disciplines is being done on the problems of deforestation, dam building, ecological damage, mining, sustainable settlement, and land conflict. See Marianne Schmink, *Contested Frontiers;* David Cleary, *Anatomy of the Amazonian Gold Rush;* Susanna Hecht, "Logic of livestock and deforestation" and *Fate of the Forest;* Barbara Cummings, *Dam the Rivers;* and David Goodman, ed., *Future of Amazonia.* Internet sites maintained by the Rainforest Action Network, Greenpeace, Amnesty International, and other conservation and human rights groups constantly update their material with new releases.

Epilogue: Lessons Unlearned, Attitudes Unchanged

1. U.S. Department of State, "Brazil-Country Report on Human Rights Practices," January 1997, 14.

2. Ibid.; Amanaka'a Amazon Network, "Brazil's Justice Minister," December 1996; Rainforest Action Network, "Brazil's Justice Minister Delays," September 1996.

3. Rainforest Action Network, "Amazon Imperiled," January 1996.

4. Beto Borges, "Brazil—Decree 1775 Takes Its Toll," June 1996.

5. Stephen Schwartzman, Report to Amanaka'a Amazon Network, December 1996.

6. Rainforest Action Network report, May 1996.

7. FUNAI, the government agency overseeing indigenous affairs, has the job of judging claims made against Indian lands. In 1996, it generally rejected such claims, although some have been substantiated. The process requires constant vigilance from watchdog organizations such as the Rainforest Action Network, and in the final analysis, the reserves are losing land. Beto Borges, update report to Rainforest Action Network, July 1996. Also, Julio Feferman, *World Rainforest Report* (summer/fall 1996).

8. Eugene Parker, "Forest Islands," and Darrell Posey, "Indigenous Management."

9. See R. E. Schultes, *The Healing Forest*.

10. See David Treece, "Indigenous Peoples in Brazilian Amazonia," and Barbara Cummings, *Dam the Rivers*. Also, Amanaka'a Amazon Network, "Brazil's Justice Minister," and unauthored e-mail report to NATIVE-L listserve, March 19, 1993.

11. See David Cleary, *Anatomy of Amazon Gold Rush*, and Gordon MacMillan, *At the End of the Rainbow*.

12. See Cummings, *Dam the Rivers*, 81–83, and Treece, "Indigenous Peoples." See also Moran, "Law, Politics, and Economics."

13. Cummings, *Dam the Rivers*, 83.

14. A great number of monographs and scholarly articles have been published on the growth of the Amazonian road system and its attendant colonization and deforestation. The reader is particularly directed to the works of Moran, Smith, Hecht, Schmink, Almeida, and Gross.

15. See Almeida, *Sustainable Settlement*, chap. 1.

16. Friends of the Earth report published to listserve NATIVE-L, June 1995. See also Brent Millikan's report to NATIVE-L in 1994; Rainforest Action Network report, 1996; and Rainforest Action Network/Amazon Coalition, "Amazon Imperiled," 1996.

17. Friends of the Earth report, June 1995.

18. See Almeida, *Sustainable Settlement*, chap. 1.

19. Ibid.

20. See Alfredo de Almeida, "State and Land," and Schmink and Wood, *Contested Frontiers*.

21. Diane Schemo, "As Research Dries Up," and EnviroNews Service report of July 26, 1996, on logging.

22. See Treece, "Indigenous Peoples," and John Heming, *Amazon Frontier*.

23. Besides continuing to burn fields to claim ownership, in Rondonia in 1991 some people were burning coffee and cacao plantations to plant food crops and pasture cattle because commodity prices for coffee and cacao were too low to be profitable. James Langston communication to listserve NATIVE-L, October 17, 1991.

24. See Schmink, *Frontier Expansion*.

25. See Schmink, *Contested Frontiers*. Also, Luiz de Oliveira, "Alert: Planaflora," 1994; Rainforest Action Network reports, "Amazon Imperiled," 1996 and "Financing Environmental Destruction," 1996.

26. Almeida, *Colonization of the Amazon*, passim, esp. pt. 2, "Frontier and State."

27. Emilio Moran, "Private and Public Colonization Schemes."

28. See Anthony Anderson, ed., *Alternatives to Deforestation*, Chris Barrow, "Environmentally Appropriate," Anthony Gross, "Amazonia in the Nineties," and David Goodman, ed., *The Future of Amazonia*. For the most recent comments on sustainable economic activity, see Rainforest Action Network reports "Economic Alternatives," 1996, and "Extractive Reserves," 1996.

29. See Douglas Stewart, *After the Trees*, Nigel Smith, *Rainforest Corridors*, and Marianne Schmink, *Frontier Expansion*.

30. Charles Wood, "Blaming the Victim."

31. Cummings, *Dam the Rivers*, 34–43.

32. Ibid., 22–28.

33. Ibid., 36.

34. Ibid., 56–61, 63–83.

35. Howard LaFranchi, "Is Burning of Amazonia All Smoke?," 1998.

36. Dr. Jose Fragoso and Kirsten Silvius report, "Amazon Fires," 1998.

37. Joelle Diderich, "Yanomami Shamans," 1998

38. Phil Davidson, "Bureaucrats Fan the Flames"; Tod Robberson, "Brazil—Politicians, Corporations Fiddle"; Joelle Diderich, "Brazil Sends More Personnel," all 1998.

39. See reports from Rainforest Action Network, "Brazil Bans Mahogany Logging"; EnviroNews Service, "Logging Contracts Cancelled"; and Greenpeace Brazil, "Rainforest Under Siege," all 1996.

40. Cleary, *Anatomy of the Amazon Gold Rush*.

41. Brasil, Ministerio de Relações Estrangeiras report, "Prospection," 1994.

42. Ted Gragson, "Fishing the Waters of Amazonia," 428–40; Michael Goulding, *Floods of Fortune*, passim. See also, Nigel Smith, *Man, Fishes, and the Amazon*.

Appendix B : Data Collection, Research Design, and Statistical Analysis

1. Bivariant correlation analysis, in this case using Pearson Coefficients, provides a single number which summarizes the relationship between two variables. The correlation coefficients indicate the degree to which variation in one variable is related to variation in another. The main disadvantage of such correlation is that it assumes a linear relationship, and economic variables are far more apt to be curvilinear. However, in the case of rubber, variation is very nearly linear, thus eliminating the problem.

2. The coefficient of determination is computed as R^2. It expresses the relative reduction in the variation of one variable that can be attributed to a knowledge of another variable and its relationship to the first by way of a regression line. Stated another way, the coefficient of determination gives the portion of the total variance

that is explained or accounted for by the linear relationship of one variable with another. Thus, quite simply, an R^2 of 0.7231 can be interpreted as 72.13% of the total variation of variable X, which can be explained by the relationship between X and the corresponding values of variable Y. Multiple R^2 works exactly the same way except that it explains the portion of variance accounted for by the relationship of one dependent variable with a group of interrelated independent variables.

3. The significance level of R was held at 0.6000 precisely because the square of R becomes far too small if R is less than 0.6000.

4. A regression equation was constructed using a set of six variables: rubber, Brazil nuts, cacao, rice, sugar, and farinha. The variables were then rotated so that each variable became the dependent variable, explained to the extent possible by the other independent variables. Stepwise regression was used so that variables assumed ranking from greatest change in R^2 to least.

5. *Mensagem*, Lauro Sodré, February 1, 1897, 21.

BIBLIOGRAPHY

Adonias, Isa. *A Cartografia da região amazónica: Catálogo descritivo, 1500–1961* (Cartography of the Amazon region: Descriptive catalogue). 3 vols. Rio de Janeiro: Instituto Nacional de Pesquisas da Amazonia, 1963.

Alden, Dauril. "Black Robes versus White Settlers, the Struggle for 'Freedom of the Indians' in Colonial Brazil." In *Attitudes of Colonial Powers toward the American Indians*, ed. Howard Peckham and Charles Gibson, 19–45. Salt Lake City: University of Utah Press, 1969.

———. "Economic Aspects of the Expulsion of the Jesuits from Brazil, a Preliminary Report." In *Conflict and Continuity in Brazilian History*, ed. Henry Keith and S. F. Edwards, 25–71. Charleston: University of South Carolina Press, 1969.

———. *O significado da produção de cacau na região amazónica* (Significance of cacao production in the Amazon region). Belem: Universidade Federal do Pará, 1974.

———. "The Population of Brazil in the Late Eighteenth Century: A Preliminary Study." *Hispanic American Historical Review* 43, no. 2 (1963): 173–205.

———, ed. *Colonial Roots of Modern Brazil.* Berkeley: University of California Press, 1973.

Almeida, Alfredo Berno de. "The State and Land Conflict in Amazonia, 1964–1988." In *The Future of Amazonia: Destruction or Sustainable Development?*, ed. David Goodman and Anthony Hall, 226–44. New York: St. Martin's Press, 1990.

Almeida, Anna Luiza Ozorio de. *The Colonization of the Amazon.* Austin: University of Texas Press, 1992.

Almeida, Anna Luiza Ozorio de, and João S. Campais. *Sustainable Settlement in the Brazilian Amazon.* Oxford: Oxford University Press, 1995.

Alves, Diogenes. "Brazil Monitors Amazon Forests." Landsat Pathfinder Project report, 1992. Available online: http://amazon.unh.edu/pathfinder/information/papers/gisworld2/index.html, accessed September 4, 1997, no longer available.

Amanaka'a Amazon Network. "Brazil's Justice Minister Opts to Legalize Theft in Indian Land," December 23, 1996. Available online: http://www.amanakaa.org/macuxi.htm, accessed July 26, 1997.

Anderson, Anthony, ed. *Alternatives to Deforestation—Steps toward Sustainable Use of the Amazon Rain Forest.* New York: Columbia University Press, 1990.

Anderson, Robin L. "A Cabanagem, a luta entre raças e classes na Amazonia, 1835–1836: Um ensaio interpretativo" (The Cabanagem, race and class warfare in Amazonia, 1835–1836: An interpretive essay). *Revista do Instituto Histórico e Geográfico Brasileiro* 307 (1975): 22–27.

———. "The Caboclo as Revolutionary: The Cabanagem Revolt of 1835–1836." In *The Amazon Caboclo: Historical and Contemporary Perspectives*. Vol. 32, *Studies in Third World Societies*, ed. Eugene Parker, 51–88. Williamsburg: College of William and Mary, 1985.

Andrade, L., and L. Santos, eds. *As hidroelétricas do Xingú e os povos indígenas* (Hydroelectric projects on the Xingú and the indigenous peoples). São Paulo: Comissão Pro-Indio de São Paulo, 1988.

d'Azevedo, João Lucio. *Os Jesuitas no Grão Pará* (Jesuits in Grão Pará). 2d ed. Coimbra: n.p., 1930.

Baena, Antonio Ladislau Monteiro. *Compendio das eras da provincia do Pará* (Compendium of the years of the province of Pará). 2d ed. Belem: Universidade Federal do Pará, 1969.

Barata, Manoel. *A antiga produção e exportação do Pará: Estudo histórico-económico* (Old production and export from Pará: Historical-economic study). Belem: Livraria Gillet, 1915.

———. *Apontamentos para as efemerides paraenses* (References for chronologies of Pará). Reprinted in Manoel Barata, *Formação histórica do Pará, obras reunidas* (Historical formation of Pará, collected works). Belem: Universidade Federal do Pará, 1973.

———. *A formação histórica do Pará, obras reunidas* (Historical formation of Pará, collected works). Belem: Universidade Federal do Pará, 1973.

Barrow, Chris. "Environmentally Appropriate, Sustainable Small-Farm Stategies for Amazonia." In *The Future of Amazonia—Destruction or Sustainable Development?*, ed. David Goodman and Anthony Hall, 360–82. New York: St. Martin's Press, 1990.

Benchimol, Samuel. "O cearense na Amazonia: Inquérito antropo-geográfico sobre um tipo de imigrante" (The Cearense in the Amazon: Anthro-geographical investigation on one type of immigrant). *Revista de Imigração e Colonização* (1945): 337–420.

Bethell, Leslie, ed. *Colonial Brazil*. New York: Cambridge University Press, 1987.

Boiteux, Lucas Alexandre. *Marinha Imperial versus a Cabanagem* (The Royal Navy and the Cabanagem). Rio de Janeiro: Imprensa Naval, 1943.

Borges, Beto. "Decree 1775 of 1996," program update to Rainforest Action Network, June 1996. Available online: http://www.ran.org/ran/ran_campaigns/amazonia/update_6–96.html, accessed July 26, 1997.

Boserup, Edith. *Conditions of Agricultural Growth: The Economics of Agrarian Change under Population Pressures*. Chicago: Aldine, 1965.

Boxer, Charles R. *The Golden Age of Brazil, 1695–1750: Growing Pains of a Colonial Society*. Berkeley: University of California Press, 1962.

Brasil. *Coleção das leis do Imperio do Brasil de 1822–1870* (Collection of laws of the Brazilian empire, 1822–1870). 90 vols. Rio de Janeiro: Imprensa Nacional, 1837–87.

———. Diretoria Geral de Estatística, *Idades da população recenseada em 31 de dezembro de 1890* (Ages of population counted on December 31, 1890). Rio de Janeiro: Oficina da Estatística, 1901.

———. Diretoria Geral de Estatística, *Recenseamento da população do Imperio do Brasil a que se procedeu no dia 1 de agosto de 1872* (Population census of the empire of Brazil done on August 1, 1872). Rio de Janeiro: Oficina da Estatística, 1873–76. Vol. 2, Pará.

———. Diretoria Geral de Estatística, *Sexo, raça e estado civil, nacionalidade, filiação, culto, e analfabetismo da população, recenseada em 31 de dezembro de 1890* (Sex, race, marital status, nationality, ancestry, religion, and illiteracy of the population counted on December 31, 1890). Rio de Janeiro: Oficina da Estatística, 1898.

———. Diretoria Geral de Estatística, *Synopse do recenseamento de 31 de dezembro de 1890* (Synopsis of census of December 31, 1890). Rio de Janeiro: Oficina da Estatística, 1898.

———. Diretoria Geral de Estatística, *Synopse do recenseamento de 31 de dezembro de 1900* (Synopsis of census of December 31, 1900). Rio de Janeiro: Tipografia da Estatística, 1905.

———. *Falas do Trono desde o ano de 1823 até o ano de 1889, acompanhadas dos respetivos votos de graças da Câmara Temporaria . . . colegidas na Secretaria da Câmara dos Deputados* (Speeches from the throne from 1823 to 1889, together with the votes of thanks from the temporary cabinet . . . collected in the Secretariat of the Chamber of Deputies). Rio de Janeiro: Imprensa Nacional, 1889.

———. Instituto Brasileiro de Bibliografia e Documentação. *Amazonia—Bibliografia, 1614–1962* (Amazonian bibliography, 1614–1962). 2 vols. Rio de Janeiro: Conselho Nacional de Pesquisas, 1963, 1972.

———. Instituto Brasileiro de Estatística. *Sinopse preliminar do censo demográfico, VIII recenseamento geral, 1970* (Preliminary synopsis of the demographic census, 8th General Census, 1970), *Pará*. Rio de Janeiro: Fundação do I.B.G.E., 1971.

———. Instituto Brasileiro de Geografia e Estatística. *Enciclopedia dos municipios brasileiros* (Encyclopedia of Brazilian municipios). 36 vols. Vols. 1, 14. Rio de Janeiro: Serviço Gráfico de I.B.G.E., 1957.

———. Ministerio de Agricultura, *Relatorios*, 1861–1912. Rio de Janeiro: various publishers, 1861–1912.

———. Ministerio de Agricultura, Serviço do Povoamento do Solo Nacional, *Relatorios*, 1907–1912. Rio de Janeiro: various publishers, 1907–12.

———. Ministerio de Estado de Agricultura, *Relatorios*, 1861–1912. Rio de Janeiro: various publishers, 1861–1912.

———. Ministerio de Estado de Industria, Viação e Obras Públicas, *Relatorios*, 1892–1912. Rio de Janeiro: various publishers, 1892–1912.

———. Ministerio de Estado da Justiça e Negocios Interiores, *Relatorios*, 1828–1912. Rio de Janeiro: various publishers, 1828–1912.

———. Ministerio de Estado de Relações Exteriores, *Relatorios*, 1852–1912. Rio de Janeiro: various publishers, 1852–1912.

———. Ministerio do Imperio, Diretoria Geral de Estatística, *Relatorios*, 1872–75. Rio de Janeiro: various publishers, 1872–75.

————. Ministerio do Imperio, *Relatorios*, 1832–1889. Rio de Janeiro: various publishers, 1832–89.

————. Ministerio de Relações Exteriores. "Prospection" (no date). Available online: http://www.mre.gov.br/ndsg/textos/garimpo-i.htm, accessed September 4, 1997.

————. Serviço Brasileiro de Justiça e Paz. "Deforestation," 1995. Available online: http://peg.apc.org/~stan/245/245p23c.htm, accessed September 4, 1997, no longer available.

Brito, Rubens da Silva, and Eleyson Cardoso. *A febre amarela no Pará* (Yellow fever in Pará). Belem: SUDAM, 1973.

Brooks, Reuben Howard. "Flight from Disaster: Drought Perception as a Force in Migration from Ceará, Brazil." Ph.D. diss., University of Colorado, 1972.

Browder, John. "Public Policy and Deforestation in the Brazilian Amazon." In *Public Policies and the Misuse of Forest Resources*, ed. Robert Repetto and Malcomb Gillis. New York: Cambridge University Press, 1988.

Brown, George P.. "Government Immigration Policy in Imperial Brazil, 1822–1870." Ph.D. diss., Catholic University of America, 1972.

Buarque de Holanda, Sergio, ed. *Historia geral da civilização brasileira* (General history of Brazilian civilization). 9 vols. São Paulo: Difusão Europeia do Livro, 1964–67.

Bunker, Stephen. "The Impact of Deforestation on Peasant Communities in the Medio Amazonas of Brazil." In *Studies in Third World Societies*, 13:455–60. Williamsburg: College of William and Mary, 1980.

————. *Underdeveloping the Amazon: Extraction, Unequal Exchange, and the Failure of the Modern State*. Urbana: University of Illinois Press, 1985.

Cable News Network. "Strong Rains Fall on Fire-Ravaged Amazon State," March 31, 1998. Available online: http://pooh.esrin.esa.it:8080/ew/brazil.htm, accessed September 28, 1998, no longer available.

Camargo, Felisberto. "Terra e colonização no antigo e novo quartenario da zona da Estrada de Ferro de Bragança, Estado do Pará, Brasil" (Land and Settlement on the Recent and Ancient Quaternary along the Railway Line of Bragança, State of Pará, Brazil). *Boletim do Museu Paraense Emilio Goeldi* 10 (1949): 123–47.

Carneiro, José Fernando. "O imperio e a colonização no sul do Brasil" (The empire and colonization in southern Brazil). *Fundamentos da cultura rio-grandense* 4 (1960): 61–96.

Carneiro, Robert. "Slash and Burn Cultivation among the Kuikuru and Its Implications for Cultural Development in the Amazon Basin." *Anthropológica* (Caracas) 2 (1961): 47–65.

"Cartas de data e sesmaria" (Documents of land grants). Vols. 842–61. Biblioteca e Archivo Público do Pará (BAPP).

CEDI (Centro Ecuménico de Documentação e Informação). *Empresas de mineração e terras indígenas*. (Mining operations and Indian lands). São Paulo: CEDI, 1998.

Chandler, Billy Jaynes. *The Feitosas and the Sertão dos Inhamuns: The History of a Family and a Community in Northeast Brazil, 1700–1930*. Gainesville: University of Florida Press, 1972.

Cleary, David. *Anatomy of the Amazonian Gold Rush.* Iowa City: University of Iowa Press, 1990.

Cooper, Donald B. "Oswaldo Cruz and the Impact of Yellow Fever on Brazilian History." *Bulletin of the Tulane University Medical Faculty* 26 (1967): 49–52.

O Colono de Nossa Senhora de Ó (Colonist of Our Lady of Ó), Belem, 1855–58.

"Correspondencia de diversos com o governo, 1733–1868" (Correspondence of various people with the government, 1733–1868). 565 vols. BAPP.

"Correspondencia original dos governadores do Pará com a corte, 1764–1807" (Original correspondence of the governors of Pará with the Court, 1764–1807). 24 vols. Arquivo Nacional (AN).

Costa, Custodio de Araujo. "O braço cearense no desenvolvimento da Amazonia" (The Cearense worker in the development of the Amazon). *Boletim da Associação Comercial do Amazonas* 120 (1951): 14–15.

Costa, Orlando. "O povoamento da Amazonia" (The populating of the Amazon). *Revista Brasileira de Estudos Políticos* 27 (1969): 151–96.

Coutinho, Gov. Francisco de Sousa. "Plano para a civilização dos indios na Capitania do Pará," 2 August 1797 (Plan for the civilization of the Indians of the captaincy of Pará). Instituto Histórico e Geográfico Brasileiro, Arquivo (IHGB,ARQ).

Couto de Magalhães, J. V. *Memoria sobre colonias militares nacionais e indígenas* (Report on national military and Indian colonies). Rio de Janeiro: Tipografia da Reforma, 1875.

Cruz, Ernesto. *A colonização do Pará* (The colonization of Pará). Belem: Instituto Nacional de Pesquisas da Amazonia, 1958.

———. *A Estrada de Ferro de Bragança, visão social, económica, e política* (The Bragança railroad, social, economic, and political view). Belem: SPVEA, 1955.

———. *Historia de Belem* (History of Belem). 2 vols. Belem: Universidade Federal do Pará, 1973.

———. *Historia do Pará* (History of Pará). 2 vols. 2d ed. Belem: Governo do Estado do Pará, 1973.

Cummings, Barbara. *Dam the Rivers, Damn the People.* London: Earthscan, 1990.

Cunniff, Roger Lee. "The Great Drought: Northeast Brazil, 1877–1880." Ph.D. diss., University of Texas at Austin, 1970.

Davidson, Phil. "Bureaucrats Fan the Flames of Amazonia." *Independent* (London), March 16, 1998. Available online: http://nersp.nerdc.ufl.edu/~arm/amazonFires.html, accessed September 28, 1998.

Dawsey, Cyrus, ed. *The Confederados, Old South Immigrants in Brazil.* Tuscaloosa: University of Alabama Press, 1995.

Dean, Warren. *Brazil and the Struggle for Rubber, a Study in Environmental History.* New York: Columbia University Press, 1987.

———. "Latifundia and Land Policy in Nineteenth Century Brazil." *Hispanic American Historical Review* 51, no. 4 (1971): 606–25.

Denevan, William. "The Aboriginal People of Amazonia." In *The Native Population of the Americas in 1492,* ed. William Denevan. Madison: University of Wisconsin Press, 1976.

————. *The Native Population of the Americas in 1492*. Madison: University of Wisconsin Press, 1976.

O Diario do Grão Pará (Grão Pará daily), Belem, 1953–92.

O Diario Oficial do Estado do Pará (Official daily of the state of Pará), Belem, 1891–1912.

Dias, Catarina V., and Manuel Mauricio Albuquerque. "Povoamento e distribuição da população, os elementos étnicos, relações entre o elemento indígena e a sociedade amazónica" (The peopling and distribution of population, ethnic elements, relations between the indigenous element and Amazonian society). In *A grande região norte* (The great northern region), 1:220–37. Rio de Janeiro: Gráfica do I.B.G.E., 1959.

Dias, Manuel Nunes. "Colonização da Amazonia" (Colonization of the Amazon). *Boletim Cultural* (Porto) 31, no. 3/4 (1969): 288–311.

————. *Fomento e mercantilismo: A Companhia Geral do Grão Pará e Maranhão, 1755–1778* (Development and mercantilism, the General Company of Grão Pará and Maranhão, 1755–1778). 2 vols. Belem: Universidade Federal do Pará, 1970.

Diderich, Joelle. "Brazil Sends More Personnel to Fight Fires." Reuters, March 1998. Dateline Brasilia. Available online: http://nersp.nerdc.ufl.edu/~arm/amazonFires.html, accessed September 28, 1998.

————. "Yanomami Shamans Try to Halt Amazon Fires." Reuters, March 1998. Dateline Boa Vista. Available online: http://nersp.nerdc.ufl.edu/~arm/amazonFires.html, accessed September 28, 1998.

Diegues, Manuel, Jr. *Imigração, urbanização, e industrialização: Estudos sobre alguns aspetos da contribuição cultural do imigrante no Brasil* (Immigration, urbanization, and industrialization: Studies on certain aspects of the cultural contribution of the immigrant in Brazil). Rio de Janeiro: Centro Brasileiro de Pesquisas Educacionais, 1964.

Diffie, Bailey. *History of Colonial Brazil*. Malabar, Fla.: Robert Krieger, 1987.

Dutra, Francis. *A Guide to the History of Brazil, 1500–1822*. Santa Barbara and Oxford: ABC-Clio, 1980.

Egler, Eugenia Gonçalves. "A zona bragantina no Estado do Pará" (The Bragantina in the state of Pará). *Revista Brasileira de Geografia* 23, no. 3 (1961): 527–55.

EnviroNews Service. "Brazil Suspends All Logging Contracts." Report July 26, 1996. Available online: http://www.envirolink.org/archives/enews/0153.html, accessed September 4, 1997.

Fearnside, Philip. "Environmental Destruction in the Brazilian Amazon." In *The Future of Amazonia—Destruction or Sustainable Development?*, ed. David Goodman and Anthony Hall, 179–225. New York: St. Martin's Press, 1990.

Feferman, Julio. "Brazil's Indians on Alert as Government Hears Final Land Rights Appeals." *World Rainforest Report* 13, no. 2 (summer/fall 1996). Available online: http://www.ran.org/ran/info_center/wrr/wrr_96_10/brazil.html, accessed July 26, 1997.

Ferraz, Manuel Joaquim de Sousa. "Memoria de alguns produtos espontáneos e não espontáneos da Provincia do Grão Pará, que fazem o comercio de exportação" (Report of certain wild and domesticated products from the province of Pará, used in the export business). Biblioteca Nacional do Rio de Janeiro, Seção de Manuscritos (BNRJ,SM).

Ferreira, Alexandre Rodrigues. "Descrição do peixe pirarucú," 1797 (Description of the pirarucú fish). BNRJ,SM.

———. "Estado presente da agricultura do Pará, representado a S. Exc. o Senhor Martinho de Souza e Albuquerque, governador e capitão geral do estado," 15 March 1784 (Current state of agriculture of Pará, given to the honorable Martinho de Souza e Albuquerque, governor and military commander of the state). BNRJ,SM.

———. "Memoria sobre a jurarareté," 1786 (Report on the jurarareté). BNRJ,SM. Reprinted in Alexandre Rodrigues Ferreira, Viagem filosófica, . . . Memorias: Zoologia e botánica (Philosophical Journey . . . Reports: Zoology and Botany), 37–43. Rio de Janeiro: Conselho Federal de Cultura, 1972.

———. "Memoria sobre as tartarugas," n.d. (Report on the turtles). BNRJ,SM.

———. "Memoria sobre as variedades de tartaruga que hão no Estado de Grão Pará e o emprego que lhe dão," n.d. (Report on the varieties of turtles in the state of Grão Pará and the uses to which they are put). BNRJ,SM.

———. "Relação dos peixes dos sertões do Pará," n.d. (Report on the fish of the interior of Pará). BNRJ,SM.

———. Viagem filosófica ás Capitanias do Grão Pará, Rio Negro, Mato Grosso e Cuiabá: Desenhos originais coligidos pelo Professor Dr. Edgard de Cerqueira Falcão (Philosophical voyage to the captaincies of Grão Pará, Rio Negro, Mato Grosso, and Cuiabá: Original drawings collected by Professor Edgard de Cerqueira Falcão). São Paulo: Gráficos Brunner, 1970.

Fittkau, E. J., and H. Klinge. "On Biomass and Trophic Structure of the Central Amazon Rainforest Ecosystem." Biotrópica 5, no.1 (1974): 2–14.

A Folha do Norte (Newspaper of the North), Belem, 1896–1912.

Foresta, R. A. Amazon Conservation in the Age of Development. Gainesville: University of Florida Press, 1991.

Fragoso, Dr. José (fragoso@zoo.ufl.edu), and Kirsten Silvius (Kirsten@zoo.ufl. edu). "Amazon Fires." March 1998. Available online: http://nersp. nerdc.ufl.edu/~arm/amazonFires.html, accessed July 28, 1998.

Friends of the Earth International—Amazonia Program. "Western Amazon: Local Communities Challenge World Bank Project." (No date). Available online: http://bioc09.uthscsa.edu/natnet/archive/n1/9507/0236.html, accessed September 4, 1998.

———. "World Bank Inspection of Planaflora Project." June 20, 1995. Report to listserve NATIVE-L from foeamazonia@ax.apc.org. Available online: http://bioc09.uthscsa.edu/natnet/archive/n1/9304/0051.html, accessed September 4, 1997.

Gentry, A. H., and J. Lopez-Parodi. "Deforestation and Increased Flooding of the Upper Amazon." Science 210 (1980): 1354–56.

Goodman, David, and Anthony Hall, eds. *The Future of Amazonia—Destruction or Sustainable Development?* New York: St. Martin's Press, 1990.

Goree, Langston J. "Re: Amazon Being Torched." October 17, 1991. Available online: http://bioc09.uthscsa.edu/natnet/archive/n1/91d/0216.html, accessed September 4, 1997.

Goulding, Michael, et al. *Floods of Fortune: Ecology and Economy along the Amazon.* New York: Columbia University Press, 1995.

Gourou, Pierre. "A região de Belem" (The region around Belem). *Boletim da Inspetoria Regional de Fomento Agrícola do Estado do Pará* 10 (1960): 3–20.

Gragson, Ted. "Fishing the Waters of Amazonia: Native Subsistence Economies in a Tropical Rain Forest." *American Anthropologist* 94 (1992): 428–40.

Greenpeace Brazil. "Rain Forest Under Siege." Project report July 26, 1996. Available online: http://xs2.greenpeace.org/~comms/cbio/brazil.html, accessed September 4, 1997.

Gross, Anthony. "Amazonia in the Nineties: Sustainable Development or Another Decade of Destruction." *Third World Quarterly* 12, no. 3 (1990): 1–24.

Gross, Daniel. "Protein Capture and Cultural Development in the Amazon Basin." *American Anthropologist* 77, no. 3 (1975): 526–49.

———. "Village Movement in Relation to Resources in Amazonia." In *Adaptive Responses of Native Americans,* ed. Raymond Hames and William Vickers. New York: Academic Press, 1983.

Gross, Sue A. "Agricultural Promotion in the Amazon Basin, 1700–1750." *Agricultural History* 43, no. 2 (1969): 269–76.

———. "Labor in Amazonia in the First Half of the Eighteenth Century." *Americas* 32, no. 2 (1975): 211–21.

Hall, Michael. "The Origins of Mass Immigration in Brazil, 1871–1914." Ph.D. diss., Columbia University, 1961.

Hecht, Susanna. "The Logic of Livestock and Deforestation in Amazonia." *Bioscience* 687 (1993): 689–92.

———, ed. *Amazonia: Agriculture and Land Use Research.* Cali, Columbia: Centro Internacional de Agricultura Tropical, 1982.

Hecht, Susanna, and Alexander Cockburn. *Fate of the Forest: Developers, Destroyers, and Defenders of the Amazon.* London: Verso, 1989.

Hemming, John. *Amazon Frontier: The Defeat of the Brazilian Indians.* Cambridge: Harvard University Press, 1987.

———. *Red Gold: The Conquest of the Brazilian Indian, 1500–1760.* Cambridge: Harvard University Press, 1978.

Hill, Lawrence. "Confederate Exiles to Brazil." *Hispanic American Historical Review* 7 (1927): 192–210.

Hunter, David. "The Planaflora Claim: Lessons from the Second World Bank Inspection Panel Claim," 1996. Available online: http://www.econet.apc.org/ciel/planafl.html, accessed September 4, 1997.

Hurley, Jorge. *Belem do Pará sob o dominio portugués, 1614–1823* (Belem do Pará under Portuguese control, 1614–1823). Belem: Livraria Clássica, 1940.

————. *A Cabanagem* (The Cabanagem). Belem: Livraria Clássica, 1936.

Hutter, Lucy Maffei. *Imigração italiana em São Paulo, 1880–1889: Os primeiros contatos do imigrante com o Brasil* (Italian immigration in São Paulo, 1880–1889: The immigrant's first contacts with Brazil). Tese de doutoramento para a Universidade de São Paulo, Departamento de Historia. São Paulo: Instituto de Estudos Brasileiros, 1972.

"Indios mandados para trabalharem na fortaleza," 1769 (Indians sent to work on the fort). BAPP.

O Jornal de Pará (Pará journal), Belem, 1837–78.

Kiemen, Mathias C. *The Indian Policy of Portugal in the Amazon Region, 1614–1693*. Washington: Catholic University of America, 1954.

LaFranchi, Howard. "Is Burning of Amazon All Smoke?." *Christian Science Monitor*, March 18, 1998. Dateline Brasilia. Available online: http://nersp.nerdc.ufl.edu/~arm/amazonFires.html, accessed September 28, 1998.

Laraia, Roque de Barros, and Roberto Augusto da Matta. *Indios e castanheiros: A empresa extrativa e os indios no medio Tocantins* (Indians and Brazil nut gatherers: An extractive business and the Indians on the Middle Tocantins). *Corpo e Alma do Brasil*, 21. São Paulo: Difusão Europeia do Livro, 1967.

O Liberal do Pará (Pará liberal), Belem, 1860–90.

Lieth, H., and M. J. A. Werger, eds. *Tropical Rain Forest Ecosystems: Biogeographical and Ecological Studies*. Amsterdam: Elsevier, 1989.

Lombardi, Mary. "The Frontier in Brazilian History." *Pacific Historical Review* 44, no. 4 (1975): 437–57.

MacLachlan, Colin. "The Indian Labor Structure in the Portuguese Amazon 1700–1800." In *Colonial Roots of Modern Brazil*, ed. Dauril Alden, 199–230. Berkeley: University of California Press, 1973.

MacLeod, Murdo J. *Spanish Central America: A Socioeconomic History*. Berkeley: University of California Press, 1973.

MacMillan, Gordon. *At the End of the Rainbow?: Gold, Land and People in the Brazilian Amazon*. New York: Columbia University Press, 1995.

Mahar, Dennis. *Frontier Development Policy in Brazil: A Study of Amazonia*. New York: Praeger, 1979.

————. *Government Policies and Deforestation in Brazil's Amazon Region*. Washington: World Bank, 1989.

"Mapa dos escravos e libertos e os rendimentos anuais dos engenhos e engenhocas existentes na Ilha de Joanes, termo de Monsarás, aos 20 de outubro de 1790" (Table of the slaves and freedmen and the annual income of the sugar mills presently on the island of Joanes, termo of Monsarás, on October 20, 1790). BAPP.

"Mapa dos escravos que a Companhia do Comercio introduziu neste Estado do Pará no ano de 1777" (Table of slaves which the Commerce Company brought to the state of Pará in 1777). IHGB, ARQ.

"Mapa dos escravos que a Companhia Geral de Comercio introduziu neste Estado do Pará no ano de 1775." (Table of slaves brought to the state of Pará by the General Commerce Company in 1775). IHGB, ARQ.

"Mapa dos géneros e escravos que a Companhia Geral importou neste Estado do Pará do ano de 1776" (Table of goods and slaves which the Companhia Geral imported to the state of Pará in 1776). IHGB, ARQ.

Marajó, Barão de. *A Amazonia. As provincias do Pará e Amazonas e o Governo Central do Brasil* (The Amazon: The provinces of Pará and Amazonas and the central government of Brazil). Lisboa: Tipografia Minerva, 1883.

Maxwell, Kenneth A. "Pombal and the Nationalization of the Luso-Brazilian Economy." *Hispanic American Historical Review* 48, no. 4 (1968): 608–31.

Melby, John Fremont. "Rubber River, an Account of the Rise and Collapse of the Amazon Boom." *Hispanic American Historical Review* 23, no. 3 (1942): 452–69.

Mello, Alcindo Teixeira de. *Os nordestinos na Amazonia* (Northeasterners in the Amazon). Rio de Janeiro: Instituto Nacional de Imigração e Colonização, 1956.

Mendonça, Albuquerque. *Estado do Pará: Administração do Dr. Lauro Sodré* (Pará State: The administration of Dr. Lauro Sodré). Belem: Tipografia do Diario Oficial, 1897.

Mendonça, Marcos Carneiro de. *A Amazonia na era pombalina. Correspondencia inédita do governador e capitão general do Estado do Grão Pará e Maranhão, Francisco Xavier de Mendonça Furtado, 1751–1759* (Amazonia in the Pombal era: Unedited correspondence of governor and military commander of the state of Grão Pará and Maranhão, Francisco Xavier de Mendonça Furtdo). 3 vols. Rio de Janeiro: Instituto Histórico e Geográfico Brasileiro, 1963.

Menezes, Adriano. *O problema de colonização da Amazonia* (The problem of colonization of the Amazon). Rio de Janeiro: SPVEA, 1958.

Menezes, José Napoles Tello de. "Condições com que são concedidos aos particulares os indios silvestres dos novos descimentos" (Conditions under which forest Indians from the new expeditions are granted to private individuals). AN. Unpublished document dated 1782.

Millikan, Brent (bmillikan@ax.apc.org). "Planaflora." Report to listserve NATIVE-L, July 5, 1994. Available online: http://bioc09/uthsca.edu/natnet/archive/nl/9407/0032.html, accessed September 4, 1997.

Miranda, Vicente Chermont de. "Molestias que afetam os animais domésticos, mormente o gado, na ilha de Marajó" (Diseases affecting domestic animals, especially cattle, on the island of Marajó). *Boletim do Museu Goeldi de Historia Natural e Etnografia* 4, no. 1 (1904–6): 438–68.

Moran, Emilio. *Developing the Amazon.* Bloomington: Indiana University Press, 1981.

———. "The Law, Politics, and Economics of Amazonian Deforestation." *Global Legal Studies Journal* 1, no. 2. Available online: http://www.law.indiana.edu/glsj/vol1/moran.html, accessed September 4, 1997.

———. "Private and Public Colonization Schemes in Amazonia." In *The Future of Amazonia—Destruction or Sustainable Development?*, ed. David Goodman and Anthony Hall, 70–89. New York: St. Martin's Press, 1990.

———. *Through Amazonian Eyes—The Human Ecology of Amazonian Populations.* Iowa City: University of Iowa Press, 1993.

———, ed. *The Dilemma of Amazonian Development*. Boulder: Westview Press, 1983.

Muller, Antonio Rubler, and Hiroshi Saito, eds. *Estudo de assimilação de imigrantes do Brasil* (Study on the assimilation of immigrants in Brazil). São Paulo: Escola de Sociologia e Política de São Paulo, 1956.

Muniz, João de Palma. *Imigração e colonização do Estado do Grão Pará, historia e estatística, 1616–1916* (Immigration and colonization in the state of Grão Pará, history and statistics, 1616–1916). Belem: Imprensa Oficial do Estado do Pará, 1916.

Neiva, Artur Hehl. "Aspetos geográficos da imigração e colonização do Brasil" (Geographical aspects of immigration and colonization of Brazil). *Revista Brasileira Geográfica* 9, no. 2 (1947): 249–70.

———. "A imigração na política brasileira do povoamento" (Immigration in Brazilian population politics). *Revista Brasileira dos Municípios* 2, no. 6 (1950): 220–44.

———. "Povoamento do Brasil no século XVIII" (The peopling of Brazil in the eighteenth century). *Revista de Historia* 10 (1952): 379–88.

Nery, Baron de Santa Anna. *The Land of the Amazons*. Translated from the French by George Humphrey. London: Sands and Co., 1901.

Oliveira, Luiz Rodrigues de. "Alert: World Bank/Planaflora/Brazil," July 5, 1994. Available online: http://bioc09/uthscsa.edu/natnet/archive/n1/9407/0032. html, accessed September 4, 1997.

Pang, Eul Soo. *Bahia in the First Brazilian Republic: Coronelismo and Oligarchies (1889–1934)*. Gainesville: University of Florida Press, 1979.

Pará. *Dados estatísticos e informações para os imigrantes, publicados por ordem do Exm. Sr. Tristão de Alencar Araripe, Presidente da Provincia* (Statistical data and information for immigrants, published by order of the honorable Tristão de Alencar Araripe, president of the province). Pará: Tipografia do Diario de Noticias, 1886.

———. *Relatorio* of Division of Obras Públicas, Terras, e Colonização, 1897 (Public works, land, and colonization). Published in *Diario Oficial*, 1897.

———. *Relatorios* of presidents of the province, 1839–89. (Various titles). Belem: various publishers, 1839–89.

———. *Relatorios* of state governors, 1889–1912. (Various titles). Belem: various publishers, 1889–1912.

Parker, Eugene. "Caboclization: The Transformation of the Amerindian in Amazonia, 1615–1800." *Studies in Third World Societies* 29 (1985): xvii–li.

———. "Forest Islands and Kayapó Resource Management in Amazonia: A Reappraisal of the Apete." *American Anthropologist* 94 (1992): 406–28.

———, ed. *The Amazon Caboclo: Historical and Contemporary Perspectives*. Vol. 32, *Studies in Third World Societies*. Williamsburg: College of William and Mary, 1985.

Peckham, Howard, and Charles Gibson, eds. *Attitudes of Colonial Powers toward the American Indians*. Salt Lake City: University of Utah Press, 1969.

Penna, Domingos Soares. *O Tocantins e o Anapú. Relatorio do Secretario da Provincia,*

. . . (Tocantins and Anapú Rivers. Report of the Secretary of the Province . . .). Pará: Tipografia Frederico Rhossard, 1864.

Penteado, Antonio Rocha. "Condições geo-ecológicas da Amazonia brasileira" (Geo-ecological conditions in the Brazilian Amazon), *Revista do Museu Paulista* 21 (1978): 1–17.

———. *Problems de colonização e de uso da terra na região bragantina do Estado do Pará* (Problems of colonization and soil use in the Bragança region of the state of Pará). 2 vols. Pará: Universidade Federal do Pará, 1967.

Pereira, Manuel Nunes. "Negros escravos na Amazonia" (Black slaves in Amazonia). *Anais do X Congresso Brasileiro de Geografia* 3 (1952): 153–85.

Pompeu Sobrinho, Thomaz. "As secas do Nordeste, 1825–1925" (Drought in the Northeast, 1825–1925). *Livro do Nordeste*, Recife, 1925.

Portugal. *Directorio que se deve observar nas povoações dos indios do Pará e Maranhão emquanto Sua Magestade não mandar o contrario* (Directions to be observed in Indian villages of Pará and Maranhão unless His Majesty orders differently). Lisbon: Oficina de Miguel Rodrigues, 1758.

Portugal. "Regimento e leis sobre as missões do estado do Maranhão e Pará e sobre a liberdade dos indios," 1686. (Rules and laws regarding the missions of the state of Maranhão and Pará and regarding the freedom of the Indians). BNRJ, SM.

Posey, Darrell A. "Indigenous Ecological Knowledge and the Development of the Amazon." In *The Dilemma of Amazonian Development*, ed. Emilio Moran, 225–58. Boulder: Westview Press, 1983.

———. "Indigenous Management of Tropical Forest Ecosystems: The Case of the Kayapó Indians of the Brazilian Amazon." *Agroforestry Systems* 3 (1985): 139–58.

Prado, Caio, Jr. *The Colonial Background of Modern Brazil*. Translated from the Portuguese by Suzette Macedo. Berkeley: University of California Press, 1967.

———. *Historia económica do Brasil* (Economic history of Brazil). 16th ed. São Paulo: Editora Brasiliense, 1973.

A Provincia do Pará (Province of Pará), Belem, 1876–1912.

Rainforest Action Network and Amazon Coalition. "Amazon Imperiled by New Generation of Short-Sighted Mega-Projects." January 30, 1996. Available online: http://www.wideopen.igc.org/ran/info_center/press_release/mega_projects.html, accessed September 30, 1997.

———. "Action Alert 118—Genocide Decree Attacks Indian Rights." March 1996. Available online: http://www.ran.org/ran/info_center/aa/aa118.html, accessed July 26, 1997.

———. "Brazil Bans Mahogany Logging in the Amazon," July 29, 1996. Available online: http://www.ran.org/info_center/press_release/mahog.html, accessed July 26, 1997.

———. "Brazil—Decree #1775 Takes Its Toll." June 1996. Available online: http://www.ran.org/ran/ran_campaigns/amazonia/update_6–96.html, accessed July 26, 1997.

————. "Brazil's Indians on Alert as Government Hears Final Land Rights Appeal." 1996 World Rainforest Report, 13, no. 2. Available online: http://www.ran.org/ran/info_center/wrr/wrr_96_10/brazil.html, accessed July 26, 1997.

————. "Brazil's Justice Minister Delays Macuxi Demarcation." Update report September 1996. Available online: http://www.ran.org/ran/ran_campaigns/amazonia/macuxi.html, accessed July 26, 1997.

————. "Economic Alternatives to Rainforest Destruction: The Liana Project." 1996. Available online: http://www.ran.org/ran/ran_campaigns/amazonia/liana.html, accessed July 26, 1997.

————. "Extractive Reserves in Brazilian Amazon." 1996. Available online: http://www.ran.org/ran/ran_campaigns/amazonia/reservas.html, accessed July 26, 1997.

————. "Financing Environmental Destruction: The World Bank and the Rainforests." 1996. Available online: http://www.ran.org/ran/ran_campaigns/world_bank/index.html, accessed July 26, 1997.

————. "Funai Rejects Claims." Update report, July 1996. Available online: http://www.ran.org/ran/ran_campaigns/amazonia/update_7–96.html, accessed July 26, 1997.

————. "Guarani-Kaoiwa Indians Keep Their Land." 1996. Available online: http://www.ran.org/ran/victories/guarani.html, accessed July 26, 1997.

————. "Mega-Projects—Roads." 1996. Available online: http://www.ran.org/ran/ran_campaigns/amazonia/mega.html, accessed July 26, 1997.

————. "Panara Brazilian Indians Obtain Land Rights." 1996. Available online: http://www.ran.org/ran/victories/panara.html, accessed July 26, 1997.

————. "Threat to the Amazon: New Mega-Infrastructure Projects Are a Red Alert to the Amazon Basin." 1996. Available online: http://www.ran.org/ran/ran_campaigns/amazonia/mega.html, accessed July 26, 1997.

Raiol, Domingos Antonio, Barão de Guajará. *Motins políticos, ou historia dos principais acontecimentos políticos da provincia do Pará desde o ano de 1821 ate 1835* (Political uprisings, or the history of the main political events in the province of Pará from 1821 to 1835). 3 vols. 2d ed. Belem: Universidade Federal do Pará, 1970.

Reis, Artur Cezar Ferreira. *A Amazonia e a cobiça internacional* (The Amazon and international covetousness). 4d ed. Rio de Janeiro: Companhia Editora Americana, 1972.

————. *Aspetos económicos da dominação lusitana na Amazonia* (Economic aspects of Portuguese domination of the Amazon). Rio de Janeiro: SPVEA, n.d.

————. "Brasileiros e estrangeiros na ocupação da Amazonia" (Brazilians and foreigners in the occupation of the Amazon). *Correio da Manhã* (Rio de Janeiro), September 18, 1970.

————. "Estrangeiros na Amazonia" (Foreigners in the Amazon). *Revista de Imigração e Colonização* 2 (1948): 3–7.

————. *O processo histórico da economia amazonense* (The historical process of the Amazonian economy). Rio de Janeiro: Imprensa Nacional, 1944.

———. "Sertanistas, missionarios e demarcadores na revelação geográfica da Amazonia" (Frontiersmen, missionaries, and map makers in the geographical discovery of the Amazon). *Anais do X Congresso Brasileiro de Geografia* (Rio de Janeiro) 2 (1952): 254–61.

"Relação das familias que existem na nova vila de Mazagão ao 7 de outubro de 1784" (Report of the families present in the new village of Mazagão on October 7, 1784). AN.

"Relação do gado vacum que se ferrou nas fazendas desta Ilha Grande de Joanes qual foram buscar aos gerais chamados bravos," 1770. (Report of wild cattle branded on the ranches of the Great Island of Joanes). BAPP.

Relação dos indios silvestres que tem descidos dos matos de estado do Grão Pará em o governo do ilmo. Sr. José de Napoles Tello de Menezes, Governador e Capitão Mor do mesmo estado," Oficio, November 19, 1781 (Report of forest Indians brought down from the forests of Grão Pará during the governorship of the honorable José de Napoles Tello de Menezes, governor and military commander of said state). BAPP.

"Relação dos presos que achão nas Cadeias de Lisboa a quem S. Magestade comuta de penas que mereciam pelos seus crimes e irem degredados para o Estado do Grão Pará até nova ordem sua, 1766" (Report on prisoners found in the prisons of Lisbon whose deserved penalties are commuted by His Majesty and who are going as degregados to the state of Grão Pará until further orders). BAPP.

"Relações dos cazais que se vão estabelecer na nova vila de São José de Macapá nos anos de 1763, 1764, 1766, 1767, 1768, e 1769 (Reports of the married couples making homes in the new village of São José de Macapá in the years 1763, 1764, 1766, 1767, 1768, and 1769). BAPP.

Robberson, Tod. "Brasil—Politicians, Corporations Fiddle as Rain Forest Burns." *Dallas Morning News.* Dateline Manaus, March 18, 1998. Available online: http://nersp.nerdc.ufl.edu/~arm/amazonFires.html, accessed September 28, 1998.

Rocha, Joaquim da Silva. *Historia da colonização do Brasil* (History of the colonization of Brazil). Rio de Janeiro: Imprensa Nacional, 1918.

Rocque, Carlos. *Grande enciclopedia da Amazonia* (Great encyclopedia of the Amazon). 6 vols. Belem: Amazonia Editora, 1967.

Russell, Joseph A. "Fordlandia and Belterra Plantations on the Tapajós River, Brazil." *Economic Geography* 18 (1942): 125–45.

Salles, Vicente. *O negro no Pará, sob o regime da escravidão* (The Black in Pará, under the regime of slavery). Rio de Janeiro: Fundação Getulio Vargas, 1971.

Sanford, R. L. et al. "Amazon Rain-Forest Fries." *Science* 227 (1985): 53–55.

Schemo, Diane. "As Research Dries Up—Amazon Burning Mounts." Report posted October 11, 1995, to listserve Latino.com. Available online: http://www.latino.com/braz1011.html, accessed September 4, 1997.

Schmink, Marianne, and Charles Wood. *Contested Frontiers in Amazonia.* New York: Columbia University Press, 1992.

———. *Frontier Expansion in Amazonia*. Gainesville: University of Florida Press, 1984.

Schultes, R. E., and R. F. Raffauf. *The Healing Forest: Medicinal and Toxic Plants of the Northwest Amazon*. Portland, Ore.: Dioscorides Press, 1990.

Skole, David, et al. "Physical and Human Dimensions of Deforestation in Amazonia." 1995. Available online: http://amazon.unh.edu/pathfinder/information/papers/bioscience/index.html, accessed September 4, 1997.

Skole, David, and Compton Tucker. "Tropical Deforestation and Habitat Fragmentation in the Amazon—Satellite Data from 1978 to 1988." Available online: http://amazon.unh.edu/pathfinder/papers/science1/index.html, accessed September 4, 1997, no longer available.

Smith, Herbert H. *Brazil, the Amazons and the Coast*. New York: Scribners, 1879.

Smith, Nigel. "Agricultural Productivity along Brazil's TransAmazon Highway." *Agroecosystems* 4 (1978): 415–32.

———. "Colonization Lessons from the Rain Forest." *Science* 214 (1982): 755–61.

———. "Destructive Exploitation of the South American River Turtle." *Yearbook of the Association of American Geographers* 36 (1974): 85–102.

———. *The Enchanted Amazon Rain Forest: Stories from a Vanishing World*. Gainesville: University of Florida Press, 1996.

———. *Man, Fishes, and the Amazon*. New York: Columbia University Press, 1981.

———. *Rainforest Corridors: The TransAmazon Colonization Scheme*. Berkeley: University of California Press, 1982.

Smith, T. Lynn. "Brazilian Land Surveys, Land Division, and Land Titles." *Rural Sociology* 9, no. 3 (1944): 264–70.

Spaulding, Karen. *Huarochirí, and Andean Society under Inca and Spanish Rule*. Stanford: Stanford University Press, 1984.

Stark, N. "Nutrient Cycling: Nutrient Distribution in Some Amazonian Soils." *Tropical Ecology* 12 (1971): 24–50.

———. "Nutrient Cycling II: Nutrient Distribution in Amazonia Vegetation." *Tropical Ecology* 12 (1971): 177–201.

Sternberg, Hilgard O'R. *The Amazon River of Brazil*. Geographische Zeitschrift, 40. Weisbaden: Franz Steiner Verlag, GMBH, 1975.

———. "Land and Man in the Tropics." *Academy of Political Science Proceedings* 27, no. 4 (1964): 11–21.

———. "Radiocarbon Dating as Applied to a Problem of Amazonian Morphology." *Comptes Rendus*, 1960, XVIII International Geographical Congress, Rio de Janeiro, 1956, 2:399–424.

Stewart, Douglas. *After the Trees: Living on the TransAmazon Highway*. Austin: University of Texas Press, 1994.

Sweet, David. "A Rich Realm of Nature Destroyed: The Middle Amazon Valley, 1640–1750." 2 vols. Ph.D. diss., University of Wisconsin, 1974.

Tambs, Louis A. "Rubber, Rebels and Rio Branco, the Conquest for the Acre." *Hispanic American Historical Review* 46, no. 3 (1966): 254–73.

Teixeira, José Ferreira. "O Arquipélago de Marajó" (The Marajó Archipelago). Anais do X Congresso Brasileiro de Geografia 3 (1952): 714–807.

Treece, David. "Indigenous Peoples in Brazilian Amazonia and the Expansion of the Economic Frontier." In *The Future of Amazonia—Destruction or Sustainable Development?*, ed. David Goodman and Anthony Hall, 264–87. New York: St. Martin's Press, 1990.

U.S. Department of State. "Brazil Country Report on Human Rights Practices for 1996." January 30, 1997. Available online: http://www.usis.usemb.se/human/human96/brazil.html, accessed September 30, 1997.

Velho, Otavio Guilherme. *Frentes de expansão e estrutura agraria: Estudo do processo de penetração numa area da transamazónica* (Expansion fronts and agrarian structure: Study of the penetration process in one area of the TransAmazon). Rio de Janeiro: Zahar Editores, 1972.

Verissimo, José. *Estudos amazónicos* (Amazon Studies). Belem: Universidade Federal do Pará, 1970.

———. *A pesca na Amazonia* (Fishing in Amazonia). 2d ed. Belem: Universidade Federal do Pará, 1970.

Vianna, Artur. *As epidemias do Pará* (Epidemics of Pará). Belem: Imprensa do Diario Oficial, 1906.

von Martius, Charles Friedrich Phillip. *Natureza, doenças, medicina e remedios dos indios brasileiros*, 1844 (Nature, illnesses, medicine and remedies of the Brazilian Indians). São Paulo: Companhia Editora Nacional, 1939.

Wagley, Charles. *Amazon Town: A Study of Man in the Tropics*. New York: Borzoi Books, 1964.

———. "The Brazilian Amazon: The Case of the Underdeveloped Area." *Four Papers Presented in the Institute for Brazilian Studies*, 9–31. Nashville: Vanderbilt University Press, 1951.

Weinstein, Barbara. *The Amazonian Rubber Boom, 1850–1920*. Stanford: Stanford University Press, 1983.

Werner, D., et al. "Subsistence Productivity and Hunting Effort in Native South America." *Human Ecology* 7, no. 4 (1979): 303–15.

Wood, Charles, and José Alberto Magno de Carvalho. *The Demography of Inequality in Brazil*. New York: Cambridge University Press, 1988.

Wood, Charles, and Marianne Schmink. "Blaming the Victim, Small Farmer Production in an Amazonian Colonization Project." *Studies in Third World Societies* 7 (1979): 77–93.

INDEX

Robin L. Anderson is an associate professor of history at Arkansas State University. She is the author of numerous articles on Amazonian history, Brazilian medical history, and Brazilian current affairs.